Ashley Kalagian Blunt is the author of *My Name Is Revenge*, which was shortlisted for the 2019 Woollahra Digital Literary Awards and was a finalist in the 2018 Carmel Bird Digital Literary Award. Her writing appears in *Griffith Review*, *Sydney Review of Books*, *Westerly*, the *Australian*, the *Big Issue* and *Kill Your Darlings*. Ashley is a Moth StorySLAM winner and has appeared at Story Club, the National Young Writers' Festival, and Sydney Writers' Festival. She lived and worked in Canada, South Korea, Peru and Mexico before moving to Australia.

Ashley loves hearing from readers.
Find her online at ashleykalagianblunt.com

Praise for *How to Be Australian*

'As a new Australian, I laughed out loud at the sharpness of
Kalagian Blunt's keen observations, the drollerie of her self-deprecating
reflections. But under the humour are strands of serious research and
earnest endeavour, a wish to address the questions we ask ourselves.
Where do I fit in? How will I find a home for my heart?'

Vicki Laveau-Harvie, winner of the 2019 Stella Prize

'This is the kind of book we need right now. It's funny and
heartwarming and I couldn't put it down, but it also makes you think …
If you like Bill Bryson, you will love Ashley Kalagian Blunt.'

Katherine Collette, author of *The Helpline*

'Wonderfully eccentric, tremendously fun and endlessly interesting,
this book reveals just how challenging Australia can be, and how much
hard work it takes to stay and – hopefully – belong.'

Walter Mason, author of *Destination Saigon* and
Destination Cambodia

'Kalagian Blunt's prose sparkles and fizzes with personality in this
hilarious memoir about migrant's dual search for home and love that
lasts. She skilfully illuminates the restlessness and paradoxical yearnings
of the human soul, and renders our familiar Australia oh-so-strange and
our strange marriages oh-so-familiar.'

Lee Kofman, author of *Imperfect* and *The Dangerous Bride*

Ashley Kalagian Blunt

HOW TO BE AUSTRALIAN

An Outsider's View on Life & Love Down Under

Published by Affirm Press in 2020
28 Thistlethwaite Street, South Melbourne, VIC 3205.
www.affirmpress.com.au
10 9 8 7 6 5 4 3

Text and copyright © Ashley Kalagian Blunt, 2020
All rights reserved. No part of this publication may be reproduced without prior permission of the publisher.

 A catalogue record for this book is available from the National Library of Australia

Title: How to Be Australian / Ashley Kalagian Blunt, author.
ISBN: 9781925972801 (paperback)

Cover design by Design by Committee
Typeset in 12.5/19 Granjon by J&M Typesetting
Proudly printed in Australia by Griffin Press

 The paper this book is printed on is certified against the Forest Stewardship Council® Standards. Griffin Press holds FSC® chain of custody certification SGS-COC-005088. FSC® promotes environmentally responsible, socially beneficial and economically viable management of the world's forests

For That Guy, and the rest

Author's note

This is a work of creative non-fiction. The events take place from 2011 to 2016. The names and identifying traits of some people have been changed, and some characters are composites inspired by a variety of people and interactions. For the sake of narrative clarity, some incidents have been condensed and some timeframes rejigged.

Contents

Prologue		ix
1	Up Over, but Hot	1
2	The Other Shoe	14
3	Sydneysiding	24
4	The Hollywood Kookaburra Con	44
5	Paranoia Solis	58
6	Fitting In	67
7	Fear Has Seven Legs	74
8	Homeland	89
9	The Reins	98
10	Down Under Burlesque	111
11	The Secret City of Melbun	123
12	Worry Box	135
13	Per Rectal	145
14	The Lesser Ocean Road	154
15	Fingerprint Break	166
16	Welcome to Tits	172
17	Perthlings	184
18	Going to the Waffle	192
19	Welcome to the Wet	201
20	The Platypus Gene	210
21	Further Down, More Under	220

22	Tasting Notes for Australia's Worst Beers	237
23	It's the Vibe	249
24	Welcome to Australia	261
25	Citizenship Sizzle	270
	Acknowledgements	286

Prologue

I had four blocks to go and I couldn't breathe. It was the middle of February 2002 in Winnipeg, Canada. The city sat a snowball's throw away from the United States border, and yet on this day, like so many days, it was indistinguishable from the North Pole.

Four blocks is a distance that, in summer, would have taken me ten minutes. In summer I would have strolled, whistling maybe. In summer I wouldn't have counted the blocks. But in mid-February, the wind that was blasting my face had come via the Arctic Circle. I could feel the cold hitting my lungs as I struggled to suck oxygen out of each breath, huffing like I was an avid smoker running a marathon instead of a university student trying to get home from the bus stop in one of the coldest cities in the world.

I held one arm up, crooked at the elbow, shielding my eyes. Still, the wind squeezed tears out of them, and when I blinked, my eyelashes frosted together. I tried walking backwards so that I could at least breathe, but I stumbled, swearing into the wool scarf that sat wet against my mouth. My winter coat was basically a doona with a zipper, which I wore along with the sodden scarf, a toque pulled low over my ears, and padded mittens that turned my hands into useless stumps. The coat's hood came up over my toque, and

How to Be Australian

the scarf wrapped around the hood, immobilising my head and eliminating my peripheral vision. If I wanted to see to either side, I had to swivel my entire torso.

I was bundled in enough material to clothe eleven or twelve children on a less inhospitable day, but the wind still stabbed through me like a steak knife through a marshmallow.

'Only a few more blocks, only a few more,' I muttered. This was the block where no-one shovelled the sidewalks. It hadn't snowed in the past few days, but the wind had whipped the winter's accumulation out of yards and piled it along my path. Some drifts came up past my knees, and I sank with each step. This was how an easy ten-minute walk stretched to a grim twenty-minute trudge.

There were plenty of things that should have occupied my thoughts as I made the arduous journey home – juggling university deadlines with my shifts at the bookstore, upcoming exams, and Steve. Normally the thought of him could distract me from anything, and often did. He had a kind smile and the athletic build of a marathon runner. He'd shown up at the bookstore yesterday and handed me a bouquet of violets for our two-month anniversary.

But at that moment, not even the thought of Steve was powerful enough to distract me from the misery of the cold. The exposed strip of flesh on each of my cheeks burned. My toes ached. Every nerve in my body screamed at me to get out of the wind. Like rubbing vinegar into a paper cut, walking into a minus 40-degree wind was a cruel mindfulness practice. My mind refused to let me be elsewhere; it figured I was about to die of hypothermia.

While contemplating how mindful I'd become, I forgot about the danger zone. During the last burst of warmth weeks before,

Prologue

melted snow had pooled in a sidewalk depression and frozen into a bathmat-sized stretch of perfectly smooth ice, poised like a landmine under a dusting of snow. That morning, when I'd left home in the dark, I'd crossed it gingerly, hands up and knees bent, like a tightrope walker.

Now, my right foot hit the ice and kept going. Still in motion, my left foot took on the right's momentum, launching me skyward. My brain reeled, trying to catch up. A moment earlier I'd been walking upright, but now I was airborne, horizontal and descending with speed. Physics was a vile magic trick.

My hip smashed into the ice. If my head had come next, the impact would have split it open. Instead, my elbow collided with the unforgiving surface. I remained miserably conscious.

I lay on the ground, shivering, afraid to move. Did I need to call for help? I had a phone in my purse. To get it, I'd have to remove at least one mitten, and there was no way that was happening. Also, I was pretty sure my purse was wedged under my butt.

As my extremities started to go numb, a feeling of peace came over me. Above, the leafless silhouettes of poplar branches shook in the wind, forlorn and eerie, undead tree skeletons. Beyond, a scattering of satellites passed for stars in the night sky. Why was I so calm? Was I dying? Had I hit my head without realising it?

It took a few more dazed seconds before I noticed the snow bank I'd practically fallen into. It crested above me like a wave, shielding me from the gale.

I could dig my way deeper into the snow bank. I could go to sleep here. That wouldn't be so bad. Better than fighting against the wind. I'd read that hypothermia was a peaceful way to die. My preferred method would have been smothered under a pile of seal cubs, but if Winnipeg had taught me anything, it was that life is a series of disappointments.

Maybe a neighbour would come along and help me up. I waited, but at this temperature, no-one was out.

Canada has a twenty-four-hour free-to-air channel devoted exclusively to the weather. It's even more boring than it sounds, a fact I knew well because of the TV in the kitchen that my mother kept permanently set to the Weather Channel. Since early December, the graph for the two-week forecast had shown a yellow line starting at minus 40 Celsius, that day's temperature, and stretching out with depressing prairie flatness until day fourteen, where it shot abruptly upwards towards the balmy temperature of zero. Despite this daily forecast, the temperature had remained stuck at minus 40 for two months. Lying on the ice, contemplating digging myself into a snow bank for shelter, I accepted the truth: the graph wasn't an actual forecast. It was an anti-suicide initiative.

Why did anyone live in this abominable part of the world, where winter could start in October and last until May? I was here because my parents were here, and my parents let me live rent-free while attending university. They were here because the Canadian Air Force had posted my dad here. Before Winnipeg, we'd lived across western Canada. It was all pretty bleak, weather-wise.

As the pain in my hip spread into my pelvis, I tried to think warm thoughts. My family couldn't afford much travel. Our most exotic vacation was crossing the US border to shop in Bismarck, North Dakota, where the mall had a Macy's *and* a JCPenney. Growing up, however, I'd passed the long prairie winters watching

xiv

an unhealthy amount of TV, so it was easy to picture myself on a tropical beach. I could see it in high definition. Bikini-clad and sun-kissed, I strolled across golden sand, hand in hand with a handsome guy – maybe an athletic one with a kind smile – as turquoise waves lapped at our feet. It was the picture of perfect happiness.

Why couldn't I do that?

When I finished my degree, I could go anywhere I wanted. I didn't have to stay in Canada. I could live in a city with beaches. I could live in a place where it never snowed at all. I'd thought this before, in the hypothetical manner of a person describing how they'd spend their Powerball winnings. Now, lying on the ice, wriggling my left and then my right toes to check whether I was paralysed, leaving Canada became my sole ambition.

I rolled onto my side, bolts of pain shooting through my knee. I crawled off the ice patch and planted my feet. The wind tried to knock me back, but I leaned into it, scowling with determination. If other people wanted to spend their lives digging themselves out of snow banks for six months a year while breathing through snot-soaked scarves, fine. If Winnipeg's housing was affordable, if taxes were reasonable, if you could reliably get a seat at any restaurant, it was only to con people into staying in what was, objectively, one of the worst places human civilisation had ever been established. But not me. I wasn't falling for Winnipeg's ruse.

Weeks later, when a professor would ask about my career plans, I'd look him in the eyes and reply with teenage certitude, 'Moving abroad.'

1

Up Over, but Hot

I caught a glimpse of Sydney's skyline in the early morning sunlight as I stepped from the jetway into the terminal. It was 2011. The sun glowed, infusing the city. Fine clouds stretched across the sky in streaks. Anticipation crackled through me. I squeezed Steve's hand, his wedding band pressing into my finger as he squeezed back.

By the time we stumbled into the immigration line, I'd been in transit and horribly awake for more than forty hours. I'd attempted to sleep during the flight by curling up in my seat. Now, every muscle in my body hurt in a specific, individual way as if injected with concrete or pummelled with a variety of meat tenderisers.

Steve had somehow managed a few hours of sleep, and was functioning with higher capacity. He scribbled responses to our arrival cards as I stood behind him, swaying slightly. I rubbed my fingers over the rough cover of my navy passport, its gold embossed unicorn and two lions striking me, for the first time, as odd. Canada was a nation of people who carried around ID emblazoned with a mythical creature beloved by five-year-old girls – and I'd never known anyone to comment on the strangeness of that. Including myself.

'You okay, sweetheart?' Steve asked, his face bleary and concerned.

I opened my mouth, struggling to form distinguishable sounds.

'Maybe let me help you,' he said, taking my carry-on bag.

Despite my exhaustion, my face puffed into a smile. Nine years had passed since the snow bank incident, and here I was, keeping that promise to myself. I didn't actually know a whole lot about Australia beyond the beautiful beaches and endless sunshine. I didn't feel like I needed to know a lot before deciding to spend a year here. As Canada's Commonwealth sibling, Australia felt distinct yet familiar. And, crucially, Steve had agreed to it.

Since applying for our visas, I'd looked forward to the transcendent moment when, starting our new life together, we'd be greeted with, 'G'day.'

I rubbed my face and stood a little straighter, trying to prepare myself. We reached the immigration desk and handed over our passports. My breath caught as the officer glanced at us, his lips parting. I gripped Steve's hand. 'Welcome to Australia,' he said, his stamp *ch-chunking* against a blank page of my passport.

I blinked. Steve retrieved our documents. 'Are you okay?' he whispered, hooking an arm through mine and guiding me towards baggage claim. 'You look stunned.'

'It's fine,' I mumbled. 'There'll be plenty of g'days to come.'

~

Up Over, but Hot

We walked out of the airport and into a bright February morning. Across the parking lot, the sun rose against the perfect blue sky.

I had the dizzying sensation that *this* was the start of my adult life. Not turning eighteen, or graduating from university, or moving on my own to South Korea, or even getting married. This act of arriving in Australia with my new-ish husband to embark on a life together – this marked a true shift from youth to maturity.

The warm, still air pressed against me like a hug and I breathed in deeply. It would never snow here. Winter wasn't bearing down on me. I was wearing short sleeves!

It felt like freedom.

Back home in Winnipeg it would be minus 25. People would be wearing hats with earflaps and spraying miniature bottles of de-icing liquid into their frozen car-door keyholes while saying things like 'Cold enough for ya?' But in Sydney it was summer. It was February and it was *summer*, which was like saying 'I was born on Jupiter.'

Someone walking by quipped, in a wonderfully Aussie accent, 'Bloody chilly this morning'. I tried to hold it together, but I made the mistake of catching Steve's eye, and we burst out laughing.

~

Our visa allowed us one precious year in Australia, and Steve had allowed me this one precious year overseas. Sometimes I felt that it had been a mistake to fall in love with a homebody with no desire to live abroad. I'd been living outside Canada for three years prior to our Australian jaunt, soaking up as much of the world as I could. Steve and I had tried to split up but we couldn't get over each other.

When it seemed he was destined to stay in Winnipeg forever, I'd sketched out how the next decade of my life would go without him, teaching in Japan, the UAE and eastern Europe. Instead, we got married, and Steve quit the window manufacturing company where he'd worked for nearly a decade, compromising on this one year aboard with me.

The clock was ticking. Who knew if we might be permitted any more time, or if Steve would tolerate it. In twelve months, we might move back to Canada for good – forever. In the back of my mind I wondered, assuming this went well, if Steve might consider another year abroad somewhere.

I didn't want to get my hopes up. I had to assume this one year was all I would get. It was imperative that we start exploring as much of this new country as possible right away – after we got some sleep. I'd been unprepared for the physical toll of getting to Australia. The airline tickets should have come with a warning.

We found the Billabong Hostel on a narrow, leafy residential street in Newtown. Collapsing into bed, I wondered blearily what a billabong was. A lesser-known cousin of the boomerang, I assumed.

I slept for twenty-four hours. Once in a while, Steve would romantically caress my neck with two fingertips, searching for a pulse.

When I finally woke, I felt like a living human instead of a microwaved corpse. Blinking, I pushed myself onto my elbows.

'Oh good, you're not dead,' Steve said. I stretched out my hand, and he helped pull me out of bed.

I rubbed my eyes. 'I thought I might die on the second leg of that flight. It's possible to die from exhaustion.'

Up Over, but Hot

'You look fine now.' Steve wasn't one to get dramatic, or emotional, or even mildly perturbed. 'Let's get lunch.'

I watched him as he pulled his shoes on. I'd spent eight years convincing him to move abroad. Impatient, I'd struck out on my own, living in Asia and Latin America, free of the debilitating depression Winnipeg seemed to manifest in me, but missing Steve every day we spent apart, waiting for the next phone call, the next email, the occasional postcard with his tight, curvy penmanship. Where I was agitated, bouncing through life like a pinball, Steve had the quiet patience of a cat. People gravitated to his broad, heartfelt smile, his prairie friendliness. When someone really made him laugh, he'd throw his head back and smack his palm on the table. Usually it was his cousins or high-school friends who elicited this reaction; I cherished the rare occasions I managed it. I loved him with every bit of myself.

And now we were in Australia, together.

~

Outside, I took a glorious joy in the sun's warmth, until I felt my skin burning within the first block. We crossed the street to walk in the narrow patches of shade. The temperature edged past 30 degrees.

'I'm so glad I finally coaxed you out of Winnipeg,' I said.

Steve smiled, wide and unreserved. 'It's nice to see you so happy.'

Checking a map he'd grabbed at the hostel, he led us to King Street. The trees vanished, replaced by stoplights and parking signs. Every second place seemed to be a cafe. In between were African restaurants, cosplay shops and an actual operating DVD rental store that suggested Newtown was situated within a tear in the space-time continuum.

We strolled among the hubbub, enjoying wafts of coffee and bacon. Bus engines idled and crosswalk signals rapped mechanically. We passed shoebox-sized shops selling fresh produce like it was 1950, and hand-holding lesbian couples with neon purple mohawks and metal chains connecting their nose and ear piercings like it was definitely not 1950. My curiosity surged.

We passed women in hijabs, a group of young Koreans speaking animatedly outside a cafe, and other people whose nationalities I could only guess at, but who could have easily represented half the United Nations, from the variety of languages being spoken. Winnipeg had its share of cultural diversity, but the suburbs I'd lived in were far-flung and largely white.

It wasn't just the diversity of people that struck me; it was the sheer number. In Winnipeg, because of how the climate shaped the city's design and its inhabitants' lifestyles, it was rare to see so many people bustling about the streets.

The first person I noticed walking down the sidewalk without shoes only briefly caught my attention. He was otherwise ordinary, wearing shorts and a T-shirt. What piqued my interest was his confident barefoot stride, as if the roughness of the pavement, the chance of stepping on a used needle or dog faeces, had never occurred to him.

The second barefoot person held my attention longer, not only because we encountered her less than a block after the first guy, but also because she was carrying her shoes. I'd have understood this if the shoes were stilettos and this was the end of a long

6

night of dancing. But it was noon, and she was holding a pair of runners.

When, a few blocks further on, I saw a barefoot man boarding a bus, I squeezed Steve's hand and gestured towards the man, whispering, 'Is that legal?'

'I thought you said we weren't near the beach.'

'I'm pretty sure this suburb is landlocked.' We both frowned. Maybe the barefootedness was a political protest.

We ran out of shade. On the hottest day in Canada, the sun had never felt so intense. 'I feel like a chicken on a spit.'

'Let's get some water,' Steve said. When I'd imagined life in Sydney, the heat had been dry, like a blanket fresh out of the dryer. Today's heat felt like a boiled sponge wrung over my head. Still, I was pleased it was sweat dripping from my nose instead of cold-induced snot.

We stepped into a convenience store, its air-conditioning set to antarctic. Steve and I looked at every brand of water, in the fridges, in the aisles, stacked by the counter, our faces growing increasingly grave. The cheapest bottle we could find cost $3.80.

In my derision of Winnipeg as a frozen wasteland, I have to emphasise this one fact: Winnipeg is cheap. The house Steve had bought – recently renovated, three bedrooms plus a detached garage – cost $175,000 Canadian, a smidge more in Australian dollars. We'd known Sydney was going to be more expensive than Winnipeg. Practically everywhere with indoor plumbing was more expensive than Winnipeg. But $3.80 for a litre of water? This wasn't artesian mineral water sourced from the French Alps and filtered through crushed diamonds. This $3.80 bottle was the house brand, probably local tap water filtered through a used cheesecloth.

'I'd rather die of thirst.' Steve put the water back and clicked his teeth, his jaw visibly tense. My own jaw clenched in response. Of course he was stressed, being unemployed for the first time in ten years, so soon after the global recession. Everything would be fine once Steve found a job, I thought, trying to brush my concern away.

We ambled on. The smell of roast garlic and lemon came from a restaurant, and we realised we were starving. We sat down at a patio table, menus in hand.

'They've got an actual espresso machine.' I pointed through the open doors. Outside proper cafes, espresso machines were only found in the fanciest Canadian restaurants. They were the Ferraris of coffee: expensive, rare and show-offy.

A server appeared, a dozen silver hoops lining her left ear.

'How're you going?' she asked, smiling. Steve and I exchanged a look.

'Uh, we've just moved here?' I wasn't sure if this answered her question. I was also starting to suspect the whole g'day thing was an urban legend.

'You're from America?'

'Canada,' we said in unison.

We ordered one entree to share, and I asked for a decaf cappuccino, since it was after my 9 am caffeine cut-off.

'And a coffee with cream, thanks,' Steve said. What he wanted, though neither of us knew to specify it, was a cup of black filter coffee with a thimble-sized serving of cream, specifically the liquid variety with 18 per cent fat, portioned in an individual plastic capsule. This was what the phrase 'coffee with cream' meant to us.

The server looked at Steve like he must be new to English. 'So, um, a flat white?'

'A what?'

'Like … with espresso?'

'Okay, with cream.'

She cocked her head. 'I guess I can bring some cream with it.'

When she left, Steve took an abandoned newspaper from another table, portioning a few sections to me.

'Hey, there's an article about hockey!' For the first time since we'd arrived, real excitement filled his voice. But hockey turned out to be a jowly politician and not what Aussies would call ice hockey.

The sports section was alien to Steve. 'I think they have … two types of rugby,' he said, like he expected the *Twilight Zone* theme to start playing.

'How old is this paper?' I flipped to the front, expecting to see a date from at least a decade ago. 'It says same-sex marriage isn't legal here.'

'That can't be right. It's 2011.'

The server returned, setting our drinks on the table. 'Is this how Canadians drink coffee?' she asked.

'Everybody has it like that,' Steve replied, his nose in the paper, and she left before he noticed his latte-looking beverage, and beside it, a tiny bowl of whipped cream. He looked from the cream to me, as if this was a practical joke I'd orchestrated.

I threw up my hands, protesting my innocence.

Steve had grown up on a rural acreage outside Winnipeg, a

descendent of pragmatic Calvinist-types, people who grew their own food and built their own homes. He considered my occasional espresso a ridiculous extravagance.

Spooning some cream into the cup, Steve sipped suspiciously. It was a flat white, the server reiterated when she returned with our food. It sounded less like a beverage and more like a teenage boy's derogatory classification of a female classmate. Steve finished the flat white in a few swigs, then tried to get a 'normal' coffee. Out of desperation, we described the filter process.

'Oh,' she said. 'Nobody serves that here. Maybe at Starbucks?'

We'd been here a single day, most of which I'd spent sleeping, and already we were faced with miscommunication and the unexpectedness of something so ingrained in our understanding of restaurants – the ubiquitous bottomless cup of coffee – being absent in Australia. The beverage options themselves didn't matter, but the underlying revelation did.

I'd assumed navigating life Down Under would be a breeze. Wasn't Australia just Up Over without the snow? As Canadians, we'd spent a good deal of time in the United States. The US was a different country, but we knew how to order a coffee there.

It was true – I'd assumed that Australia would be at least as familiar as the US. But perhaps I didn't know what to expect. A muddle of excitement and uncertainty rushed through me, like the first shot I'd swigged on my 18th birthday, a prairie fire – tequila and tabasco sauce.

Over our shared chicken skewers, Steve and I discussed logistics – purchasing cell phones, opening bank accounts, the everyday necessities we'd avoided during the three months we'd spent travelling through Europe en route to Australia. Real life was about to kick in again.

But then two facts centred themselves in my mind: it was February, and we were in Sydney. What *was* real life, when you lived in a city of beaches, in a country of kangaroos?

I pulled some paperwork from my purse and noted the address of the apartment we'd be moving into tomorrow.

I pointed to it. 'I still think this is a mistake.'

It read 1/2-4 Metropolitan Road, Enmore. This seemed less like an address and more like a math equation, the answer being -3.5 Metropolitan Road.

I felt likewise uncertain about the Enmore bit. When my mother had asked for our mailing address, I'd told her to write Sydney. Back home, she lived in St James, we'd lived in St Vital, my friends lived in Wolseley, Corydon and East Kildonan, but it was all Winnipeg as far as the post office was concerned. Winnipeg was the collection of neighbourhoods packed into its city limits. What was Sydney? The postal definition of a city seemed like a basic question, but I felt as confused as I had in Seoul when my Korean colleagues patiently explained that no, of course the streets didn't have names.

Besides, 'Enmore' wasn't sexy. No-one dreamed of living there. Giving people your Sydney address, however, felt like a mark of success.

Steve glanced at the address, likewise puzzled.

We left the restaurant, still hungry but keen to explore more of King Street. I practically dragged Steve along. Who knew what we might see? A polo-shirted man barbecuing suspiciously oversized shrimp, a gigantic venomous spider, or a dingo eyeing a baby carriage. Nearly everyone had joked about these ancient memes before we left Winnipeg, as if all of Australia's vastness contained only this handful of things.

It was the inverse, I suspected – with Australia so far away, people's brains could only hold a few random, repetitive tropes about it. I wanted to stuff my brain full of Australiana – flat whites and billabongs and so much more.

Consulting his map, Steve led us to the University of Sydney, where I was about to start a one-year Master of Cultural Studies. Because Steve was older than me, and because it had taken so long to convince him to move outside the 25-kilometre radius in which he'd lived his entire thirty-three years, he'd no longer been eligible for a working holiday visa by the time we got married. But there was a solution. If I agreed to pay a mere $27,000 in international student tuition, Steve was legally permitted to tag along on my student visa and work full-time in order to fund the endeavour.

I'd planned to do a master's degree regardless, as a way to kickstart an actual career – in what exactly, I still wasn't sure. But everything had worked out so far, and I trusted that by the time I finished the degree, a clear career path would open up.

We turned into the campus, strolling towards the sandstone quadrangle that beckoned from a hilltop. This was the austere, Oxfordesque building splashed across the university's marketing material. Green lawns surrounded the quad, each blade of grass cut to uniform height. For a moment it felt like we'd been transported to a very sweaty day in England.

Up Over, but Hot

'It feels really … English here,' Steve said, like he'd been reading my mind.

'Do you remember people talking about how English Canada used to be?' It was something I'd heard often, but was always framed in past tense.

He nodded. 'Toronto has some buildings like this.'

Canada and Australia must have been more similar in the past, when they were still English colonies. Now Canada had the United States to define itself in opposition to.

For the first time, I wondered about Australia's identity. Tucked down in the bottom corner of the Pacific, it couldn't still think of itself as English. Could it?

Then I looked up.

Among the quad's run-of-the-mill demonic gargoyles, a kangaroo stared down at us. It wasn't an exaggerated gargoyle kangaroo, just an ordinary roo mixed in with the gothic beasts. Its mouth curved down like it was experiencing digestive discomfort, but it otherwise looked cuddly.

Perched over the front entrance of such a venerable building, the roogoyle promised Australia would be full of surprises.

2

The Other Shoe

I woke with a start in the night, fearing the woman we'd planned to meet that day wouldn't show, that maybe I'd dreamed her up. But she arrived outside the Billabong at 10 am sharp. She was around Steve's age, mid-thirties, with short black hair, a cigarette between her lips, and flowery tattoos poking out from her skirt hem and neckline. Like many Aussie women I'd meet, she was taller than me. She also happened to be a fellow Sydney Uni postgrad student.

'How're you going? I'm Kay.'

I nodded, still confused by the question. *Going where?* She shook my outstretched hand, then Steve's.

'The place is this way.'

Kay was our one bit of good luck. Back in Winnipeg, Steve had started searching for an apartment in Sydney. As he showed me a few possibilities, I'd glanced at the rental rates.

'$450? That's pretty good.'

'That's per week.'

'Per week? Who charges rent by the week?' I thought a second further. 'That's $1800 a month!'

'It's $1950 a month. Because there's fifty-two weeks in a— '

'That's insane!' In Winnipeg, the rent on Steve's two-bedroom apartment had been $650 a month. The mortgage on our three-bedroom house was $775 a month. 'Who charges rent by the week?' I repeated, feeling dizzy.

By then it was too late. We'd paid my tuition and booked our flights. We were going to have to live in Sydney somehow, perhaps in the back of one of those dwarfish trucks I'd learned were called utes.

Thankfully we found Kay online. Her PhD research was taking her overseas for a few months, and she was subletting her apartment for the more humane price of $250 a week. We couldn't afford to be suspicious.

We trailed Kay down King Street, me staggering under the weight of my backpack. Humidity thickened the air and washed out the sky.

'Let me give you the grand tour.' Kay shouted at us over her shoulder, competing with the rumble of four lanes of traffic. She pointed out a twenty-four-hour bakery, a gym adorned with rainbow flags, a local food co-op.

'And that is *the* tattoo place, I highly recommend them.' If Kay had noted the lack of visible tattoos on Steve and me, perhaps she assumed ours were more privately situated. I might have had a tattoo if not for a fear of needles, but the Pope will be showing off his ink before Steve considers one.

A flash of white caught my eye. A flock of bald birds, their faces like old men, crept in loose formation across a stretch of park space. Black beaks sprouted like curved tongs from their undersized heads, and their feathers were greasy and stained. They snuck through the grass with ginger steps like they were leaving the scene of a crime. One of the alien birds turned its narrow head, catching my eye. My heart bounded.

'What are those?!'

Kay shrugged without slowing. 'Bin chickens.'

We split onto Enmore Road. A few blocks on, Kay paused in front of a chicken shop that occupied the ground floor of a two-storey building painted a creamy yellow. 'Here we are.'

We rounded the corner onto Metropolitan Road, where Kay opened a door indecisively marked 2-4. We followed her up a narrow staircase, my pack threatening to topple me backwards. At the top of the stairs, Kay swung open another door.

'Like I said on the phone, it's cheap because it's crap as.'

As what? Kay had emphasised this point via email as well, but glancing around, the place seemed fine. As the photos had promised, there was a dark wood table with benches in the kitchen, a bedroom area sectioned off from the living room by a rose-gold curtain, and two dark leather couches that had let themselves go. Surprisingly, considering its location directly above the chicken shop, there wasn't a whiff of chicken.

'Let me show you the bathroom.'

Steve and I dropped our backpacks to the floor and followed. The black-and-white-tiled room was just large enough for the three of us to stand inside without being forced into a group hug.

Kay pointed to the high ceiling. A piece of cardboard the size of a bathmat was duct-taped above the sink.

The Other Shoe

'There's heaps of pigeons living up there and their shit has corroded the ceiling. A few weeks ago a pile of it crashed into the sink.'

Ah, I thought. Sometimes when the other shoe drops, it's full of pigeon shit.

'And the cardboard is supposed to stop that?' Steve asked, his eyes fixed on the duct tape.

'A bloke came, stuck that up and said he'd come back. That was last week.' She narrowed her eyes. 'So remember, when the tradie comes back, you're mates taking care of the place for me, yeah?'

We didn't know what a tradie was, but even considering the potential biohazard, this was all we could afford. Steve's face was grave. The cooing of pigeons and scratching of clawed feet filled the silence. We nodded.

Kay looked up again. 'I just hope the bloke will come back before any more shit starts raining down.'

~

'Okay, it's not ideal,' I said when Kay left. 'But look, we're here! We started planning this, what, two years ago? And now we're in Australia, together!' I wrapped my arms around Steve's chest and kissed his stubbly cheek. For a moment, he melted into the hug. I felt centred in the world, calm and comforted.

Then he pulled away.

'I should start checking out jobs.' He dug our laptop out of his bag. My guts tightened, as if I were bracing, and my teeth sunk into my bottom lip. I went into the other room to give Steve some time alone.

Back in Winnipeg, he'd had recruiters calling him, begging him to hear them out about some new position. In Canada he could have had a new job by the end of the day. But we'd arrived in Australia not knowing anyone. It would take him time to settle in, make useful contacts, and apply for jobs, so we'd budgeted for him to be unemployed for three months. That, I'd later learn, was longer than the term of several Australian prime ministers.

The only thing for me to do was unpack the crumpled contents of our backpacks. Through the open windows, screeching brakes, honking car horns, and the insistent pulsing of the crosswalk signal melded into a symphony of urban angst. Boisterous conversations escaped from mouths crammed with roast chicken. The noise crept under my skin, a constant agitation.

I thought of the stylish bungalow Steve had bought in Winnipeg, tucked away on a quiet residential street. There, both before and after our wedding, we'd shared meals with our parents and hosted parties with friends.

Then I thought of how much time I had spent lying on the kitchen floor of that house, crying. I'd called it seasonal affective disorder, though it had lasted well into summer. The misery that sat on me like a physical weight, the panic that sizzled through me whenever I thought about the future – I'd left that all behind in Winnipeg. 'Australia' was practically a synonym for happiness.

I shoved a handful of socks into a drawer. Reaching into the bottom of my backpack, I found my journal and the heavy notebooks I'd refused to risk shipping with the rest of our clothes. They summarised interviews I'd done in Canada with my father's family, the beginnings of a book I wasn't sure I could write, but

The Other Shoe

that might follow on from the thesis I was about to attempt.

Movement in my peripheral vision caught my attention. I jerked my head and screamed.

Steve sprinted through the doorway. 'What is it?'

The curtain separating the lounge space from the bed hung from a taut wire. A massive brown insect was scaling it like a tightrope. It made awkward progress, clinging to the wire every few seconds as its various legs slipped off.

I barred my teeth. 'Is that a cockroach?'

'Looks like it,' Steve said. Taking a shoe, he knocked the bug to the floor. It scuttled towards me and I jumped onto the couch. One benefit of Winnipeg's extreme cold was a lack of roaches (though it compensated for this with black swarms of disease-bearing mosquitoes in the warmer months). I'd battled ant infestations in Mexico, but never roaches.

And this wasn't any roach. It was the Godzilla of roaches.

Steve karate-chopped the shoe down on Roachzilla. I expected it to shake itself off and scramble away. Instead, creamy yellow roach puree, the same shade as the building paint, coated the shoe sole and puddled around the crunchy corpse.

'Are you sure it's a cockroach? I thought you couldn't kill them.'

'It looks pretty dead.'

'Haven't you heard that about roaches – you can't kill them?'

Another roach, less monstrously sized, crawled from under the dresser. Steve raised an eyebrow at me. 'I'll let you deal with that one.' He headed back to the kitchen.

I sank onto the couch. I thought again of our house in Winnipeg, the stained-glass windows in the living room, the maple tree we'd planted in the backyard, the spacious deck my dad had built off the kitchen as our wedding present. The lack of cockroaches. We'd sold the house to fund my tuition and, in turn, our new life here. To me, a house was the prison you paid for, but not to Steve. Even when we'd spent our weekends painting the basement or replanting the lawn, he'd taken genuine delight in the house.

It wasn't until the taste of iron hit my tongue that I noticed I'd been chewing my lip.

~

After unpacking, I headed to the kitchen, hoping Steve had found some jobs he was excited about. I knew this apartment would drive him nuts, that we'd have to move somewhere quieter and less vermin-infested as soon as we could afford it. Still, there was something electric about being at the centre of so much urban hubbub. If I'd been here on my own, I might have still felt the burbling excitement of our King Street walk.

But there was Steve, looking like he'd been smacked in the face by a two-hole punch. I sat beside him at the table. Overhead, the ceiling pigeons cooed and jostled.

'How's the job search going?'

'Terrible.'

'What?' My heart twitched. 'I thought there were lots of accounting jobs.'

'There are. But I have to write some kind of essay to apply.'

I frowned. Steve pushed the laptop towards me, showing me his attempt to structure a paragraph describing his spreadsheet

The Other Shoe

formatting abilities. Most Canadian job applications required a cover letter and a multi-page resume. Both required tailoring to fit specific application requirements, but since the cover letter was a maximum of one page, you could do this fairly efficiently, even if you were an accountant who found concepts like grammar and punctuation as cryptic as UFO blueprints. Here, however, the job application process, and specifically the additional selection criteria component, seemed to have been designed by Satan, or one of his more competent interns.

'You have to do this for every application?' I leaned back from the screen, stunned.

Steve sighed, then pulled the laptop back and resumed typing.

~

Cleaning up after dinner, I realised the brown crumbs scattered across the kitchen countertops were tiny roaches. When I brushed my teeth, a thumbnail-sized roach crawled out of the bathroom drain. Climbing into bed, I pulled back the covers, and there was another Mothra-sized roach, crawling across my pillow. It was like we were invading *their* space, not the other way round. I couldn't stop thinking about that episode of *ER* when Noah Wylie extracts a live cockroach from a patient's inner ear.

'Are you still working?' I called.

'Yep.'

'Okay, goodnight.' I waited for a response. 'Goodnight!'

'Go to sleep.'

'Goodnight to you, too, sweetheart,' I grumbled to myself, pulling the sheet over my head for added roach protection.

Suddenly I remembered the date. We'd arrived in Sydney on 12 February and spent two nights at the Billabong Hostel, which made today 14 February. We weren't into Valentine's Day gifts or cards (the best gift was saving money), but Steve and I normally did something to celebrate. I thought about going back to the kitchen to let him know we'd missed it. Then I recalled the look on his face, his sunken eyes and tight, downturned mouth.

He was barely recognisable as the handsome man in the long-tailed tuxedo I'd married little more than a year ago at a national park called The Forks, where Winnipeg's two rivers meet. The spot was beautiful except for the murky brown rivers, which featured agricultural washout and sewage overflow that could sometimes be smelled several hundred metres away. 'You'll be upwind from the river,' the man who organised the ceremony assured us. He was right, and the day had been a joyous blur of orange bridesmaid dresses, fresh-cut gladiolas and a piñata iced in white crepe paper that was easily mistaken for a genuine, four-tiered wedding cake until we strung it from the ceiling and let its sugary bounty rain down on the dance floor.

Steve had never done this before, I reminded myself. He'd lived rurally until his early twenties, then moved into his grandmother's basement in Winnipeg's lifeless suburbs, and finally into his own suburban apartment, where he'd lived for nearly a decade.

In contrast, I'd lived in three provinces by the time I was four years old.

My breath was coming quick and shallow. I tried to ignore it. Steve would find a job soon, and once he relaxed, I could relax.

The Other Shoe

Right now, the ideal Valentine's gift would be not pestering him.

I must have fallen asleep. Police sirens startled me awake as two cruisers stopped below our window. Steve had come to bed at some point, and now we both went to the window to watch the cops break up a group of brawling drag kings. Kay had mentioned this. It happened weekly, following the local drag king show.

'It's kind of exhilarating, isn't it?' I said. Below us, one woman tackled another and they crashed to the ground, fists and feet flailing.

'What, the pub fight?'

'Living somewhere different.'

'If you say so.' Steve brushed a cockroach off the sheets.

We flopped back into bed, sticky with sweat. The shouts and banging continued below. Bar music thumped. Above us, something skittered.

'Happy Valentine's Day,' I whispered.

If Steve heard me, he didn't reply.

3

Sydneysiding

On our first visit to what Steve and I referred to as downtown Sydney, a pearly white cruise ship was docked in Circular Quay. It dwarfed every other boat in the water, and some of the office buildings as well. The Harbour Bridge and the Opera House flanked the ship, as if this was a tableau arranged for our benefit.

We had come to Australia via Europe. I'd never been, and Steve had only gone once, before we met. Our trip included an off-season cruise from Barcelona with stops in Rome, Athens, Istanbul and Malta. At each stop, I dreaded getting back on the ship. I longed to stay in each destination for a year or two. These places were fascinating and striking, which was why cruise ships stopped there. No cruise ships ever visited Winnipeg. It was a landlocked city in the centre of the continent, but that was beside the point. Winnipeg didn't even have a double-decker bus tour.

'I remember this view from the 2000 Olympics,' Steve said, the sun lighting up his face. 'The Canadian broadcasters couldn't get over how beautiful the city was.'

Sydneysiding

Taking in the busy splendour of Circular Quay, I felt like someone had handed me the crown jewels. Standing here, I could hardly remember the stranger who'd spent her 27th birthday crying under the covers in Winnipeg. Life felt full of promise and delight.

Even the ride from Newtown Station had felt cosmopolitan. Because the Canadian prairies had no commuter trains, my impression of them came from movies set in Europe. Riding the train felt as sophisticated as visiting the Louvre. Sydneysiders like Kay complained about Sydney's transit, but I thought it was wonderful. I'd never get frostbite waiting for a bus, and I could stroll along a shaded train platform like someone who spoke three languages and vacationed in the Alps.

From the quay, we walked across the Harbour Bridge, greedily admiring the skyline, the Opera House eggshells, the lush pocket of the Botanic Garden, the blend of nature and cityscape.

'Are the people here New South Welsh?' Steve asked.

'I guess so?' I'd learned this wasn't the New Wales of the South, but rather a new South Wales. In other words, the cliffs around the harbour had reminded Captain Cook specifically of the south of Wales. This explained the lack of resemblance to anything else in Original Wales, one of the stops on our European jaunt.

Australia, it seemed, was full of mysteries to puzzle through.

We returned over the Harbour Bridge, traffic rattling the girders, the salt-scented wind tousling my hair into knots. The cruise ship horn bellowed, three long mournful blares as it pulled out of the harbour. *Those poor people on the ship,* I thought, *sailing away from all this.*

~

As the summer heat roasted the city, I settled into the routine of classes and thesis research, as well as the online course I was running for the University of Winnipeg. Steve applied for dozens of jobs. So far every email response he'd received had included the word 'unfortunately'. Thinking about this, my chest ached, as if there were a metal band around my ribs, cinching ever tighter.

To celebrate our first month in Sydney, we returned to Circular Quay. The university's international student orientation day had featured a Welcome to Country, where I'd learned we were on the traditional lands of the Gadigal people of the Eora Nation. If First Nations groups had a similar custom in North America, it hadn't been integrated into Canadian society. Looking out to the harbour and wondering what life was like when only Gadigal people lived here, I realised I didn't know which tribes had traditionally called the land that was now Winnipeg home. The Cree? The Ojibwe?

Across the water, packs of ant-like figures scaled the Harbour Bridge. Yellow and green ferries rocked against the wharves as passengers boarded. People posed for photos with the Opera House and the bridge. Their happiness felt contagious. I made a game of guessing, from their displays of enthusiasm and the width of the smiles, who was here for the first time, perhaps achieving a long-cherished dream or life goal – to be in this city, with this view. It was no-one's life goal to visit Winnipeg.

Trying to broaden my perspective on our new city, I'd started Peter Carey's *30 Days in Sydney*. But I'd thrown the book to the floor when Carey noted a friend's comment: you're not a true citizen of Sydney unless you own a boat.

I struggled with Delia Falconer's *Sydney*, too, blinking in confusion when she described the city as haunted, with 'an attachment to the feral, undisciplined and harsh'. Steve and I thought we were holding the crown jewels, and along came Falconer to tell us those jewels were hollowed out and filled with maggots.

We were charmed by Sydney's waterways and 'bush'. In Falconer's view, all this messy nature made it hard to determine where the city began and ended. She described a city I didn't recognise. 'No other major city is as penetrated by remnant wilderness as Sydney.' I thought of Kuala Lumpur, where the jungle seemed determined to reclaim the city, to subsume it. In contrast, Sydney's natural setting felt harmonious.

Falconer's kicker was this: 'It has been hard, at times, for its inhabitants to believe that they live in a "real" metropolis.' She pinpointed a 'niggling insecurity about whether Sydney is truly a city'. The place she described felt a universe apart from the city I was in now, a city that featured the world's most famous opera house, regular cruise ship visits, and the skyscraper that blew up in *The Matrix*. (Number of tallish Winnipeg buildings fictionally destroyed in Hollywood productions? Zero.)

From that first visit to the inelegantly termed 'CBD', I pondered Falconer's perspective as Steve and I explored her city. Because of our mortification of spending any money until Steve found a job, we spent our free time pursuing the cheapest hobby going: walking. We strolled the golden expanse of Bondi Beach hand in hand, like I'd envisioned for years. Feeling the sand under my feet, I tried to telepathically reach back to the version of myself lying frozen in that snow bank, to assure her everything would work out.

Baffled both by Sydney's unpredictable streets and by our instinctive sense of direction insisting that the sun transited across the southern half of the sky, we were often lost. Still, we rambled past the tombstones of Waverley Cemetery to Coogee, marvelling at the individual character of each beach. We trekked further south to Maroubra, along more beaches, where the houses became less ostentatious. We crossed the harbour on the Taronga Zoo ferry, bypassing the zoo itself because we assumed, based on the entrance fee, that the animals each had personal butlers. Instead we walked the North Shore coastline, past the mansions of Mosman, gazing across the harbour to the Opera House and the Sydney skyline from a dozen vantages, the golden bulb of Sydney Tower often peeking over a hill to orientate us. We crossed the unfortunately named Spit Bridge, a setting so distractingly breathtaking, I was surprised none of the cars whizzing past crashed through the barricades and into the water. Were the drivers accustomed to this view?

In Manly, we were astounded to discover we could keep going, to Freshwater Beach and on over the rising cliffs and sandy interludes another 28 kilometres north to Palm Beach.

From our first view of the harbour, we thought Sydney was the most glorious city in the world. Our ambulatory explorations proved us right.

Granted, with its two yellow-brown rivers, flat nothingness, and an aesthetic that a fellow Winnipegger once described as 'a poverty of vision', our hometown might not have been much for comparison. But Steve and I had done our share of travelling before we rocked up in Australia. Sure, Chicago had more impressive skyscrapers, Mexico City would win on public art, and Barcelona was infused with the vision of Gaudí. Sydney, however, had an effortless beauty I'd never encountered before.

I struggled to imagine the city of Falconer's youth, the harbour grey with pollution from industrial use, downtown buildings left empty and crumbling, the wheat-filled goods trains and warehouses abandoned around Blackwattle Bay.

Still, I learned from her. 'Perhaps the most wonderful thing about Sydney during those years was the unauthorised uses neglect encouraged.' One of these was 'bridging' – clambering up the Harbour Bridge supports after dark. Here was something definitively Australian: romanticising a life-threatening activity. The more one risked death, I realised, the greater the accomplishment staying alive became.

I came to understand our biohazardous apartment as a glimpse into another quintessentially Australian experience: the filth-ridden share house. Canada has no equivalent. Some Canadians share houses (with 'roommates', although I now realised how inaccurate the term is, since roommates almost always have individual rooms), and some live in poor conditions. But the relative squalidness of others' living conditions are of little interest to most Canadians, and if they were to delve into them, people would be disgusted and perplexed. Raise the topic of biohazardous share houses in Australia, as I'd come to learn, and many people would gleefully relate a time in their youth when the pride of their living conditions was a curation of rotting food and a mould build-up that had evolved from vegetable to animal. This cultural touchstone, the 'fetish of filth', was also nostalgic for Falconer. She described the dismal living conditions of her young adulthood wistfully. I thought she was nuts. But what were a few hundred cockroaches spread through our Newtown apartment? (And presumably the chicken shop below; we never did eat there.) The sign of a true infestation was walls that shimmered in the moonlight. Maybe this was another aspect of the national survival ethos – if you had to live in an urban centre and not in the life-threatening bush, you could at least risk death through mould inhalation.

~

As the cultural chasm between Australia and Canada widened, a niggling insecurity began, a psychological scratch just under the level of consciousness. The more I learned about Australia, the less I understood it.

In our first month though, everything sparkled, new and exciting.

'What's that coffee called?' Steve asked as we stood in line at a cafe. 'A plain white?'

We were postponing celebratory drinks until he found a job. Instead, we ordered flat whites. I also indulged in the most delicious surprise I'd encountered in Sydney so far – caramel slices. The thick caramel, chocolate top and crumbly base made for creamy bliss, the epicurean equivalent of the gleeful rush the city gave me.

'And I'll have one of those buns,' Steve said at the cafe counter, pointing to a scroll with chocolate swirled into its crevices.

Sydneysiding

'Cheers,' I said, and we tapped our takeaway cups together. He smiled, but not as broadly as that first day at Circular Quay.

We found a bench near the Opera House, angled towards the bridge. Steve stared into the distance, not saying much. I wondered again what was going on inside his head. If I asked, he'd only rehash his frustrations about the job search. A twinge of pain shot through my jaw, a knot of tension forming. Steve bit into his scroll. His face turned sour and he jerked away, holding the bun at arm's length. 'This has gone bad.'

'How does a chocolate scroll go bad?' I sniffed it, getting a heady whiff of something that was not chocolate. Tearing off a tiny corner, I touched my tongue to it and got a bitter, salty jolt.

'This might be Vegemite.'

'Why would they ruin a bun like that?' He took a sniff himself, then tossed it in the garbage. Two seagulls squawked in protest.

Steve sipped his flat white. 'At least the coffee's good.'

Settling into silence, we took in the bustle of Circular Quay, the city's beating heart. Joy swelled through me. For the next year, this was all a quick train ride away.

In reading about the city, however, one thing had become clear: my bursting love for Sydney went against the ethos of our new home. 'Join our lightheartedness … or be too serious at your peril,' Falconer warned. 'Sydney is allergic to earnestness.'

So let me try to express my deep feelings about this incredible city in a more culturally appropriate way.

Ahem.

Yeah, Sydney's all right I guess.

How to Be Australian

~

By mid-April, a chill had set in, and grey rain sloshed over the city. It was Friday, and as usual, I spent the morning in Fisher Library reading dense philosophical arguments and scratching out thesis notes. I'd narrowed my topic to diasporan cultural identity – in other words, how a cultural group dispersed from its homeland attempts to maintain its unique identity. The global Jewish community was the classic example of diaspora, but my research focused on Armenians. Or would, if I could make any progress with it.

Through March, the stress of Steve's job search had masked the stress of my classes, like one bad odour covering another.

My bachelor's degree in journalism hadn't required any essays longer than a few thousand words. Maybe that was why this 14,000-word thesis made me feel like I was caught in an academic riptide, struggling not to drown.

In the afternoon, I headed into the frigid rain, hurrying to my supervisor's office. The cultural studies department was in the Oxfordesque quad, the one Steve and I had discovered on our first day in Sydney. I passed under the roogoyle, taking several wrong turns through the quad's labyrinthine corridors before finding the right door.

Professor Wilson called me inside, gesturing for me to sit. Then she turned her attention back to her computer, to finish whatever was more important than talking with me. I clutched my hands in my lap, trying not to tear my cuticles. A small orange sofa gave the high-ceilinged, book-strewn room a touch

32

of personality, but our meeting wasn't sofa-based. Instead, I sat across the desk, my attention focused keenly on the human embodiment of my academic distress.

She signed off her emails with 'Regards, Bron', a strange mix of formality and casualness. She'd worn summer dresses until the weather had turned, and then switched to jeans and layered shirts. The teaching staff's casual dress code delighted me. *Look how relaxed we Australians are*, it announced. But I was habituated to addressing professors more formally, and when she insisted on Bron, I avoided addressing her by name. She was from Brisbane, but her accent was mild, more English to my ear than Australian. She made up for this by using a variety of cryptic phrases, like 'knock-on effect', 'fortnight' and 'take a squiz'. I guessed their respective meanings as the startled feeling of an unexpected knock at the door, a night measured with military precision, and something toilet related.

Professor Wilson turned to me, clasping her bony hands on the desk and smiling as though it pained her. 'What can I help you with today?'

'I was hoping to ask about the grade on my last assessment.' I held the stapled pages out to her, an assignment in the thesis preparation course she also taught.

She glanced at the paper, but didn't take it. 'What's the issue?'

The issue was obvious – I'd barely scraped by with a credit. We were ostensibly speaking the same language, but the more meetings we had, the less I felt like she was understanding me. Maybe it was time to be more upfront.

'Look, I've always done well in classes. I won the university gold medal for the highest grades in my undergraduate program.'

Her eyes widened. *I must be getting through to her.* Her face remained tense and pensive while I went on about how I was working hard, but I felt like I was missing something.

'And how's your research progressing?'

I updated her on my thesis. She responded by listing a few theorists and books to consider. They were the same ones she'd suggested last month.

I was about to point this out, but her phone rang and she excused me from her office abruptly. If she noticed the dismay on my face, she skilfully ignored it.

I trudged down the stone stairs, still holding my paper with its shameful grade.

~

Coming around a corner in the quad, I ran into Noelle Kurland, who I recognised from a few of my lectures. She was standing in one of the sandstone archways, staring at the pounding rain.

'Ashley, hi.' She waved me over. 'I'm not too keen to head home in this. Want to grab a coffee?'

We opened our umbrellas and dashed into the rain.

I'd assumed my classmates would be mainly locals, but it was more common for Aussies to jump from honours to PhD studies; my master's program was almost entirely international students, Noelle among them. She had a quiet, thoughtful manner, and offered insightful comments in class. I was chuffed by her invitation; I'd assumed I wasn't interesting enough for her. Noelle was born in Uruguay, but her parents had worked around the world. During her school years, her family had lived in Chile, Germany and Brazil. She'd attended university in Boston, married an American, and moved to New York. She and her husband had arrived in Australia a year ago. Her global upbringing made my three years in Asia and Latin America seem paltry.

Noelle led the way, bypassing the closest cafe for another further on.

'This is my favourite place.' She dropped her sodden umbrella into a bucket by the entrance. 'It has the thickest caramel slices.'

We were going to get along just fine.

We ordered coffees and a slice each, and took a seat by the window. Noelle was right. The caramel was a solid block, and the chocolate topping had beach-like ripples adorned with a few delicate salt flakes.

'So how did you end up in cultural studies?' I asked.

'I'd worked in marketing for a few years and thought it was time for a career shift. This seemed interesting.' She gave her coffee a stir. 'How about you?'

'I'm considering writing a book about the legacy of the Armenian genocide. My great-grandparents were survivors. I thought this degree might be helpful. My husband thinks I'd make a good professor, but I think I ... might like to be a writer.' The only consolation for sacrificing my nomadic lifestyle for Steve – other than marrying the person I loved most in the world – was that I'd decided to take a risk and pursue the career I'd dreamed of since childhood. 'Anyway,' I said quickly, 'how's your thesis going?'

Noelle was researching the concept of home for people like herself, who'd lived in multiple countries. It turned out we had the same supervisor. I mentioned the meeting I'd just left, and how Bronwyn kept suggesting I look at the same books.

'Maybe it's not a suggestion.'

I frowned. 'She says "You might want to take a look at so-and-so." I did take a look. Then I moved on.'

'But if she's directing you to the same people every time ...'

'If I have to include them, why wouldn't she just say that?' Exasperation swelled in my voice. If I couldn't figure out what Bronwyn wanted, I had no hope of writing a passable thesis. For the first time it occurred to me that I could pay $27,000 and not end up with a degree. Pain crunched through my shoulders as my whole body tensed.

Noelle took a bite of her caramel slice. 'I don't find her hard to talk to. I had a good chat with her a few weeks ago. We came here for coffee. Arrived too late though – they had sold out of slices.'

'You went for coffee with Bronwyn?'

'I assumed she did that for all her thesis students.'

'She seems to grit her teeth around me.'

Noelle tapped her spoon against her coffee cup. 'She's so nice though. I can't see why she'd have an issue with you.'

'Me either! I won a university gold medal in my BA, and now I'm getting Cs. I tried to explain that to her, but it's like we're speaking different languages.'

Noelle's eyes widened at this, just as Bronwyn's had. 'You told her you won a gold medal?'

When I nodded, she started to laugh, then put her hand to her mouth when she saw my confusion.

'Have you heard of tall poppy syndrome?'

It sounded like a disease.

'I think I know why you got on her nerves.' She explained the national disdain for tall poppies. 'It's like Aussies want to … punish anyone who's successful. So when you announce, with your friendly Canadian smile and your natural North American confidence that you won a gold medal –'

'I don't feel confident,' I interrupted. 'That's why I was asking for help.'

'Trust me, when you talk about yourself here, it comes off as brash. I read about it in a cultural guide to Australia – I'll lend it to you, if you want? My husband has the same problem, except it's worse – he's American. Because of the tall poppy thing, Aussies tend to talk themselves down. Listen for it, you'll catch on.'

What a neurotic way to live. I remembered Falconer's admonition – Sydney is allergic to earnestness. I'd oozed earnestness all over Bronwyn's desk, thinking I was sharing contextual facts when, if Noelle was right, I'd just been talking myself up, a tall poppy gone mad.

Maybe I wasn't the one who needed to do the listening.

Then again, I was the outsider here – and I was surprised to find myself feeling that so powerfully. I hadn't fit in when I lived in Asia or Latin America, and I hadn't expected to. Had I assumed Australia was a thawed-out, sun-dried version of Canada, and therefore I would fit in easily? That because I was a white, middle-class Canadian, I could slot into white, middle-class Australia and feel perfectly at home?

~

The pelting rain hadn't slowed. As I said goodbye to Noelle, she mentioned she was planning a daytrip to the Blue Mountains. 'If this rain ever stops, I mean. You should come.'

'Sounds great.' Hoisting our umbrellas, we waved goodbye and darted in opposite directions.

My shoes were soaked through before I made it across campus. I sloshed along King Street, despondent at the thought of returning to the apartment. My enthusiasm for our new life was crumbling in the face of Steve's job hunt, my thesis struggles, the constant cockroaches, our lack of sleep. We tried to reassure ourselves — everything would be better when he was employed, when we could afford a different apartment, when I figured out my thesis, when, when, when. I was twenty-seven and still waiting for life to properly start.

Steve had now applied for 120 jobs. He knew the figure exactly, because he tracked his applications in Excel to prevent himself from suffering spreadsheet withdrawal. He'd also met with several recruiters. But he hadn't had a single interview.

The lack of interest in Steve as a potential employee baffled us. Australia was supposedly in need of experienced accountants, and Steve's CV was nothing but accounting. Was there some secret job application code we didn't know about? Was his cover letter supposed to mention drop bears?

Vehicles splashed past. The wind grabbed my umbrella and flipped it inside out, breaking two of its flimsy arms. I tossed the umbrella in the trash — the 'rubbish', I reminded myself — and dashed under the shop awnings. The cafes closed mysteriously early, but the bars were open, and through the windows, patrons sipped pale ale and swirled pinot gris. A passer-by pushed open a pub door, and the smell of beer rushed out, mingling with the rain.

Stopping for a drink was tempting, but I'd already spent too much on the coffee and caramel slice. Our budget was getting tighter by the day. Steve had started bringing home on-the-verge-of-expired discount groceries from the Marrickville mall (the one that closed at 5 pm like it was definitely the 1950s). We set our change aside for bus fares. And we were barely drinking, perhaps the most un-Australian thing we could do.

Outside a newsstand, the papers offered variations on the same daily headlines, Prime Minister Julia Gillard and Opposition Leader Tony Abbott snarling at each other, as though the nation's parents were in the midst of a nasty divorce.

Too soon I'd reached Metropolitan Street, the meaty scent of roast chicken filling the air.

I climbed the narrow stairs, stopping outside our apartment door to squeeze my eyes shut and silently wish for good news before sliding my key in the lock.

'I'm home!' I pumped faux-cheer into my voice.

As usual, Steve sat hunched in front of the laptop at the kitchen table. Today though, his head was in his hands and the laptop screen was blank. I'd quit asking if he'd gotten any job-related calls. Instead I smiled and said, in a disgraceful attempt at an Aussie accent, 'How're you going?' I hoped Steve would respond with our private response, 'by foot', or at least a laugh.

He didn't laugh. Lately he'd been laughing less and less, and not smiling much either. Or leaving the house. Or wearing clean clothes.

His funk had come on gradually, like the shifting seasons. Suddenly, I recognised the despair in his eyes as the same look I'd had through Winnipeg winters.

How was this possible? Depression was my thing. If Steve was depressed, the whole universe was at risk of becoming destabilised. I put my hands on the table to steady myself.

In the decade I'd known Steve, he'd been a poster boy for stable mental health. I'd been both envious of this and frustrated by it. He never understood my low moods. He'd sit on the floor with me when I cried, he'd stay home when I needed him, but when I tried to explain, his eyes glazed over. Maybe now he'd be able to better relate to me, if things got bad again. Maybe in the long run, this would be good for us. As long as Steve got a job and psychologically recovered enough not to hold it against me.

'Maybe we could go to the pub up the street, the Bank Hotel?'

Steve had sat in the apartment staring at the laptop all week, like every other week since my classes had begun. Whenever I'd started to feel down in Winnipeg, he'd encouraged me to go out. Occasionally this had resulted in me curled in child's pose, crying through a yoga class. Often though, a change of scenery could distract me from myself, at least for a while.

He said nothing. Outside, traffic splashed through the growing kerbside puddles. The ceiling pigeons scratched and flapped.

'I got paid yesterday. We could go for a beer. One wouldn't be a big deal.' I was only teaching one online course ten hours a week, but it was keeping us afloat for now.

Steve sighed. His elbows were still on the kitchen table, his head still in his hands.

'C'mon, don't give me the silent treatment.' The table had two long benches instead of chairs. I slid in beside him.

'Can you call my cell phone?' It sat beside the laptop.

'They call them mobiles here,' I said before I could stop myself. 'But sure, you mean now?'

He shrugged.

I pulled my phone from my pocket and found his number.

For a half-second after I pressed the green call button, nothing happened.

Time slowed, giving us a glimpse of hope that all these weeks, the problem had been Steve's phone. That was why, after 120 applications, he hadn't received any calls about job interviews. If we simply got the phone fixed, he'd be gainfully employed in no time.

The phone rang. It cut through the room like a scythe.

I ended the call. The pigeons seemed to sense the tension and hushed their cooing.

Finally Steve looked at me. Deep purple circles lined his eyes, and his shoulders slumped lower.

'I need to start thinking about going back to Canada.'

I huffed out a startled breath and grabbed his arm. 'The three months aren't up yet!'

'What's the point?' His face sank closer to the table. 'I could apply for 500 jobs. I haven't gotten a single call.'

I couldn't argue with that. A cockroach scuttled across the table. Neither of us reacted.

'You can stay and finish your degree,' Steve said. 'I'll find a job back home and we'll figure it out from there.'

My heart spasmed.

How to Be Australian

There's a moment in Guy de Maupassant's *A Woman's Life* when the main character discovers her beloved husband is cheating on her with the maid, and she realises the impossibility of ever knowing what's going on in another person's mind, even a person who sleeps beside you every night. We didn't have a maid for me to worry about, but now I wondered how long Steve had been thinking about going back to Canada without me.

This was my fault. I should have researched the cost of living in Sydney, should have figured out which city would have the best job opportunities for Steve. I'd thought only about finding a suitable degree program. In hindsight, a better choice would have been literally any program in Melbourne, where rent was less extreme. Or I could have applied in Perth, assuming it had a university. Instead I'd brought us to one of the most expensive cities in the world, blithely assuming Steve would be fine.

But maybe Steve wasn't regretting Australia – maybe he was regretting me. He tolerated interpersonal conflict like the average person tolerated a house full of wasps. If Steve had decided he was unhappy with me, moving back to Canada would be a perfect exit strategy, letting time and distance soften the blow when he delivered the bad news, an entire ocean shielding him from the messy barrage of my emotions.

I wrapped my arms around his shoulders, as though everything would work out if only I could hug him hard enough. How could he think about leaving? We hadn't even seen a kangaroo.

'Please wait at least – at least one more week.'

'Um, you're crushing my chest.'

I slackened but didn't let go. 'Please?'

42

4

The Hollywood Kookaburra Con

On Monday morning, I headed across campus towards the quad, where my cultural diversity class took place in a lecture hall decorated with murals of old white men. Steve had agreed to wait one more week before he shifted his job search to Canada.

Maybe it would be better to move back with Steve before his job hunt destroyed him. His self-worth was deeply entrenched in his professional identity, and that identity was proving meaningless in Australia. But moving back would mean withdrawing from my program and sacrificing the tuition we'd paid. I could finish my thesis by distance, but not the coursework.

More than that, it would mean accepting defeat. *If we go back to Canada now*, I thought, *that would be it*. I'd never convince Steve to move anywhere ever again. My chest tightened, my lungs constricted.

That's when I heard it. The noise came from the trees behind me. Starting low, it grew louder, filling the air.

A pack of monkeys! That's what the raucous hooting must be, my brain deduced. I froze, one foot mid-stride. Was I back in the

Mexican jungle, the last place I'd heard monkeys? I scanned the park, seeing nothing.

The ruckus stopped.

Huh. I didn't know Australia had monkeys. They must be invasive, another creature the British had imported, probably because they made for lively hunting, or because monkey fur garter belts were all the rage among 1830s society ladies.

I started to walk away, my mind spiralling back to Steve, to my thesis, to my bad grades. But within a few steps, I was interrupted by a thought too powerful to contemplate while in motion, and I stopped again.

That wasn't monkeys. *It must have been kookaburras!*

Pulling my phone from my pocket, I called Steve. 'I just heard kookaburras!'

'I'm in the middle of a job application, is this important?'

I sighed. This was classic Steve. He'd never come out and say that he was feeling stressed. Instead he'd passive-aggressively pretend that kookaburras weren't worth getting excited about.

But they were.

Growing up in Canada, I'd heard of kookaburras, but that did nothing to prepare me for the wondrous, bounding monkey laughter that was still filling the air. At that moment under grey skies on the University of Sydney campus, it was the soundtrack of pure delight.

I'd later discover that kookaburra laughter was part of the literal soundtrack of jungle scene-setting in numerous movies, from *Raiders of the Lost Ark* to *Jurassic Park* to *Jumanji*. At some point, a Hollywood producer decided kookaburras sounded more

44

The Hollywood Kookaburra Con

like monkeys than monkeys themselves, and they've been creating jungle ambiance in American blockbusters ever since. Hence why, having grown up on pop culture, I was so sure I'd heard monkeys that day.

~

Some Australian animals were more familiar to me. In every animal alphabet book of my childhood, K was for kangaroo or koala. The global fame of a handful of Aussie animals meant Steve and I supposed we knew something of Australia when we arrived.

And, in a way, we were right; our knowledge of the country's natural diversity was as sophisticated as a child's alphabet book. Fearing my year in Sydney might be cut short, I strived to change that.

It started with the birds, those fabulous strutting ibises I'd spotted in Newtown. I'd long considered birdwatching a hobby for people who couldn't find any wet paint to entertain themselves with. Winnipeg's avian soundtrack ranges from the crow's grating *caw* to the more distinctive *chick-a-dee-dee-dee*, with generic cheeps and twitters in between. In other words, the birds sound like birds. In winter they mostly vanish, though the occasional sparrow can be seen puffed-up and shivering on a bare branch. Plumage-wise, the Canadian prairies have a few stand-outs – majestic red cardinals, handsome but cranky blue jays, the darting yellow streak of a gold finch. But I rarely saw these, and took their reclusion personally.

In contrast, Australian birds refused to be ignored. Their neon rainbow plumage demanded attention, as did their dawn to dusk trilling. *Listen to our madcappery! Are we capuchins? Pterodactyls?*

45

A time-travel sound effect in a cartoon? How could anyone resist becoming a twitcher in Australia?

Steve and I needed a common vocabulary to discuss the avian brilliance around us. We developed a shorthand that included clacka-clackas, groaner birds, krunkies and sci-fi birds. Over time I discovered that the pair of long-legged sneaks silently creeping across the grass and piercing the sky with their *clacka clacka clacka* were masked lapwings. The bird groaning mournfully like his girlfriend had left him for his brother was a raven, though they sounded nothing like Canada's ravens. And the bird that sounded like a car engine refusing to turn over, the grinding *kr-unk*, was the wattlebird.

For months we knew the sci-fi birds by call only, their distinctive time-travel sound effect. Finally on one of our bird-spotting walks, a magpie looked us in the eyes, cocked its head, and made the time-travel sound. Up close, its call was so complexly melodic, I would have believed this was an alien species asking its companions what the bleating noises coming out of these pale, flightless flesh creatures could signify.

The trees took longer to grab my attention. At first, they didn't factor into our conversations beyond, 'Wow, a lot of these trees have some sort of bark disease.'

I once would have said that a tree is a tree is a tree. As an elementary school student on the prairies, I'd had to collect leaves, glue them to paper, and draw and label the trees those leaves were once part of, like the world's most boring *CSI* episode. The exercise ensured that my adult self knew Canada's birch and oak, pine and Douglas fir. Still, I was accustomed to these trees. They filled the background like TV re-runs. For the three weeks of the typical prairie autumn, some trees put on a colourful show before dumping their leaves in a frost-induced panic. The spruce, pine and cedar, however, looked the same all year. They weren't even trying.

Australian trees burst into brash, vivid bloom in a year-round show. But I was tree-illiterate. Walking through my neighbourhood surrounded by anonymous greenery was a reminder that I was a stranger here. No-one in Sydney was going to force me to collect leaf samples and label them, though I wished they would. I kept telling myself I'd buy a book on Australian trees, but I was drowning in academic theory.

'Do you think they'd let me audit a grade three class for a few days?' I asked Steve towards the end of May, peering at him from behind the textbooks piled on the kitchen table. 'Just to learn about the birds and the trees?'

'Shhhh!' He pointed to the window and I shut up, alert to the faint cackling of kookaburras.

Of all the flora and fauna we'd encountered in Sydney, the kookaburras enthralled me most. Author David Sedaris described their aesthetic as brutish gym teacher, but to me they had regal airs. I loved their blue-flecked wings, their striped tails and the gorgeous brown streaks fanning back from their eyes, as if they'd gotten carried away with the eye shadow.

Across the street, a pair of the birds swayed on a powerline, calm and self-assured, until they threw their beaks back and laughed with abandon.

Steve and I had never owned a Christmas tree. We rarely bought each other birthday gifts. There wasn't much in the world we held sacred. Yet without discussion, we established a new ritual. Whenever we heard a kookaburra, no matter how far in the distance, we stopped mid-sentence, revelling in the sublime sound.

Now, we held our breath in the kitchen, heads cocked, as the brassy laughter filled the air with the holiness of a reverberating gong.

I glanced at Steve's entranced face, and my joy faded, replaced by a longing that sat heavy on my chest. *This is what our time in Australia could be*, I thought, *if only things worked out*.

~

Exactly three months after we arrived, Steve's taciturn cell phone rang. He'd applied for an accounting position with the State Government, and only now, two months later, were they finally responding to applicants. He ironed a checked dress shirt, I kissed him good luck, and he went off to the interview.

Later that week, I arrived home from campus to find Steve had changed out of his usual bleach-stained sweatpants and put on jeans and a knit sweater.

'You got the job!' I half-asked, leaping on him. 'When did you find out?'

'They called this morning.'

'You didn't call me! I've been on edge all day.'

He winked. 'I wanted to tell you in person.'

With a regular pay cheque and a server full of spreadsheets to tinker with, Steve returned to his level, pragmatic self. We celebrated by visiting all the King Street restaurants we'd passed longingly for months, and made up for lost time at the cafes and

The Hollywood Kookaburra Con

bars as well. I felt redeemed. I had brought us here and, despite the stress and uncertainty, it was coming good.

We also celebrated by moving to a quieter apartment. I was flat out like a crushed lizard, or whatever the expression was, so Steve went apartment hunting. He found a bright, spacious one-bedroom place in Camperdown, a quieter suburb on the other side of the university. The rent was more than double, there were no nearby train stations, and the elevator played a looped muzak version of the Carpenters' 1973 classic 'Yesterday Once More' (a choice clearly made in response to the question, 'What song will make people wish this elevator would suddenly malfunction and plummet to the ground, killing everyone inside?'). This was all worth it. There were no rapping buskers, no drag king brawls, and no threat of pigeon shit cascading into our mouths as we turned our faces up to gargle.

~

'The Blue Mountains trip is finally happening! Can you make it this weekend?' Noelle asked via email. 'It's a great group. You'll love them.'

I desperately wanted to go out of town with Noelle and her friends, especially because I'd still hardly met any Australians and hadn't established much of a social group.

The trip would take a full day, however, and I didn't have the time. Between moving, attending classes and teaching online, I'd made little progress on my thesis.

'Just go. It's one day,' Steve said. 'You'll be grouchy if you miss out.'

So early on Saturday, I headed to Central Station and boarded the Blue Mountains train.

Noelle and I had started spending a lot of time together on campus, reading each other's essays and thesis drafts, interpreting Bronwyn's feedback, and indulging in caramel slices. Now, seated among a cluster of women, she greeted me warmly and made introductions as the train rattled out of the city. Two of the group were from Italy, the others from Ireland, Belgium, Austria, France and Germany. They were in their late twenties, and with one exception, were fellow postgrad students. We bonded over our difficulties with our thesis supervisors. They seemed lovely, but my lack of Australian friends was beginning to feel strange.

The air was brisk when we disembarked at Katoomba Station, the sky moodily overcast. Noelle had been here before, so we followed her along the town's main street, which plunged into a steep valley. Katoomba looked like it had seen better days. A few of the shopfronts sat empty, and those that were open had dated signage and cracked paint. It was surprising, so close to the Blue Mountains' biggest attraction.

The wind nipped at my ears. Australian winter had apparently started on 1 June. I liked that the seasons changed on the first of the month, rather than on the more random dates of the solstices and equinoxes. According to the Canadian calendar, winter didn't officially start until 21 December, though the cold and snow could settle in by October.

I pulled my toque on. There were some words I couldn't acquiesce to, and beanie was one of them. It sounded like a word for preschoolers.

50

The Hollywood Kookaburra Con

Soon we arrived at Echo Point. At least, according to the sign. Clouds had blown in, obscuring the view of the valley.

'The Three Sisters should be right there.' Noelle pointed to the left, past the handful of tourists milling about in the cold. All I could see was cloud.

'This wasn't worth the trip,' an Italian named Fabrizia said, her voice flat.

But then the clouds shifted and three vegetation-spotted spires jutted out of the hidden valley like ancient skyscrapers. The rock formations were impressive, but what most captured my attention was the magic trick – that something so immense could be hidden right in front of me, then suddenly revealed.

Noelle herded us towards the hiking trail. We passed a sign that read Giant Stairway. I realised I hadn't asked Noelle for any details of this hike.

'How giant is this stairway?'

'Something like 997 steps. Don't worry, we're going down.'

Arranging ourselves in a line, we started down the stairs. Some were carved into the stone, others were ladder-like metal steps drilled into the rock. I stepped carefully. The fog obscured the view below us and, soon, above us as well. The further we descended, the more my thighs burned. Still, it felt good to be moving instead of sitting at a desk. By the time we reached the bottom, trees and ferns surrounded us, offering a reprieve from the biting wind.

Noelle led us along the Federal Pass trail. We drifted into clusters of twos and threes, stopping to take photos of interesting moss, impressive mushrooms and the crimson rosellas that darted through the trees. The forest smelled fresh and woodsy, and was luxuriously quiet, except for occasional bird call. It was as beautiful as any Canadian forest, and with its vivacious parrots, more interesting. I'd never imagined places like this in Australia. I felt a renewed swell of delight at being here.

'So what made you choose Sydney?' I asked Fabrizia.

'Scholarship. I applied to a few places, and this is where I ended up. I've been here three years.'

'How are you liking it?' I asked.

'This country.' Her exasperated huff surprised me. 'You know the first week here, we went to Bondi – you're not allowed beer there. Why? I'm an adult, don't tell me where I can drink.'

I was about to tell her that in Canada you couldn't have open alcohol in public places, with very few exceptions, and what a pleasant surprise it had been in Sydney to see people picnicking in the local parks with sparkling wine.

Elise, our Belgian companion, cut in. 'I adopted a rescue dog when I arrived here, before I knew they had so many stupid laws. She can't go on the train, she can't go to most of the beaches, these national parks,' she gestured around us, a hard jabbing motion. 'She can't even go inside the pubs with me. It's such idiocy.'

'Dogs can go inside pubs in Belgium?'

'Of course! In pubs, restaurants, shopping malls – almost everywhere. Why not?'

'And then they have a parade here, and they put up barricades everywhere, like the people are too stupid to be allowed to cross the street,' Fabrizia said.

'Maybe that's the problem!' Elise said, and they laughed. 'We

52

have to watch what we say now, since our friend started dating an Australian. But really, it's such a police state.'

I had no idea how to respond. Their attitudes were jarring to me, perhaps because they echoed an inherent sense of European superiority that felt outmoded and inappropriate now.

I was spared as we came around a curve in the trail. The creature blocking our path was grey and brown, with an undersized head and a tiny grey beak. It would have been an unassuming bird, except for the grandiose tail feathers folded over its back. If there were a tall poppy among birds, this would be it.

Startled, it scrabbled into the bush, vanishing as quickly as the Three Sisters had appeared.

'Was that a lyrebird?' Fabrizia asked.

'I think so!' Elise replied.

For the first time that day, they sounded impressed.

We marched on, stripping off our jackets and shoving them into our bags.

'What about you?' Fabrizia glanced at me. 'Did you come on a scholarship?'

'I'm more of a climate refugee,' I said, trying for a tongue-in-cheek tone.

She gave me a stinging look. 'What a First World problem. Especially considering this country's offshore processing policies.'

I didn't know what offshore processing referred to, but her accusatory tone made me queasy.

'I just meant I needed to get away from winter,' I said quickly. 'And I wanted my husband to try life outside Canada for a while. You know, broaden his world view.'

Elise laughed. 'You chose Australia to broaden his world view?'

'He wanted to be somewhere English-speaking, for his work.' Even to me, it sounded like a poor reason. These women were each fluent in multiple languages. Canada might be nationally bilingual, but less than 20 per cent of the population was. And that didn't include Steve and me.

The pair didn't say much to me after that. Soon we were dragging ourselves out of the valley. The Furber Steps were less severely vertical than the ones we'd descended, but they had to get us back to our original altitude. I huffed and panted my way up, relieved that no-one was talking to me.

'That was a gorgeous hike, Noelle,' I said, when I caught up with her at the top. 'Thanks for organising it.'

'The sunshine never came out,' Fabrizia said, scrolling through images on her phone. 'These photos are terrible.'

On the train ride back to Sydney, most of the group closed their eyes. Everyone seemed spent from an excess of exercise and fresh air. I retrieved a textbook from my backpack, one of Bronwyn's 'suggestions'. But I was too tired to wade through academic theory on identity negotiation. Trees flashed past the window, offering the occasional glimpse of towns I'd never heard of, but now wanted to explore, tempted by their mysterious names – Bullaburra, Blaxland, Emu Plains.

I was still puzzling over the Europeans' comments about Australia. I'd wanted to protest, to defend Australia. *The beaches! The beautiful city! The wide availability of espresso!* But I supposed Europe had these things, and you could bring your dog to the pub.

Meanwhile, I'd made myself out to be a selfish, insensitive

person who joked about being a refugee. It was a stupid comment, but I couldn't understand Fabrizia's biting response. Maybe this was her standard reaction; she'd complained about everything that day, including her own photos.

The sun set quickly, leaving nothing to see out the windows. I picked at my bleeding cuticles until I saw a folded newspaper on an empty seat across the aisle. 'Offshore processing' jumped out from a headline. I leaned across to grab the paper.

The article focused on asylum seekers in Australian detention centres, some of which were offshore. It described suicides, hunger strikes and riots. It mentioned detainees suturing their own lips. I read on, my shock growing.

The past year in Winnipeg, I'd volunteered with a Colombian family: a couple and their two young daughters. They were from Bogota, where the husband had worked for the national congress. Although he had a low-level role, a guerrilla group had attempted to extort him. When the guerrillas made good on their threat to murder his brother, the family fled. As asylum seekers in Canada, they were officially termed refugee claimants. The girls attended school while their parents worked, took English classes, and awaited the outcome of their refugee claim. I'd met the mother through a language exchange program, and saw her regularly for months. It was a stressful time for the family, facing an uncertain future. But they were able to get on with their lives and begin to work through the trauma that had forced them to leave their home and extended families behind.

If you'd asked me how Australia treated refugees, I would have assumed the system was pretty much the same.

55

But now, as I read, I learned that Australia was locking up people like my Colombian friends in conditions that weren't far removed from concentration camps. *That can't be right. This is Australia, not North Korea.*

Fabrizia's reaction to my thoughtless comment came into sharper focus. There were comments I'd heard on campus, too, references to asylum seekers. I hadn't paid attention. This immensity had been in front of me since I'd arrived, invisible until it was suddenly revealed. Steve and I had moved to a country – and were now paying taxes to a government – that was locking up people fleeing persecution and violence.

I thought of my family, and a pang tore through my heart.

5

Paranoia Solis

'Are you ready?' Steve called, holding the apartment door open.

'Yep, I'm almost—' I shoved my towel into our beach bag and slid into my flip flops. 'All good!'

When I'd envisioned life in Australia, it was in a beachside suburb. Once in Sydney though, I wasn't willing to commute to campus via two buses and a train. It might have been different if the train line had extended to the beach, a realisation that gave me insight into why Sydneysiders considered their transit system so dismal. Steve and I lived 10 kilometres from some of the world's most beautiful beaches, but when the tyranny of daily life kicked in, we may as well have been in Alice Springs. We hadn't seen the beach in months.

October had arrived, bringing hot and cloying afternoons. After weeks of foiled plans, we finally had a day without rain, without Steve's work demands, without a looming thesis deadline. I thought back to the atrocious winter day when I'd fallen on the ice, the day I'd promised myself I'd live somewhere warm and scenic. Things were coming together – Steve's job, our new apartment, even my gradually improving grades. Today held the promise of everything I'd imagined.

Heading along Campbell Parade, I stopped to revel in the view. Bondi was the world's most striking city beach, a sunken crescent of stripes – aquamarine water, foamy surf, white-gold sand, and the steep, grassy hill that buffered the beach from the blacktop of the car park and the city sprawl beyond. From the top of the hill, Bondi looked like all my fantasies of Australian life.

Steve kept walking, then realised I'd stopped. He took the few steps back to the pavement's edge.

'What are you waiting for?'

'I'm trying to savour the moment.'

He slung his arm over my shoulder, and looked pointedly from one end of Bondi to the other. 'There, savoured. Let's go, the beach is waiting!'

As we stepped onto the sand, the waves that had looked so scenic from above became huge and rageful, like Poseidon had finally realised it was us dumping all that plastic in his oceans and was coming for revenge.

Steve pulled off his shirt and tossed it on the sand. 'You coming?'

The beach was packed. 'I think I'll stay with our stuff.'

He shrugged and raced into the surf. I stood at the edge, holding our bags and trying not to lose sight of him among the horde of swimmers.

Suddenly, he vanished under a monstrous wave. I searched for him frantically, preparing to scream for the lifeguards.

Steve popped up, waving cheerfully. He emerged dripping and

buoyant. We found a spot and spread our towels on the sand. *Okay,* I thought. *You can start enjoying yourself.* This was the whole point of living in Australia – fun, easygoing, beach-centric happiness.

Following a stretch of rainy weekends, it seemed all five million Sydneysiders had decided to spend the afternoon at Bondi. People poured in around us. To our right, a group of guys in board shorts and tank tops spread towels and bags. The speaker they dropped onto the sand blasted reggae. On our left, two blonde girls propped themselves on their elbows and lit cigarettes. They were model thin and topless, and their sweat-free skin was impervious to the heat. A magenta tent sprang up in front of us. Pain shot through one of my back molars; I'd been clamping my jaw again.

Steve sprawled on his beach towel beside me. I tapped him on the arm.

He pulled his earbuds out. 'What is it?'

'I thought we could talk.'

'Okay.' He paused. 'What do you want to talk about?'

I huffed. 'I don't have an agenda.'

He waited. I didn't remember long stretches of silence between us when we were dating. What had changed? Was Steve growing more taciturn? Was I less interesting?

'Remember on our third date,' I said, 'you took me to Star Grill, that little restaurant across from Assiniboine Park that offered psychic readings? We were there for over three hours.'

'The psychic wasn't working that day.'

'Do you remember anything we talked about?'

'It was ten years ago.'

I nodded. The waves crashed.

Steve shrugged. 'Lemme know if you remember any of it.' He popped the earbuds back in. Blood seeped along my lower lip; my teeth had cut it open again.

The sun bore down like a laser. Despite my sunscreen, the outer layer of my skin felt like it was about to melt off and reveal flesh the colour and texture of roast beef. I dug the sunscreen out of our beach bag, slipped my wedding rings off, and started slathering the cream on.

Whereas the sunscreens of my childhood had been uniformly coconut-scented, this brand was fragrance free. It was also paraben and SLS free, had cost $45, and was as spreadable as tile grout. Over the years I'd fantasised about life in Australia, about strolling empty beaches hand in hand with Steve, I never considered the harsh reality of sun protection. Now that I was here, it was impossible to think about much else.

'Here,' I said, shoving the tube towards Steve.

He was stretched out, face-down on a towel in the sand. The dozens of moles on his back, legs and arms peered at me like misshapen brown eyes, glowing with cancerous potential.

'I put some on,' he mumbled from his towel.

'That was an hour ago.'

'That sunscreen is terrible. I wish you'd buy some normal stuff.'

'The "normal" stuff is full of chemicals. Your skin is your body's largest organ, you can't go smearing a bunch of chemicals on it. They absorb into your bloodstream and poison you.'

The air shifted between us. Steve said nothing. I tried for a deep breath, but could only manage ragged attempts. I leaned over and ground the pasty sunscreen into his slimy, glistening back. His moles appeared to have grown several centimetres since my last glance. I could practically see the cancer cells.

I struggled to breathe. The beach and everyone on it seemed to press up against me. *You're supposed to be enjoying yourself.* I held the heel of my hand against my sweaty sternum, trying to force my heart to slow through sheer will.

Another couple about our age sat a few metres away. They had the same pecan-brown hair as Steve and I, though hers was stylish, somehow tame in the humidity. They sat side by side, facing the waves. Though I couldn't overhear them, it was clear they were having a lively conversation. He was telling a story, making animated gestures. She threw her head back, laughing. I doubted they were talking about sunburn.

Closer to the water, a girl of about three played with her mum. Wearing purple water wings, she hovered on the edge of the surf, splashing in the shallow water, giggling and racing away when the waves approached. Maybe that was the secret – to have that level of beatific ease, you had to be born here.

Next to us, someone reached over and turned up the music. Reggae pounded in my ears like tiny rhythmic jackhammers.

Teeth gritted, I poked Steve in the arm. 'I can't handle this.'

He pushed himself up on his elbows. 'We've only been here an hour.'

'You're burning.' I pressed my fingertip harder on Steve's arm. The patch of tomato-red skin turned bright white, then re-reddened as I raised my finger.

'It took us ages to get here, Ash. Let's just move somewhere quieter.'

We gathered our towels, flip flops and bags, and picked our way through sprawled limbs and naked toddlers and frisbee games, walking unevenly over the hot sand. At the beach's south end, where the sand met the rocky cliff edge, we dropped our things.

'Oh, hey, I do have something to tell you – good news.' Steve said as he spread his towel out. 'I talked to my boss yesterday, about how your student visa expires next year, and he thinks he can get me a work visa.'

Australia was perfectly happy to let me pay international student fees for what was turning out to be a largely useless degree – heavy on French philosophy, light on practical application. I'd enrolled thinking I could leverage the degree to start a career in intercultural workplace training, but in hindsight I'd based this on little more than wishful thinking. My job prospects felt dismal. There was a slight chance I could get an academic position if I went on to a PhD, but I doubted I'd have the marks to do so. As an accountant, however, Steve could apply for a four-year work visa through his office.

'Oh,' I said, unease creeping through me. Was this good news? It should be. I loved living in Australia. Didn't I? I definitely loved Sydney. Maybe I was getting sunstroke, not thinking clearly.

'I'm relieved. I'd hate to go through another job search any time soon,' Steve said, as if the visa was already submitted and approved.

I shook my towel and let it drift onto the sand. My left hand felt oddly light. Despite being crusted in sand, my fingers felt naked. I glanced down.

My wedding rings – the rings Steve had custom designed and engraved with our names and wedding date – were not on my finger.

Despair punched through me. I could forfeit most of my material possessions easily, but I loved those rings. The engagement ring's wide band of white gold curved upwards on either side of the stone, hugging it in place, and a row of smaller stones studded the thinner wedding band. More than feeling distressed at my own stupidity, I felt the symbolic significance of losing my rings on the beach.

I sank to my knees, crying into my hands.

Steve's Englishness went on red alert. In his view, crying in public is barely acceptable behaviour for babies, let alone grown women. (Crying in private was likewise unacceptable, but at least there was no audience.) He stood in front of me, trying to conceal my rampant emotions.

'Stop it,' he said. 'What's wrong?'

Before we'd left the apartment, Steve had reminded me to take my rings off. Twice. I'd still forgotten. How could I admit I'd lost them?

I waved my hand and gestured towards where we'd been siting. I stumbled to my feet. I needed to get back up the beach as fast as possible.

'Stop crying, I can't understand you. Did you step on a stone?'

This made me cry harder.

I flapped my hand at him again. 'My rings! They're – I don't know – on the beach I think.'

Steve slapped his hands onto his head as if to keep the top from popping off in frustration. He grabbed our beach bag and started back towards the magenta tent. I struggled behind him, suffocated by the noise and heat and people. My thoughts tumbled over themselves.

'I said *don't* wear your rings to the beach.'

'I know.'

'Then why did you take them off here?'

'The sunscreen makes them slimy.'

Less than ten minutes had passed by the time we arrived back at the patch of sand between the reggae lovers and the bronzed blondes. My rings weren't in sight.

'They must have fallen when I grabbed the towels.' We knelt and ran our hands through the sand, finding nothing, my despair deepening.

This wasn't about the cost of the rings or whether insurance would replace them. It was about the specific ring Steve had given me on our engagement, the specific ring that he had slid on my finger after we exchanged wedding vows surrounded by family and friends. Insurance couldn't replace that.

'Are you sure they're not in your bag?'

I was sure, but I emptied everything out of the beach bag anyway. Steve went through it, his rate of head shakes per minute increasing rapidly.

'Hey,' he said, pointing towards the water. 'There's a guy with a metal detector.' Steve ran down the beach, waving towards him.

~

Before the shaggy-haired man with the metal detector came and worked his way back and forth across the sand, I wasn't sure we'd find the rings, but I was certain they were there somewhere, just out of sight.

Twenty minutes later, when the guy gave up and left to continue his search for loose change or landmines or whatever, I accepted that the rings were no longer there. Someone had taken them, and that was it.

They were gone.

Which wasn't an ideal precursor to me telling Steve that I wasn't sure I could stay in Australia.

6

Fitting In

The Friday after our beach excursion, I pushed myself out of bed at the first blush of dawn, determined to shift my mood. I pulled on gym clothes and forced myself to smile at my bleary reflection while splashing water on my face. Then I headed for the elevator, preparing myself for the muzak torture of the Carpenters.

When the doors slid open, I startled. It was rare to see another person at this hour, particularly someone in a crisp white collared shirt and a grey pinstripe skirt and blazer, carrying two thick binders. A neighbour, I presumed. I had on fluorescent orange sneakers and the same T-shirt I'd worked out in yesterday. I hoped its stink radius was minimal.

We mumbled good morning to each other as I stepped inside.

Then it happened.

It was barely 6 am, but my brain evaluated the situation and determined this was a perfect opportunity for me to 'be the change I wanted to see', in this case a change to a world where neighbours have friendly chats in elevators instead of standing in awkward silence.

Fitting In

Except all I could come up with in the 0.39 seconds between when my brain declared me the Gandhi of Residential Elevators and when sounds started coming out of my mouth was to gesture towards the woman's binders and say, 'Where do you work?'

The look she gave me – surprised, mildly horrified – was as if I'd asked how many abortions she'd had. Her eyes darted from me to the floor-number indicator.

'I'm a lawyer,' she muttered.

'Oh, no!' I said, my face flushing like an overripe tomato. I wasn't prying! I'd meant the question geographically: *Do you have far to go? What's your commute like? In what area of the city do you spend the majority of your time when you're away from the building in which this elevator is contained?*

The doors opened and the woman darted past me into the foyer. I called to her back as she hurried away. 'I meant on a map!'

~

'Steve,' I said that night after spitting a mouthful of toothpaste into the bathroom sink, 'Are you sure you want to apply for the work visa?'

He yanked his toothbrush from his mouth and looked at me like I'd asked if he was sure he wanted to keep both his eyeballs in their sockets.

'Why are you asking that?'

My teeth were clean, but I kept brushing. Ever since we'd agreed to move to Australia, I'd been certain of one thing: when I finished my degree, Steve would want to return to Canada. We would argue back and forth about this, and maybe I'd knock a

67

stack of folded laundry to the floor and stomp away in frustration. Then I'd graciously relent and we'd move to Vancouver or, well, anywhere not as arctic, remote and dull as Winnipeg, and we'd just be ordinary, boring Canadians for the rest of our lives.

It never occurred to me that Steve might want to stay in Australia. Now that he did, I had to confront my own feelings.

Living in Sydney, we may as well have been on the moon. Even calling our parents was difficult because of the 17-hour time difference. The longer we were away from them, the guiltier I felt. When I left Canada at twenty-two years old, I'd been living with my parents my entire life, and the expanse of the Pacific Ocean wasn't enough space between us. After three years in Asia and Latin America, however, I moved back to Winnipeg to discover my parents had become two of my favourite people, tied for second place only behind Steve. My in-laws, Pam and Rick, ranked highly, too. We often spent our weekends with his parents or mine, or all together. We played cards and talked gardening while Steve's dad mixed us Blunt Instruments, his personal blend of rum and lime soda. It hurt to admit how much I missed them. Our parents, I mean. Also the drinks.

If we could have hooked Australia up to some kind of intercontinental winch and hauled it next to, say, Hawaii, it would have been reasonable to think about staying here indefinitely. With the current geography though, getting home involved thousands of dollars and twenty-four hours in transit. What if my dad had a heart attack? What if Rick fell off a ladder – again? Next time maybe he wouldn't be joking about how Pam had rushed to the safe to check their insurance policy before he'd hit the ground.

68

Fitting In

We also had two siblings between us, one sister each. Steve's sister had recently had a second baby and mine was due to have her first. We were about as close with our sisters as the US and the USSR ever were (i.e. we had semi-regular phone contact). Relations weren't going to thaw if we stayed in Australia, missing out on christenings, birthdays and Christmases.

I wiped the toothpaste off my chin and met Steve's eyes in the mirror. 'You didn't want to move overseas in the first place.'

'We're here now. It took me three months to find a job. And we finally got all our mail coming to this address.' He headed into the bedroom. I followed.

'I'm just worried ...'

Steve rubbed his face. 'You're always worried. You're worried about your grades and your thesis. You're worried if we spend two seconds in the sun, we've got skin cancer. You worried that I wouldn't leave Winnipeg, and when I did, you worried that I wouldn't get a job—'

'You worried about that, too!'

'It didn't look like I was going to get a job. But I did, that's my point. Actually, no, my point is that you worry about everything and it's extremely frustrating.'

I threw my arms up. 'You're covered in moles and the UV index goes to fifteen here! I didn't know it went above ten. I thought it was a score *out of* ten! We may as well paint our walls with uranium.'

'It's bedtime.' Climbing into bed, he switched off his bedside lamp.

'But I—' I grimaced and squeezed my hands together. 'I saw

69

one of our neighbours in the elevator this morning and I asked her where she worked and all I meant was, you know, where she was headed, because if I wanted to know what she did, I would have asked that.' The shame of this conversation still burned inside my rib cage. It had played on a mental loop while I ran on the treadmill, while I had breakfast, and while I was in class and working on my thesis and making dinner. 'It was like I'd suggested we get naked together and press the elevator buttons with our butts.'

'Aussies don't ask that,' Steve said.

We'd read this in the book of handy tips to cultural etiquette in Australia that Noelle had lent me. The book warned that in small talk, Aussies don't ask new acquaintances about their professions. The problem couldn't lie with Australian reservedness, the underlying attitude that framed my neighbourliness as an attempt to pry. The problem was clearly with me and my inability to adapt.

'At home I always asked people what they do. I could have spent all day in an elevator in Canada asking people what they do, and I probably would have won a medal for friendliness.'

'No-one likes talking in elevators.' Steve flopped onto his pillow and stared at the ceiling.

'What I'm trying to say is, I'm worr ... concerned that I don't fit in here.' This was the first time I'd admitted this, even to myself.

'What are you talking about? You love it here.'

'Just because you love ... plastic vampire fangs doesn't mean you should make them a regular part of your wardrobe.'

He closed his eyes. Was he falling asleep? Was that how little I mattered?

'Steve?'

70

He sighed. 'I'm concerned that you're concerned about every damn thing.' He reached out to me, as though to stroke my cheek, then stretched his arm past my head and switched off my lamp. 'Go to sleep.'

Within minutes he was emitting tiny snores.

I stared at the ceiling, the evening's thick heat like a smothering blanket. Now that I had named the cluster of fears lurking in my mind, they crystallised into one distinct paranoia.

I didn't fit in.

It wasn't only that I couldn't relax on the beach, that I didn't understand how it was possible for any sane person to ever relax with sand wedged between their butt cheeks. It was my outsiderness, scratching at me like a woolly cardigan.

I'd arrived with the assumption that, except for the climate, Australia and Canada were basically the same. The language was the same, give or take some slang; the same queen was on the money, and the same history of colonial atrocity was pointedly ignored. We knew we'd have to exchange 'eh' for 'mate' in our speaking and bison for kangaroo in our burgers, and that for some reason the 's' had been taken from 'sports' and added to 'math'. We knew that in Australia the direction of traffic on the streets was reversed, but once here, we were shocked to discover that *everything* was reversed – the flow of pedestrians, the position of escalators, even the direction keys turned in locks. Australia ran along a different current, and I couldn't read the water.

It wasn't only that morning's debacle in the elevator. Every time I opened my mouth, someone asked if I was American. If roles were reversed, I'd have asked the same thing, but being on the receiving end of the question felt like a constant reminder that I didn't belong here. My thesis supervisor was still speaking in code, saying one thing when she meant something else. I couldn't bring myself to say 'Cans' when I meant 'Cair-rns', I felt compelled to insist 'sport' should be plural, and I found the term 'bush' lewd. On the rare occasions I drove, I would terrify Steve by attempting to turn into the oncoming lane, before noting the traffic barrelling towards us and wildly veering away. I couldn't remember which of the Arnott's assorted were the Monte Carlos and which were the Kingstons. And I couldn't tolerate the term biscuit for what was clearly a cookie. None of these things mattered much on their own, but combined they were a powerful phalanx, making me constantly question myself.

I lay awake, feeling homesick for a home I hadn't yet found. A home I was beginning to realise might not exist.

7

Fear Has Seven Legs

We had two months before we'd have to make a decision about Steve's work visa.

Whenever I tried to pin down my thoughts about it, they swirled into a vortex of uncertainty. For the moment, I had bigger things to think about.

My parents were visiting.

It was a big deal. They hadn't visited me in Mexico, or Peru, or Korea. My dad loved travelling, and so by the law of opposite attraction underpinning all romantic relationships, my mother preferred to stay home, generally within the bounds of her own property. She had a spacious garden to tend, so what reason was there to leave? But for the first time since leaving Winnipeg, I was living somewhere reasonably safe from drug cartels, violent revolutionaries and nuclear-armed communist regimes. My mother had no excuse. Though she did have one concern regarding our safety in Australia.

When Steve and I had announced our move to Sydney, everyone at home ritually invoked the Australian Trinity of

Terror – snakes, sharks and spiders. The way Canadians talk, you'd think Australia's coasts are frothing with sharks, and you have to check under your seat at the Opera House for taipans. 'I could never visit Australia, I'm too afraid of the spiders,' Canadian friends had said. 'How are you going to handle the spiders?' they'd insisted, as though daily life in Australia required a spider-preparedness plan.

There was once an African safari park outside Sydney that advertised its lions and tigers and bears with a commercial jingle featuring the refrain, 'It's scary but nobody cares.' While I can't imagine the phrase inspired many theme-park visits, such nonchalance in the face of potential death would be the perfect national motto for Australia. Sure, some Aussies do care, but the national attitude is pride in not caring.

The Terror Trinity grew wearisome before we'd left Winnipeg. Once in Australia, I took a hard stance of refusing to be afraid. This turned out to be easy. After ten months in Sydney, we'd encountered a severe lack of deadly creatures. Steve and I only knew when the latest Australian shark attack had happened because my mother would call.

'I guess you haven't been to the beach lately,' she'd say.

'We went on the weekend.'

'What about the shark attack? Don't you read the news?!'

Shark attacks in Australia routinely made the Canadian news. They were always in another city, near Newcastle or Byron or Perth. I insisted to Mom (I couldn't think of her as 'Mum') that it was statistically unlikely I'd ever encounter a shark, particularly as I was in Australia to write a thesis, a predominantly desk-based activity.

74

'Don't worry,' I said on the phone in the weeks before their trip. 'We haven't seen any snakes or sharks, and only some boring spiders. It'll be fine.'

My largest concern wasn't the wildlife attacking my parents. It was our housing situation. Knowing we'd likely only be here one year, Steve and I hadn't invested in much furniture. We'd bought a bed and desk second-hand, and found discarded chairs and bookcases on the pavement. We didn't even have a couch. Worse, my parents were arriving in December, which led to this depressing real-life maths problem: if 4 adults spend 1 month in an apartment featuring a total of 1 bedroom and 0 air-conditioning units, how long will it take before 1 of them murders the other 3? High-school calculus did not prepare us for such equations.

After nearly a year apart, I was overjoyed to see my parents, and the first few weeks passed without anyone resorting to murder. We drank cold beer on a hot Christmas morning, zipped ourselves into onesie windbreakers to clamber over the Harbour Bridge, and watched the New Year's Eve firework spectacular from the water. It was magical and it was grating. We got on each other's nerves in the sweaty apartment. Dad was doing well keeping his grizzly-like temper in check, but the hot sleepless nights were adding up. I wanted my parents to stay forever, and I wanted them to leave immediately.

It was mid-arvo, with only a few days before their flight home to Winnipeg. Dad was in the bedroom, catching up on sleep. Steve was at work. Mom and I were alone in the lounge, spending quality time together while both on our iPads.

Out of nowhere, she pointed to the living room wall. 'What's that?'

Lurking near the ceiling, its dark body contrasting with the white paint, crouched my nightmare: a fur-covered huntsman the size of a fist. I'd never seen a live one, but I'd spent enough time memorising spider identification charts to know it immediately. It looked exactly like the chart picture, except larger, like it was wearing the pelts of other hunstmen it had killed.

Mom and I froze. The spider froze.

Directly beneath the spider was the air mattress where Steve and I had been sleeping.

'They're not poisonous,' I whispered, trying to avoid startling the spider into action. I was also trying not to hyperventilate. This was my apartment. I had invited my mother here. Now I had to be an adult and deal with this abomination, even if it resulted in years of therapy.

'Why does it only have seven legs?' Mom whispered back.

I counted. Seven.

'Do they normally have seven legs?'

'I don't ... think so.'

The most bothersome wildlife Mom had to deal with in Winnipeg were squirrels and the occasional burrowing vole – fluffy rodent variants that dug up her garden but also fled at the sight of humans. This spider was not fleeing. I'm sure Mom was deeply unimpressed that my life choices had led her into our current predicament. But she was also not the type of person to panic. She would deal with this crisis with calm stoicism, then return home and simply never visit me anywhere in the world ever again.

Fear Has Seven Legs

I'd worry about that later. Now, we needed a plan. We weren't going to try to squish this thing any more than we'd try to squish a raccoon, and even if I could have reached the spider to use the bowl-and-a-piece-of-paper trick to take it outside, that wasn't going to happen. I had no interest in enacting a heartwarming made-for-TV-movie scene where I release an amputee huntsman into the wilds of the Camperdown nature strip, just for it to scuttle right back into my apartment after dark.

This meant we had to kill it without spider guts splattering onto our faces.

Or, option B: wake Dad mid-nap.

'Better to take our chances with the spider?' I whispered. Mom nodded.

While she kept reconnaissance, I moved towards the closet, tai chi slow, and retrieved the vacuum. The nozzle wasn't long enough to reach the spider. Using hand signals to communicate, Mom slid the air mattress away while I climbed onto a chair, vacuum in one hand, nozzle in the other.

It still wasn't long enough.

The huntsman was onto us. It started scuttering towards the ceiling. If it got away, we'd have to vacate the apartment and possibly burn it down. Shaking with adrenaline, I turned the vacuum to maximum suck and leapt off the chair, lunging towards the spider. It started to bolt, then stopped. Time slowed as the spider tried to flatten itself against the wall before it was suddenly dragged backwards, vanishing into the nozzle.

I nailed my landing, like an Olympic gymnast in the domestic implements event.

'How do we know if it's dead?'

Mom looked around. 'I guess the place could use a vacuum.'

She spent the next two hours vacuuming the lounge room, until Dad finally woke up and we put him in charge of Phase Two: removal of the vacuum from the premises for content evacuation a minimum of three blocks away.

I'd just started to feel safe again when, preparing for bed that evening, we found the spider's missing leg – a curled, furry hook with a pointed tip, lying under the sheets of the air mattress.

Staring at it, I could feel spider talons creeping along my skin. I shivered. I tried to think of the noble kookaburra, the clacka-clackas, my beloved skulking ibises. Of the Moreton Bay Figs, which I'd finally learned the name of because they were the most handsome trees in the world. Of all the Australian creatures that I loved. But my brain kept returning to the spider.

The giant spider that all evidence indicated had been in my bed.

I thought about how, if Steve got his work visa and we stayed a while longer in Australia, I now had my own spider anecdote to share with Aussie friends. How one day, maybe, I could relate the experience with enough bravado to distract from my trembling hands. I thought this long after my parents had retreated to the bedroom and Steve, insisting there was no way we were sleeping with the lights on, left me sitting awake, my back to the wall, a flashlight in each hand, vowing to never admit that I had become somebody who cares.

~

My parents left. Steve and I saw them off at the airport, their luggage trundling away on the conveyor belt. We'd been saying goodbye at airports for years. Still Mom cried. The tears welled against the rim of her glasses, then spilled down her cheeks, which made me cry.

Of course they wanted me close, but they'd never suggest I move back to Winnipeg. *We want you to be happy*, they'd say.

Life would have been simpler if my parents lived in a place I could imagine staying in. I wondered what it would feel like to be born in a beautiful city with a reasonable climate, to grow up picturing your future there, with your family. Would you recognise the lottery you'd won?

Winnipeg wasn't home, and never had been. I was generations dislocated. Like me, my mom had grown up in a military family, and spent her life pinballing from province to province. On my dad's side, my great-grandparents had stayed where fate tossed them, a town called St Catharines, near Niagara Falls. There, they'd created a sense of Armenian community, living among fellow genocide survivors, teaching their language and history to their children, and building a church. But within two generations their family had outgrown the town; Dad and three of his sisters had all left.

It was my great-grandparents' story I was striving to tell in my thesis research. I'd just started connecting with my Armenian family when we'd moved to Australia, and it felt strange to be writing about them from so far away. Maybe this was also adding to my dislocation.

My parents turned to wave one more time before vanishing into the crowd. An ocean of loneliness crashed through me. I wished I knew how to articulate my uncertainty to them. *It's not that I want to stay here, but I don't know where else to go.*

And it's getting harder to be so far from you.

I caught myself thinking, *was Winnipeg really that bad?*

~

'Okay, first question: do you know the term "budgie smugglers"?'

Aram, a data analyst from Steve's office, had invited us over for drinks. He'd welcomed us in, introduced us to his partner, and whisked Steve off to the balcony. Jules poured two champagne flutes from the bottle of chilled prosecco we'd brought while she quizzed me about my knowledge of Australian culture.

I smiled as I took one of the glasses. 'That was one of the first things we learned. When we told people we were moving to Australia, someone said, "You need to know this term."'

'Really? Holy Christ.'

We headed onto the balcony. Steve and Aram had started on bottles of Victoria Bitter. The late-afternoon sun was soft and golden, the UV below cancer-causing levels.

Aram was taller than Steve, and Jules was taller than me, and they were both broad-shouldered, with defined cheekbones, open faces and wide smiles. We were grateful they'd invited us over. Finally we had a chance of becoming friends with some actual Aussies.

We tapped glasses to beer bottles. I took a cold, dry, bubbly sip.

'Ashley's keen on learning how to be more Aussie,' Jules said to Aram with a cheeky expression.

80

'Hmm.' He drummed his fingers on the patio table. 'Have you had an iced vovo?'

'I've seen them.' I had declined to try them, not because the pink-striped biscuits were covered in desiccated coconut, which looked like an elderly person's pubic hair, but because the biscuits themselves looked unsettlingly like women's private parts, and the term 'vovo' didn't help.

'You need to try iced vovos,' Jules said.

'I don't like coconut.'

She pointed to the door. 'Get out!' The outrage on her face and in her voice startled me so badly that I was about to apologise, but she and Aram laughed. I gave a little laugh, too, as if I were in on the joke all along. This was another way I failed to fit in – Australian deadpanning was so dead serious that I couldn't identify it.

Jules poured herself another glass of prosecco, topping mine up as well. Aram opened a second beer for Steve, though his first was still half full.

'What else?' Aram mused. 'We love big things. The Big Banana, the Big Mango.'

Jules snapped her fingers. 'The Big Lobster in Victoria.'

'I think there's a Big Macadamia Nut ... Well, there's heaps.'

I didn't share my feeling that Australia overestimated the uniqueness of its big things. One of the delights of the summer trips my family took across the TransCanada Highway was the oversized landmarks we greeted like old friends. These included the giant teepee outside the town of Medicine Hat, the giant moose outside the town of Moose Jaw, and the giant head of a Native American

81

chief in a feathered headdress outside the town of Indian Head. (Yes, there's a town called Indian Head. It's in Saskatchewan – look, the point isn't to determine who is more culturally insensitive to genocide than who, but that Canada also has a lot of big things, and we don't make such a big deal of it.)

That said, Australia was culturally distinct in myriad ways, as I was learning. My latest source of insight was Nino Culotta's *They're a Weird Mob*. From 1957, it was supposedly the memoir of an Italian visitor in Sydney who decides, after getting a job as a brickie, to stay permanently. In fact, it was written by an Aussie named John O'Grady. He ended the book with advice for 'bloody new Australians'. I read it eagerly. Return all shouts, O'Grady advised. Don't be a bludger. Don't lose your temper when your workmates ridicule you – and if they're Aussies, they will. If someone does you a favour, return it, but don't overdo generosity. Abuse your friends to their face, but not in private.

I tried to create an equivalent list of Canadian cultural advice, but it was a struggle. Even with Steve's help, I'd only come up with three things: If you drop people off in the winter, make sure they get inside before driving away (this was pragmatic, to ensure no-one froze to death). If someone bumps into you on the street, be the first to apologise. Cheek-kiss greetings are for family only, and hugs are for close female friends and sports teams; otherwise, shake hands and keep your damn distance.

Off the balcony, magpies gathered in nearby trees, conferring in fluty melodies. I pulled *They're a Weird Mob* from my purse. Aram and Jules indulged me as I read O'Grady's advice. They agreed with every point.

82

Fear Has Seven Legs

'Definitely don't be a bludger. Or a piker!' Jules said. 'Bloody pikers.'

Okay, I thought. I was naturally disinclined to laziness, and though I wasn't keen for colleagues to ridicule me, I wasn't one to lose my temper. I could return shouts, though the complexity of shouting was still murky. If six of us went out, did we each have to consume six drinks? I had no idea how to abuse my friends to their faces, and where exactly was the line for overdoing generosity? I was about to launch into these concerns, but Aram spoke first.

'There's an essential part of being Australian missing from that list,' he said. 'Cultural cringe.'

'What is that, exactly?' I asked.

'Well, hmm.' He frowned. 'Okay, I did a semester of uni in Houston, and I couldn't believe how proud everybody was. Of the uni, of their fraternities, of being American.' He spread his hands wide as if trying to show the magnitude of their pride. 'Their faces, like, glowed with it. It was strange. It's not something we do here.'

I thought back to the mumbled way the woman in the elevator had told me she was a lawyer. No pride there. Perhaps this was strategic. If you had no pride in your community or yourself, if you cringed at everything around you, if the only thing you boasted about were the squalid conditions of your share house, no-one could accuse you of being a tall poppy.

'Why wouldn't you be proud of Australia?' Steve said. 'It's great.'

'Nah, it's shit,' Jules said with a smile, and she and Aram clinked glasses. The more I learned about mandatory detention for asylum seekers and other federal policies, the more I understood their perspective. Maybe if the country wasn't so busy cringing at itself, it could make better decisions.

'Canada's pretty great,' Jules said. 'People there don't lock their doors!'

'Why do you think that?' I asked, though I knew exactly why.

'That Michael Moore doco, where he goes to people's houses in some Canadian burb.'

People around the world had told me this, as though American citizen Michael Moore was the ultimate authority on Canada. In fact, every Canadian I know keeps their doors locked, with the sole exception of one couple who live in the middle of rural nowhere and reason that if someone has gone to the trouble of finding their place with the intention of robbing it, a locked door won't stop them. I'd tried for years to dissuade people of the Moore Myth, but I'd given up. People wanted to believe in a Canada where everyone was so well mannered that no-one needed to lock their doors. Maybe Australia's misperception of other countries was one of the reasons it cringed so harshly at itself, like a teenage girl staring at the photoshopped magazine cover model.

'How cold does it get in Winnipeg anyway?' Jules asked.

'It goes to minus 30 or minus 40.'

'That's Fahrenheit though?' Aram asked.

'We use Celsius, but at that temperature it makes no difference. Minus 40 is the point where Fahrenheit and Celsius are equivalent.' This is the sort of numerical trickery that made maths impenetrable to me, but the takeaway remained clear: however you measured it, minus 40 was bone-chilling.

'Some winters are only minus 15,' Steve added. He was more loyal to Winnipeg than me.

'I've never been in anything colder than 3 degrees,' Aram said. 'What's winter like there?'

'There are a lot of storms, and driving is scary, especially when there's black ice.'

'Black ice?' Jules raised her eyebrows. 'Sounds exciting.'

'It's dangerous,' Steve said. 'It's like glass, so you can't see it.'

'Winter is exhausting,' I said. 'You have to keep your car plugged in, and if you forget to unplug it, you rip the extension cord out and drive away with the busted cord trailing behind you.'

Jules and Aram cocked their heads in unison. 'The cars are electric?'

'No, they have little heaters in the engines to keep them from freezing,' Steve said.

'I'd love to live in Canada for a year, especially to experience the winter,' Aram said.

Jules gazed towards the pink-striped sunset. 'We've talked about that a lot.'

Had they heard nothing we'd said? They were like millionaires musing that it would be easy to be skinny if only they didn't have enough money for food. From what I'd experienced that year, Australia didn't have winter. Sure, it got weirdly cold indoors for a few months, but outside there were trees flowering.

'Winter isn't merely a lack of summer,' I said, stabbing my fingertip against the tabletop. 'It's a horrible nexus of cold weather events, indignities and torture. Winter is washing your car so the road salt doesn't rust through the metal and having the doors freeze shut, then connecting four extension cords to a hair dryer so you can stand in your driveway defrosting them. Winter is finding your car buried under half a foot of snow, so you turn the engine on to let it warm up enough to run properly while you clear away the snow with your snow brush, but underneath the snow is an inch of solid ice, so you have to use a scraper to chip away enough of the ice to see through the windshield. Winter is then realising you've locked your keys *and* your mobile in your car with the engine running, so you trudge three blocks to a payphone to call your dad and he is not impressed.'

Aram tried to say something, but I barrelled on, ignoring the apprehensiveness creasing Steve's face. 'All this time you've been picturing a cityscape coated in fresh white snow, pristine, romantic, the way it looks in movies. Sure, freshly fallen snow is picturesque. On sunny days, it reflects the low slanted winter sunlight to cast a soft glow. And in the country, the snow stays virginal, only disturbed by the tracks of jack rabbits, deer and snowmobile enthusiasts. But in the city, vehicle exhaust blackens the snow banks. Traffic churns the snow into a muddy slush that spatters over everything as tyres spin across it, and everyone's vehicle is coated in thick clumps of brown muck that freezes solid. Within twenty-four hours of a fresh snowfall, the city looks like it slipped and landed face down in a pigpen.'

I'd shifted into a rant, my voice shrill. Aram and Jules stared, open-mouthed. Steve kicked me under the table. But I'd had one-and-a-third glasses of prosecco and I needed to make a point.

'And don't get me started on spring! I grew up with all these picture books that made spring look like the God of Pretty Flowers comes prancing through the city. In spring, six months' worth of black, disgusting snow has to melt! Six months of dog urine that's been frozen in yellow chunks, six months of animal crap and litter that people have kicked snow over – it melts into squalid lakes that spread across the roads. Cars splash through them and soak everyone on the sidewalks. For six months the city has spread literal tons of gravel to give the roads traction – gravel doesn't magically melt away. You track it into your car and house. It ends up in your bed. Spring is the most disgusting, foul time of year, and a few crocuses and baby bunnies do not make up for it!'

Steve put his hand over his face. There was a moment of silence.

Jules gave a polite cough. 'You're saying Winnipeg didn't make the world's top ten most liveable cities.'

I forced myself back in my chair, clasping my hands in my lap. I was nervous about staying in Australia, but I knew I couldn't survive Canadian winter. I'd been running from it for years – and Steve wasn't going to keep running with me.

8

Homeland

I was on the train again, heading to Sydney's western suburbs to visit a new friend. Even these few early friendships offered tentative comfort. I hadn't had such a difficult time meeting people since high school. It had been easy in Asia and Latin America, where English-speaking expats bonded quickly and Steve's absence had forced me to be more social. Steve didn't mind our lack of social group; spending time alone or with me was enough for him. I'd invited him along today, but after an early-morning half-marathon training run, he was now at work, spending his Saturday finalising monthly financial statements. A draft chapter of my thesis was due to Bronwyn that week but, I reasoned, I could work on the train. I ignored the suburbs flashing past, focusing on my textbook instead. While I'd done a lot of research the previous year on the Armenian genocide itself, I was working to put it into a larger context. The best book I'd found for this was Norman Naimark's *Genocide: A World History*.

Halfway through my train ride, I encountered the Black Line, the colonist-organised effort to clear Tasmania of its remaining Indigenous population.

One of the things I'd known about Australia before we moved here – or thought I'd known – was that its history of colonisation was similar to Canada's. Before we left, my colleagues at the University of Winnipeg had mentioned, a little enviously, how much better Australia was doing with Truth and Reconciliation. Canada's last federally run 'residential school', the euphemistic term for our Stolen Generations, closed in 1996, four years after Paul Keating's Redfern Address. It was 2008 before Canadian Prime Minister Stephen Harper made a similar acknowledgement; he effectively recanted the apology not long after, announcing at a G20 summit that Canada has 'no history of colonialism'.

I thought I had a decent overview of our nations' colonial violence. But there was nothing like the Black Line in Canadian history. 'Though divided into distinct groups, as were their cousins on the Australian mainland,' Naimark wrote, Tasmania's Indigenous peoples 'could be considered a separate ethno-national unit that was slated for elimination by the settlers, supported and sometimes initiated by the local government, and were therefore victims of genocide.'

Maybe in a country where thousands of ordinary people had once come together to form a human chain so they could capture and forcibly relocate Aboriginal people, the policy of mandatory indefinite detention wasn't all that surprising.

~

When I stepped onto the Campbelltown platform, the crisp blue sky arching over the brick houses seemed wider than it had at Central Station.

Ani Vardanyan and her father, Senik, met me at the station. Petite with long dark hair, Ani wore a burgundy dress that seemed fancy for a Saturday arvo. In jeans and a black T-shirt, I felt underdressed. A bear-shaped man, Senik had a worn but smiling face and a gravelly smoker's voice.

'You made one mistake,' he said as I got in their car, its back seat covered by a woven rug. 'You didn't bring your husband.' My first visit to an Armenian home, and I'd forsaken one of the essential aspects of Armenian culture – family togetherness. But Senik smiled, and I suspected we would get along.

I'd met Ani on campus at Sydney Uni, where she studied medical science. Happening past my stack of research texts, she'd exclaimed in a library-soft voice, 'You're reading William Saroyan! Do you know he's Armenian?'

When I said that was my reason for reading him, she replied, 'Oh! I'm from Armenia.' Few friendships start so beautifully.

We arrived at a red brick house. Lush grapevines hung over the front door. Senik ushered me in, his meaty hand sweeping across the lounge room. 'Now, this is your house. Do whatever you like.'

The first Armenian I'd met in Australia, Ani had only lived there a few years herself. Her family had migrated piecemeal, her father and grandmother first, and then, seven interminable years later, when their paperwork came through, herself and her mother and siblings. Although she'd started university in Armenia, she'd had to return to Year 11 when she'd arrived in Sydney. Ani's shoulders rolled in, and her quiet laugh was edged with nervousness, but her eyes glowed with passion when she talked about literature, her honours research, or her homeland.

90

Homeland

The family spread across the open space of the kitchen, dining room and lounge, chatting. A clock hung perpendicular to the wall, its two faces displaying the time in Sydney and Armenia. A pet ring-necked parrot flew through the house, then snuggled up to its girlfriend, a picture of a model cut from a box of hair dye.

While Ani's teenage siblings, Meri and Mgo, had Australian accents, Ani's English had kept its charming Armenian inflection. Her elderly grandmother, who sat huddled in a recliner, spoke no English. Senik and his bright-eyed, charming wife Lala conferred in Armenian, then turned and apologised for doing so.

'I'm happy to hear it,' I said, though I didn't understand a word.

From a photo album, Senik retrieved a black-and-white photo of a long-haired child, five or six years old. 'Guess who this is. Guess!'

The child sported two long, bushy pigtails and a cherubic grin. 'It must be Ani.'

Senik shook his head.

'Lala?'

'It's me!' Senik exclaimed, his voice booming. I wondered if this had been a popular boyhood hairstyle in 1970s Armenia. But no, Senik had been the only boy with flowing locks, which earned him relentless teasing.

When he was born in Soviet Armenia, his doctors spoiled the occasion with the news that he would die as an infant. Unable to accept this, his father bartered with God, promising not to cut Senik's hair for seven years if God spared his son's life.

'In Armenia, seven is a divine number,' Senik said, his eyes lifted heavenwards.

91

Inevitably, his hair had grown to his waist. When he reached his seventh birthday, alive and healthy, the church held a special ceremony. The Catholicos, Armenia's Pope, baptised him and trimmed pieces of hair from four different spots on his head. He wrapped these in paper and gave them to Senik's father, with the instruction to hide the paper in a hole somewhere in the church.

'This is very common, so part of you is always with the church. It becomes sacred.'

The doorbell rang, and three middle-aged couples came inside, speaking Armenian and bearing food. One of the men carried long metal skewers. The genders separated like oil and water, the women to the kitchen, chopping and spicing, and the men outside, smoking and barbecuing. I broke ranks so Senik could lecture me on the importance of wood charcoal for smoked flavour. Australian barbecues didn't compare to Armenian *khoravats*, he said.

When the food was ready, everyone gathered back inside. Under Lala's direction, the table filled with tabouli, Greek and Russian salads, spinach-filled pastries, caviar, skewers of meat, and piles of salmon steaks and stuffed chicken breasts. The banquet's largesse was surprising – there were only twelve of us.

'That's the Armenian way,' Senik said, his deep voice reverberating through the room. 'If you invite ten people, you cook for thirty.' With that, we toasted with vodka shots.

This is what I imagined my great-grandparents' home might have been like. My Armenian genes came from my father's grandparents, Mariam and Paravon, whose surname I'd also inherited. Growing up, I'd spent little time with my father's family; St Catharines was a long journey from Winnipeg. Geographically

92

Homeland

cut off from the family, I hadn't known my grandfather spoke Armenian until his funeral, when I was fourteen.

I didn't move to Sydney with the intention of getting closer to my Armenian heritage through anything but textbooks. For the first time in my life, however, I was living in a city with an Armenian community, mostly based on Sydney's north shore.

I was sitting between Ani and Taline, a slight woman in her mid-forties with deep-set eyes and an abruptly tapered chin. Like nearly everyone around the table, myself included, she had dark hair, which curled around her face.

'Taline was born in Sydney,' Ani said. 'She attended public school during the week, and Armenian school on Saturdays.'

Like much of my dad's family, I thought. His aunts, uncles and older siblings had attended Armenian school in the evenings. I'd learned this on the research trip to St Catharines that I'd made before leaving Canada. I'd long been interested in the Armenian genocide and how it laid the blueprints for the Holocaust, and now that interest had expanded to include the genocide's broader legacy. After World War I, Armenians had forged communities across the world, in North and South America, in Europe, across the Middle East, as far as Tajikistan and China. Coming to understand that I was part of this story had inspired my thesis research.

'My parents moved from Egypt in '67, and I was born at Royal North Shore Hospital the next year,' Taline said. Her Australian accent carried a hint of Armenian inflection.

At home that morning, I'd been reading sociological studies about the development of the Australian Armenian identity. The

93

Antipodean community was formed by families displaced by the genocide, who had resettled as refugees across the Middle East and then, a generation later, migrated again in search of security and stability. It was like Taline had stepped out of my textbooks.

'Can I ask how you think about your identity? I mean, do you feel more Australian or more Armenian?'

'Armenia's my homeland,' she said without hesitation. 'I know it in my heart, though I've never visited. I've always lived in Australia, and I love it, too. The smell of gumleaves, you know, cicadas at Christmas. I guess I'm both, but also … not enough of either.'

'There's a quote in the Saryan Museum – do you know this painter, Martiros Saryan?' Ani asked.

I shook my head.

'There's a museum dedicated to him in Yerevan, and when you come in the entrance, there's a quote on the wall. "The earth like a living thing has its own spirit, and without one's native land, without close touch with one's motherland, it is impossible to find one's self, one's soul."'

Several people around the table nodded. Taline put her hand to her heart. My great-grandparents, and probably my grandfather, would have felt the same, I realised.

Perhaps because we moved so much at the whim of the Canadian military when I was a kid, and because another move was always on the horizon, I couldn't locate my soul in any particular swathe of land. With effort though, through my research, I was starting to understand how Armenians could. Their historical homeland, stretching across modern Turkey and

94

Homeland

the Caucasus mountains to Azerbaijan, was where they traced their ancestry, where their heroes had fought and their kings had ruled, where they had built their cathedrals, fortresses and castles. It was where they buried their dead, where their gravestones have stood for as long as 1500 years. That specific land was where they'd faced attacks on every side, where the souls of victims of hatred had lain unburied. What remained of that territory, the tiny nation of Armenia that existed today, was a reminder that they had survived the worst of humanity's evils.

It occurred to me that Armenians and Australia's Indigenous peoples had more than a little in common. If Armenians in the far-flung diaspora felt this strongly about their ties to homeland, which dated back roughly 3000 years, I could only imagine the depth of feeling of Australia's Indigenous peoples, with their close cultural ties to land that dated back tens of thousands of years.

'What about your family, Ashley?' Taline asked. 'When did they end up in Canada?'

'Right after the genocide, in 1920.' Sometimes it was hard to tell this story without my eyes welling up. I shared the details I'd learned as a teenager, of my grandfather Paravon hiding in a tree in the middle of the night while his family was murdered and his village burned to the ground. He was young at the time, maybe seven or eight. He'd stayed hidden in the tree long after the soldiers had left, then made his way to a nearby town. If he saw anyone coming, he hid under the corpses that lined the road. He ended up in an orphanage. Mariam's parents had left her with Turkish neighbours, who risked their own lives by pretending she was their daughter. This must have become too dangerous for them, because

95

she ended up in the same orphanage as Paravon. She spent her life searching for her lost family, hoping one day she might discover that one of her siblings had survived.

They were among hundreds of thousands of Armenian refugees, among the millions displaced after World War I. Paravon's one stroke of luck was a sojourner uncle, who, years before, had landed a job in St Catharines. After the genocide, the uncle tracked down Paravon and Mariam and brought them to Canada, paying the $400 visa fees; the only way they could get into Canada was through a family connection. Canada wasn't accepting refugees in 1920, especially not 'Asiatic' ones, not even from Armenia, the world's first Christian nation.

Shift the geography, shift the timeline, and it was easy – painfully easy – to imagine Mariam and Paravon in detention on Manus Island or Nauru.

I cringed at the thought, and remembered the phrase Aram had taught me. It felt shameful to go on living in a country that behaved so egregiously, especially when I thought about Mariam and Paravon. Luck had brought them to Canada, where their courage and resilience had enabled them to establish a home and a family in an unfamiliar and unwelcoming country. Three generations later, Steve and I had the privilege to move around the world on a whim – my whim.

I couldn't cajole Steve to leave when I was the one who'd brought us here. The least I could do was try to cultivate even an ounce of the resilience my great-grandparents must have had.

9

The Reins

Despite the emotional upheaval and uncertainty I'd grappled with over the past few months, I managed to scrape together and submit my thesis. In it, I concluded that diasporan Armenian identity was both globally conscious, connected to the broader Armenian story, and locally rooted, influenced by its surrounding community. The other significant learning I took from the process was that I never wanted to write a thesis again.

The morning after I'd officially completed my master's program, Steve and I sat on our balcony, having coffee together before he strode out the door and into his work day. He'd matched a striped pink tie to his faintly checked grey suit. With his professionally cropped hair and clean-shaven face, an office was his natural environment. He'd remained his steady self since his first day of employment in Sydney, secure in his identity and at peace with life.

In frustrating contrast, I wasn't even sure what I'd be doing with myself that day, beyond the online course I was still teaching part-time, in my pyjamas. I supposed it was time to transition from writing a thesis to writing a book. The book might take a year, I figured. Maybe two.

Early-morning sunlight crept across the treetops. So many gum trees, jacarandas and palms filled our swathe of Camperdown that the houses beneath were barely visible. Rainbow lorikeets darted about, chattering. Every thirty seconds, a plane appeared in the distant sky and drifted towards us, engines gently roaring. I wondered where all those people in the sky were coming from.

'I suppose you're going to have to apply for that work visa soon,' I said.

Since our evening with Jules and Aram, when I'd tried to convey the reality of Canadian winter, my feeling of homelessness had increased. Steve couldn't relate. Sometimes I ran my fingers along his hairline, wondering where I had to press to pop open his skull and reveal the mess of wires and blinking lights inside.

He tapped his fingernails against the metal arm of the patio chair. 'Is there any reason not to apply for it?'

We hadn't talked about this since the afternoon on Bondi, when I'd lost my wedding rings. Steve had tried to bring it up, but I'd changed the subject.

Our one-year student visa had given us the chance to be locals for a while. The work visa felt like a wholly different creature. One year was an adventure; four years was a commitment.

'If we left Sydney now, it wouldn't be heartbreaking,' I said, tentatively, rubbing at the untanned stripe on my finger where my rings should have been. 'If we stay, I'll get a job, our professional networks will be here, we'll make more friends.'

'I've got a good job here,' Steve replied.

The Reins

It was true. He was already up for a promotion.

'If we could live in Arizona or New Mexico …' We'd considered this. The US seemed headed in a better direction now that Obama was president, but it was surprisingly difficult for Canadians to get US work visas.

This was what I'd realised, lying awake night after night, my heart racing: I knew how to move. I didn't know how to stay.

My childhood had been spread across western Canada, and since moving out of my parents' house, I'd never lived in the same city for two consecutive years. I moved to South Korea on a one-year contract. I moved to Peru, where I volunteered for half a year, then spent several months travelling. I moved to Mexico on another one-year contract. I returned temporarily to Winnipeg to get married on the agreement Steve and I would move to Australia. Now that my latest one-year visa was expiring, and my thesis was complete, I found myself, for the first time in my life, with no concrete plans.

What I wanted was for Steve to say, 'You know, I bet I could get a job in Ireland. Let's apply for working holiday visas.' It wouldn't have solved any problems, but it would have felt like we were in motion. We would have been preoccupied with figuring out where to live in Dublin, sorting through our belongings to pack what was most precious and discard everything else, and hosting a going-away party. We wouldn't have had to think beyond the excitement of that new place, that one year.

Steve was about as likely to announce, 'You know what? I think we should each cut off one of our legs, then have ourselves surgically sewn together. Look, I bought a hacksaw.' He'd suffered

99

the misery of unemployment in Sydney because of me, his cretin wife who never thought anything through. His career was the source of his happiness, the centre of his universe. Consternation creased his face as he drank his coffee, his mouth a hard line because who knew what I was going to say next – that I wanted to move to Antarctica? To the moon?

'It's minus 25 in Winnipeg right now,' I said, 'and we're sitting on the balcony – in January.'

Steve looked at me expectantly.

'I mean, it makes me nervous, but … you like your job, and I guess I can write a book anywhere.'

'Well. Good.' He stood up, stretching his arms over his head. 'I'll get it sorted. See you tonight.'

I sighed, wishing Steve had some capacity for emotional nuance, that he could see what a major life shift this was for me. Here I was, handing over the reins. Saying, *okay, you steer our lives for a while. You apply for the four-year work visa. You tell me when you're ready to leave your job and move on.*

Marriage was about compromise, I reminded myself, as the apartment door banged shut. The noise reverberated through me. I got up and began to pace circles around the balcony table. I'd had too much coffee, I thought. I sat down, then got up and continued pacing. The empty day stretched out before me.

If we were staying in Sydney for the foreseeable future, I had to face my other fear – that I didn't fit in. That, even after reading a growing stack of books on the country's history and culture, I didn't know how to be Australian, how to make myself likeable to Australians, or what Australia was really about.

Maybe I could change that. Maybe I could become resoundingly, brilliantly Australian. I needed to learn more about this place and how I could feel part of it. I needed to meet more Aussies. I needed to ask more questions. And I needed to see the country beyond Sydney, as much of it as possible.

Maybe if you couldn't find a home, you could make one.

I wish I'd had the chance to ask my great-grandparents how they'd felt about the new home they'd forged, but they'd died a few years after I was born. In the 1970s, they'd visited Soviet Armenia, and must have imagined what their lives would have been like, had they ended up there instead of Canada — if they even would have survived Stalin's purges and the hard years of starvation the country had faced. For all my interviews with family members, I'd never got a sense of what Mariam and Paravon had truly thought about the twist of fate that had brought them to Canada. They'd loved the country, they were grateful. But had they felt at home?

Another plane angled across the sky, rumbling in the background. I tried taking a deep breath again. This one came slower. I opened my laptop and searched 'how to be Australian'. The most relevant result was a book titled *The Australian Shepherd: A vet's guide on how to care for your Australian Shepherd Dog*. I ordered it, just in case.

~

A couple of weeks later, I met Noelle at the Clock Hotel in Surry Hills, Sydney's trendiest neighbourhood. A verandah wrapped around the hotel's first storey, and a clock tower sat on top.

When the high noon sun bore down, Sydney summer could be unbearable. The evenings, however, were perfect. The western sky glowed orange as I crossed Crown Street and hurried inside. According to the clock, I was running late.

'Congratulations!' I said, when I found Noelle at the bar. She'd submitted her thesis that afternoon. In it, she concluded that for some people, home exists 'as a brief moment that is difficult to attain and impossible to retain'. I knew what she meant.

I was relieved I had someone to talk to about the decision to stay indefinitely in Australia. Opening Facebook that morning, I'd discovered that an American couple I'd met in Korea had accepted a two-year Peace Corps posting to Mongolia. In a few months, they'd be living in Ulaanbaatar. I felt itchy with envy, especially because Canadians weren't eligible for the Peace Corps. When I'd mentioned it to Steve, he'd rolled his eyes. But Noelle would understand. It wasn't about Mongolia. It was about the adventure.

'Congrats to you, too,' Noelle said, smiling broadly. 'Though I guess the work has just started for you, writing your book.'

'I told you about that lovely Armenian gal I met, Ani? She's helped me line up a dozen interviews with the Armenian community here.' I pointed at the menu in Noelle's hand. 'Let's get drinks.'

'And then I've got some news for you.'

'Bigger news than submitting your thesis?'

She grinned. We ordered negronis, then found two free seats on the verandah. Its wooden rafters were strung with fairy lights. Funny, I'd never heard the term fairy lights before we'd moved

The Reins

here, and now I couldn't remember what we called them in Canada.

We clinked our glasses. The drinks had the same deep orange hue as the sunset. Dried orange slices floated on top.

'Stop holding out on me,' I said. 'What's the news?'

Noelle took a breath. 'We're moving to San Francisco.'

'What?' My stomach sank. I should have seen this coming, knowing that Noelle's love of travel ran as deep as mine. I hadn't realised how much I'd come to rely on her friendship here, how essential she felt to my life in Sydney. At the same time, a shard of jealousy cut into me.

Noelle laughed wryly. 'I'll miss you, too. You can come visit in California.'

I tried to rearrange my face in the approximation of a smile. 'I'm happy for you, really,' I said, swirling my glass around. 'I know Ben wasn't loving it here.' Her husband was an emergency physician from the north-eastern United States. He'd been working at a Sydney hospital since they'd arrived, and found the workplace culture surprisingly challenging.

'He's lined up a good job in San Fran, and then, I don't know, we might go to Dubai or somewhere in Europe in a couple of years.'

It wasn't so long ago I'd been in Winnipeg, counting down the weeks until Steve and I would be in Sydney. Now I was here. And for the most part, it was wonderful. But thinking about San Francisco, about Ulaanbaatar or Dubai or Europe, I felt like life was slipping past me. And the only person in my life who understood that – who'd just written a thesis on it – was slipping away as well.

103

How to Be Australian

~

'Trust me, everyone is friendly. It'll be fine.' I'd finally managed to coax Steve out of the apartment, and now, halfway up the block, he was about to turn back. Traffic rushed past us, the headlights shining into my eyes.

'You know I hate public speaking.'

'If you practise, you might not hate it.' I put my hand on his arm. 'Or just come along to meet some Aussies. There's a whole bunch of them here.'

Steve gave me a tight grimace, and resumed walking in silence.

Now that Noelle and her husband had packed up and left for San Francisco, we needed to meet some new people. Learning there was a public speaking club in our neighbourhood, I figured I could meet some locals while developing my presentation skills, in case I had the chance to speak about my research on the genocide. The club was an American convention that had spread internationally. It would have been more Australian to take surf lessons or join a lawn bowls league, but public speaking appealed to my inner nerd.

We wandered the bowels of Royal Prince Alfred Hospital until we stumbled on the windowless conference room where the club met twice a month. Under the buzz of fluorescent lights, a group of people chatted cheerfully as they arranged trestle tables and chairs around a podium.

An older blonde woman in corporate wear spotted us coming through the doorway. 'Ashley, welcome back! You're on the agenda for your first speech tonight, right? And is this your husband?'

104

I'd attended the previous three meetings, and had now officially joined the club. 'Yep, I finally cajoled him into attending. Steve, this is Ruth.'

Ruth had founded the club twenty-three years ago. She shook Steve's hand warmly, and he gave her a broad smile. Despite his introversion, he had a special magnetism. Everybody loved him, immediately.

Taking Steve around the room, Ruth made introductions before the meeting kicked off. I recognised a handful of people. Viti was an older Indian Australian woman, a retired nurse who'd spent most of her career at RPA, and gave polished speeches and incisive feedback. Kyle was a mature-age engineering PhD student who took beta-blockers before his speeches. Chaoxiang had a postdoc position at Sydney Uni in genetics research, and often apologised for his English, though he had a wider vocabulary than any of us native speakers. The retired couple, Bea and Burt, had attended regularly for twenty years. I wondered if they'd resembled each other when they met, or if, over time, they'd grown more alike. They wore similar wire-framed glasses, perhaps interchangeably, and styled their grey hair in flat bowl cuts. But while Burt had a booming laugh, the most Bea would reveal of herself was a demure chuckle.

Ruth called the meeting to order, and I took a seat next to Steve. He seemed calm enough to enjoy himself now. The first half of the meeting was devoted to impromptu speaking. Chaoxiang had brought a list of open-ended questions, and called on attendees to speak in response to each for about a minute. He invited Steve to answer the last question, adding, 'It's okay to opt out. First-time guests often do.'

'I'll give it a crack.' Steve walked to the front of the room, shook Chaoxiang's outstretched hand, and then spoke for fifty-seven seconds about his favourite hobby.

'This year, I've signed up for City2Surf,' he concluded. 'I think it's going to be fun, if I can make it up the hill.'

Everyone applauded with enthusiasm.

'Good job,' I whispered when he sat down.

'My heart is racing.'

'No-one could tell.'

During the break, Viti opened a packet of Arnott's cookies. I still didn't know which ones were the Monte Carlos. I took an orange cream, then retreated to the hallway to review my speech notes. After the break, Steve squeezed my hand under the table as Kyle introduced me and invited me up the front. After years standing at the front of classrooms trying to explain English grammar to perplexed students, speaking to a friendly audience like this was a breeze. My goal, other than meeting people, was to sharpen my delivery.

For the next seven minutes, I talked about Mariam's and Paravon's survival of the Armenian genocide, how I'd learned about it as a teenager, and how it had driven me to complete my master's degree and now attempt to write a book. I ended by explaining the connection between Armenian Genocide Remembrance Day on 24 April and Anzac Day.

'It was the Anzac ships approaching Gallipoli that prompted the start of the genocide in 1915. This doesn't shift any of the responsibility from the Ottoman government, who had been planning the genocide for weeks. But it does inextricably link these two histories. In fact, they were sometimes commemorated together at past Australian events.'

From the looks on everyone's faces, I could tell this was news to them. No surprise, since the Turkish government continued to deny the genocide.

After another enthusiastic round of applause, Kyle invited Burt to give feedback on my speech.

Burt hiked up his pants as he stood, then shook Kyle's hand and planted his feet. 'Ashley gave a well-prepared speech, and I learned a lot from it. She's going to make a great addition to the club, despite having the wrong accent.' The audience gave a few quiet laughs.

I went rigid, the comment ringing in my ears, the laughter like tacit agreement. Burt continued, pointing out what had worked well in the speech structure, and what I could improve on in my delivery, but I struggled to process what he was saying. *The wrong accent? Was that what people thought?*

As soon as the meeting ended, I shoved my speech manual into my bag and tapped Steve on the shoulder. 'Let's go.'

'You don't want to say goodbye?'

Ruth was headed our way. Pretending not to see her, I hurried out the door. Steve followed a moment later. Outside, the street was quiet. In the tree branches, bats squabbled.

Steve jogged a couple of steps to catch up with me. 'What's gotten into you? I had to tell Ruth you were feeling sick.'

'That stupid comment – is that what people here think?'

'The accent thing?'

How to Be Australian

I swiped at my eyes before tears started slipping down my face.

'You're overreacting, Ash. It was just a typical Aussie comment – they say mean stuff, but they don't mean it. It was in that book you read.'

'It said abuse your friends to their face – not insult someone during a public evaluation.'

'You should take it as a compliment. It's like Burt saying, "Hey, you're one of us."'

I slowed down and dug a tissue from my pocket. 'I get this vibe that people think I'm American. Sometimes when I say I'm Canadian, this look of relief crosses their face. So are other people thinking I'm American, and inwardly grimacing?'

I had no vocal skills; I couldn't change my accent any more than I could change my face or skin colour. I had a brief glimpse of how difficult it must be for others to feel accepted here. If I couldn't do it, how could Chaoxiang – or even Viti or Aram, who were born here?

We reached our apartment. Steve held the front door open for me.

'I guess you got lucky – I don't want to go back to the club.'

'Don't give up on the club, you were enjoying it.' Steve patted my hand. 'People say stuff like that at my office all the time. One of the interns said I looked handsome in that burgundy blazer I got, and the CFO heard her and started calling me Handsome Steve. Now half the office is doing it. They're just giving you the gears. If they didn't like you, they wouldn't do it.'

I wiped my nose again. Intellectually I could see that, in his own weird way, Burt had been welcoming me. But I felt wounded,

108

The Reins

almost childishly. Maybe this was the true reason Aussies abused those closest to them – you had to be tough to survive here, you had to get over yourself and get on with things. Being earnest and showing real feelings were weaknesses, liabilities.

No wonder that Steve, with his aversion to any hint of emotion, seemed to be getting on just fine.

10

Down Under Burlesque

There's a lot that makes Australia a wonderful place to live, even without considering the weather. Take the national attitude to vacation time. The United States is known for providing just enough time off to ensure employees aren't technically slaves. Standard US vacation time, what I was learning to call 'annual leave', starts at two weeks. Canada is less renowned for this same trait, but there's a reason it's sometimes called the 51st state. In the first year of work at many Canadian companies, annual leave isn't permitted. You earn it by going a year without, surviving on the scraps of national holidays. For the first five years at a typical Canadian job, you have two weeks of annual leave per year. After that you might negotiate a miraculous third week.

Discovering Australia's standard four weeks of annual leave was like getting a raise, a bonus and a high-five from the boss, all on the same day. Plus your employer might also provide some extra leave at Christmas, just for the hell of it. I didn't think Australia could top that.

Then Steve came home from work one day and shared the

legend of leave loading, in which a bunch of brave Aussie workers refused to take leave if it meant they would lose their overtime pay, and a great battle ensued, probably involving boxing kangaroos, and somehow resulting in magical bonus pay.

'You're saying you get paid *more* when you're on vacation?' I asked Steve, not sure I was following.

'Yes!' he laughed, slapping his palm on the countertop. 'And get this – if you work for ten years with the same company, there's something called long service leave, have you heard of this?'

I shook my head.

'Three months of paid vacation.'

'This country has 87 per cent of the world's beaches and you can get three months of vacation? And Canada has what? Snow and moose?'

Steve laughed.

Of course, this wonderful aspect of Australia was only wonderful if you had a job, and particularly the right sort of job, which you may be more likely to get depending on relevant professional factors like the colour of your skin.

When we'd arrived in Sydney, Steve met with a recruiter a few weeks into his job hunt. The recruiter talked through Steve's experience, and at the end of their meeting, told him they'd be able to find him a job. 'You won't have any trouble,' the guy said. 'You're white.'

At home, Steve told me this in disbelief. 'It was nonchalant. "Hey, no worries, employers here are racist, but you're on the right side of it."'

'That's ...' Awful barely began to describe it.

When the recruiter pointed out Steve's whiteness as beneficial to his job search, he assumed Steve would agree with the comment, not see it as a gross revelation about the society we'd moved to. The recruiter didn't hint at Australia's racism or step gingerly around it. He announced it, like the weather.

Huh, I thought as I grappled with this unpleasant realisation. *I wonder if this is cultural cringe.*

That's when I started to learn about Australia Day.

~

Steve received his four-year work visa. It came as an email, without fanfare.

What had been fresh and surprising during our first year unfolded in a familiar pattern in our second year. Here came the rain and sudden chill of May, followed by the Queen's Birthday, a holiday that struck us as odd (though Canada still celebrates Victoria Day, honouring a monarch who died in 1901). Then came the peculiar, indescribable scent of the flowering golden wattle, its bursts of yellow paired with red poinsettia blooms, and the interminable stretch of winter days without a long weekend in sight, until we turned the corner into spring, and there was Labour Day, followed by November's wafting jasmine and the riotous colour of the jacarandas and flame trees.

To mark our second year in Sydney, we bought a seafoam-green couch. The couch was second-hand, but still, it was a significant milestone. When I was young and transitory, a bed was couch enough. Now here I was, a couch owner.

We started talking about permanent residency. Not because

we planned to reside permanently, but because of the instability of Steve's work visa. A work visa was tied to a specific job. If you lost that job for any reason, the Australian Government gave you twenty-eight days to find an equivalent one – not any job, but the same job – before they started chucking your stuff on the lawn. If Steve was made redundant, we didn't want the government forcing us to abandon our couch. Applying for permanent residency made sense from a pragmatic view, especially because Steve's work would pay the several thousand dollars in application fees. Still, I felt vaguely uneasy whenever we discussed it. Maybe it was the word 'permanent'.

Or maybe it was something deeper.

I'd moved from one First World country to another, choosing to live and pay taxes in a country where the government's detention of asylum seekers was a blatant human rights violation.

Australia Day didn't make things any easier. It should have been a chance to celebrate what was great about my adopted home. Instead, it doubled down on my unease.

As a holiday, Canada Day was simple. On 1 July 1867, the Dominion of Canada was created through the unification of four regions: Ontario, the original English bit; Quebec, the original French bit; Nova Scotia, the 'New Scotland' bit; and whatever New Brunswick was. Every year since, the country has celebrated Canada Day on 1 July. Families throw backyard barbecues because it's summer, and that alone is worth celebrating, and there are fireworks and little red and white flags. People say 'Happy Canada Day' to each other. The biggest controversy surrounding 1 July is that technically, until 1982, it was called Dominion Day. Even now, a handful of Canadians feel the name change is an unforgivable break with tradition, and politicians occasionally bang on about this national disgrace in parliament. Unsurprisingly, this doesn't get people in much of a fervour. No-one refers to it as National Dickhead Day out of protest at this shameful rewriting of history. People just continue politely barbecuing and then move on with their lives.

Australia Day's history was much more difficult to get my head around. People told me the date marked the arrival of the First Fleet in 1788, but when I looked it up, I learned it marked the raising of the Union Jack as a declaration of British sovereignty. For the first few decades, the newly formed colony ignored 26 January, probably because most of the colonists were starving or suffering from heat stroke. In 1818, Governor Macquarie celebrated the Anniversary of the Institution of the Colony by giving government employees an extra allowance of one pound of fresh meat. NSW continued to recognise the date, but it wasn't until 1888 that the rest of colonial Australia got in on the act, except for South Australia, which did its own thing until 1910. Depending on the state, 26 January was called Australia Day, Federation Day or the admirably bland Anniversary Day.

'The country didn't agree on a unified public holiday until 1994!' I told Steve at dinner one night in January.

'Sounds about right. Who hands out the pound of fresh meat?'

'I had assumed that Australia Day had a similar history to Canada Day, but it's only become popular since the 80s.' The timing happened to coincide with the progression of Aboriginal rights.

'I don't understand why people get so riled up about celebrating on that particular date,' Steve said.

'I don't think it's even about the date. It's like some Aussies define their national identity in opposition to Aboriginal communities – and if they acknowledged the trauma of 26 January, the floodgates would open and they'd have to reckon with the whole brutal history.'

The next day I ran into a neighbour we knew from the public speaking club, a guy in his late forties, white-haired and ruddy-faced. 'You have plans for Australia Day?' he asked.

I shrugged, not wanting to get into how conflicted I felt about the holiday, or about the country and our choice to stay here. 'No-one's invited us to a barbecue.'

'Nah, me neither.'

'Was Australia Day a big thing when you were growing up?'

'I don't remember it being a thing at all. My first memory of Australia Day was in the nineties, when I was eighteen. It was the middle of the day, and I was walking through the Rocks, and there was a guy passed out drunk on the lawn. People were tying helium balloons to him, trying to see if they could get him to float.' He smiled. 'That's Australian.'

How could Australia be simultaneously more mirthful and more viciously factious than Canada? I was never going to understand this country.

~

On our first Australia Day, Steve and I planned to avoid the festivities. Instead, we headed into the punishing summer heat to trek a section of the Northern Beaches coast walk. We expected to shamble barefoot across the sand, then lace up our hiking books to clamber over the rocky headlands. We expected to strip down to our swimmers and cool off in the seawater pools.

We did not expect to inadvertently stumble into a bizarre cultural ceremony in a golf course car park, but then again, who does?

The golf course and its car park sat at the top of a hill at the south end of Collaroy Beach. From there, a paved road wound down to a smaller car park. Dozens of people lined the road, drinking beers. As Steve and I watched on in confusion, they began to cheer and applaud, their attention focused on the top of the hill. Coming down the road with increasing speed was a worn navy two-seater couch, what Canadians romantically call a loveseat – except this one was on wheels.

A young shirtless guy was kneeling on the cushions, grasping a can of VB. Beside him was a cooler. As he drank, the loveseat rumbled over the bitumen, picking up speed, heading for the crowd. The rider leaned as if on a sailboat, and the loveseat's trajectory shifted, narrowly missing the laughing onlookers. At this point it was heading down the hill sideways, its rider pounding his beer.

The loveseat passed a chalk line at the bottom of the hill, and continued on, crashing into the kerb and tossing the guy onto the lawn. He leapt up, holding his beer over his head victoriously. The crowd cheered louder.

'What is this?' Steve whispered.

'No idea, but I really want to put wheels on our couch,' I said. 'Maybe it's an Australia Day thing.'

Steve gestured towards the trail and gave me a look, suggesting we start our hike. I wavered, wanting to be part of whatever happy craziness this was while remembering that this was a day of mourning for some Australians. It didn't seem unreasonable to respect that.

At that moment, a barefoot guy at the top of the hill clambered onto what looked like a cooler duct-taped to a skateboard. Steve and I locked on to him as if hypnotised. Two ropes were attached to the front of the skateboard, and he held these in one hand like reins, straddling the cooler, knees high. He cracked a beer.

As soon as his feet left the pavement, the skateboard-cooler contraption started moving fast. The crowd laughed as the guy's beer splashed onto his face. He pulled uselessly on the reins, leaning too far to the left and almost toppling. He righted himself, but overcompensated.

Suddenly, like the runaway locomotive of a train for hobbits, he was coming straight at me.

I have the trained reflexes of someone who spends most of her free time reading non-fiction. When my brain processed the fact that I was about to be hit head-on by a high-speed esky on wheels, its reaction was to freeze in place, like a moose in traffic.

Luckily Steve is much more athletic than me, and with typical quick thinking, he shouted, 'Ash, look out!'

Other people were shouting now, too, waving their arms towards the open road as if the only issue was that the esky rider had forgotten which way to go. Moving as if underwater, I managed to lift my right foot enough to take one tiny step back.

Still barrelling towards me and flailing widely, the rider

toppled. His forward momentum was cut short as his shoulder bit into the pavement. The skateboard-esky flipped over his body and crashed into my shins. The lid fell open, and a cascade of ice and beer cans spread over my feet.

If there were gods looking down on me – the God of Appropriate Festiveness, perhaps – this was a clear rebuke.

~

By the time 26 January came around again, I was politically aware enough to know that I should have gone to a protest. This year, I planned to avoid possible run-ins with the esky riders by spending the long weekend inside, reading Stan Grant's *The Tears of Strangers*.

But in early January, I happened to spot a poster for Down Under Burlesque, a show promising to artistically portray the history and culture of this vast, sun-baked country via feathers and sequined G-strings – on a date that wasn't 26 January.

I'd never been to a burlesque show. My squeamishness to anything even vaguely sexual is most accurately described as Victorian (the era, not the state). I get nervous typing the word 'peninsula', because what if I forget that second 'n'? And don't talk to me about 'analogy'.

On the other hand, I'd never seen a burlesque show pitched as a comedy.

'Explain this thing to me again?' Steve said as we got off the bus in Marrickville.

Down Under Burlesque was billed as tracing Australia's history. It was only after I'd booked the tickets in a burst of

118

you-only-live-once enthusiasm that I realised the show was a burlesque catch 22. You couldn't claim you were tracing Australia's history if you ignored 80,000 years of Aboriginal culture. But, as far as I could imagine, you also couldn't address a complex, nuanced subject via comedic stripping. Frankly, I was nervous.

'It seems … quintessentially Aussie. Just go with it,' I said. Steve was used to me dragging him along to museums, theatres and other cultural events that don't typically attract large crowds of accountants.

The theatre we arrived at was one of those condemned warehouses that is, with a splash of fresh paint, Fit For Art. Scattered tables featured platters of Vegemite sandwiches with the crusts cut off and packets of Wizz Fizz.

As dusk settled on a muggy night, a mixed-age crowd filled the theatre. The lights dimmed as the host, a larrikin grin on his sun-damaged face, strode on stage.

'Alright folks, let's be honest. Round of applause – who came for the dick?'

The crowd roared. I sat tense, and shoved my hands under my thighs to keep from tearing at my cuticles.

The host introduced the first act, an Aboriginal performer named Matty Shields. The curtains pulled back to reveal a pole in the centre of the stage. A sombre, bluesy song played.

Matty strode onto the stage, wearing clingy short-shorts and strips of white body paint. Exquisitely muscled, he moved with a ballerina's grace, climbing the pole and spinning down while holding on with one knee, hanging upside down with the pole gripped between his thighs, and twirling around the pole before sliding onto the floor. His body paint shimmered in the soft blue stage lights. In between twirls, he sprinkled a powder across the stage, an aspect of Aboriginal dance, I intuited. This modern interpretation of what I imagined to be ancient captivated me.

When Matty stood to bow, the crowd cheered, stamped and howled.

'That was the most amazing thing I've seen in Australia – maybe anywhere,' I whispered in Steve's ear.

He gave me a strange look. 'It was a dude pole dancing.'

I searched for words that could describe the swelling joy in my chest, the sense of possibility and wonder. But the music had already started blasting again.

After the pole dancing, Aboriginal history was ignored. The show launched into a sweeping overview of Australian pop history as set to INXS and Cold Chisel: a cross-dressing Ned Kelly, a strip-teasing Lindy Chamberlain, a prawn-mermaid writhing atop an oversized barbecue, a dancing jar of Vegemite, the girls from Picnic at Hanging Rock also stripping, and more green and gold nipple tassels than you ever imagined existed. But by that time, I was hardly paying attention.

Australia Day could be 8 May, for the 'Ma-ate' connotation, or 1 July, since that would be easy to remember, or a random day selected each year by one of those lottery-ball machines. And yet it's still 26 January, and people protest and march, and others make a hateful raucous, and what it means to be Australian becomes clanging noise and pitchforks, while other people go on blithely attaching wheels to loveseats and eskys.

On a day like 26 January, one might objectively conclude that

Down Under Burlesque

it's more complicated to be Australian than to be Canadian. My burgeoning Aussie identity felt raw and nerve-racking, like a cheese grater pressed against bare skin.

But in the opening act of Down Under Burlesque, I discovered an Australia I could love unreservedly. Alone on stage, Matty Shields was something new and unique and stunning, and from the enraptured look on his face, he was doing what he loved. The hybrid cultural performance of an Aboriginal bloke spinning upside-down like some poetic fuck-you to gravity, cheered on by an exuberant crowd on a day that wasn't 26 January – this was the Australia I wanted to celebrate. This was the Australia I wanted to belong to.

11

The Secret City of Melbun

We'd been waiting for a reason to go to Melbourne, but the timing never worked. Finally, we decided to go whenever we could get discount flights. I put Steve in charge, and he booked tickets for a weekend in July.

A few days before our Melbourne getaway, Steve and I were at the gym, stumbling bleary-eyed through our workout. The breakfast news was on (it was always on at the gym, like some sort of curse). The weather announcer pointed to his map. 'And in Melbourne, a high of only 10 degrees today and through the weekend!' He hugged himself, miming shivering.

I caught Steve's eye, and we started laughing. '*Only* 10 degrees!' we repeated. Through Canadian winter and into spring, 10 degrees was a heatwave. Manitobans wore T-shirts when the temperature was as low as zero. I'd done it myself. Zero degrees felt amazing when the previous day had been minus 20.

Boarding our Friday morning flight, I reflected on the two things we consistently heard about Melbourne. Noelle and her friends, like most expats and tourists, raved about the

The Secret City of Melbun

city. Melbourne was more European than Sydney was, more sophisticated, it had a better vibe. Australian opinions varied, but they were unanimous on one point – Melbourne's winters were terrible. We'd met a bloke who'd moved to Byron Bay to escape Melbourne winters. 'Bryon's great,' he said. 'I wear shorts all year.' This seemed the truest definition of Australian winter: a season without shorts.

As our flight landed in what seemed to be the middle of a field, with no city in sight, I leaned over to share my shorts insight with Steve.

'You know what I'm excited about? Waking up in a heated room,' he said, rubbing his hands together.

This was our third Australian winter. I'd come to think of it as an inverse phenomenon: while the outdoor temperature was reasonable most days, we'd never been so cold indoors. When the autumn air started to get nippy in Winnipeg, we'd turn up the central heating. Buildings stayed heated throughout the winter, because otherwise the cold would burst the plumbing – Canadian winter could destroy your house. In Sydney winter, I woke up wondering how I'd fallen asleep in a meat locker. I expected icicles to form on our bookshelves. I triple-layered my socks. I didn't go so far as to purchase a pair of uggs, but I finally understood what they were for. When the brand had become an international fashion icon in the mid-2000s, fellow Winnipeggers had clomped through snowy streets in sodden uggs, and I'd assumed they were poorly designed winter boots. In Australia, uggs made sense.

Our plane landed and we disembarked into a one-room terminal. 'This can't be Melbourne's main airport.'

'It was cheaper to fly to this one,' Steve replied. Of course.

A bus was waiting to take us to the city, the traditional lands of the Kulin Nation. Coming into Melbourne from the south-west, over the West Gate Bridge, the skyline appeared, grey and blocky. This wasn't the vantage the breakfast news weather graphics chose to spruik. Still, a familiar rush of excitement filled me, the sense of possibility in arriving somewhere new.

Naked-branched London plane trees lined Collins Street. It was Friday afternoon, and the city bustled with pedestrians and traffic. We passed an eclectic mix of modern buildings with lots of glass, and historic buildings featuring brick and stonework. Trams glided past, chiming politely.

Melbourne had reached its high of 10 degrees as we strode out of Southern Cross Station, but the sun was shining. Still, it was definitely chilly. Steve and I dug our toques from our bags. No-one else on the street was wearing a hat. *You wouldn't be so cold if you dressed for the weather*, I thought, as a bare-headed man walked past, his jacket flapping open. Maybe he was also dreaming of a move to Byron.

We found our hotel, tucked away on Little Bourke Street. Dropping our bags off, we took a moment to appreciate a properly heated room.

The windows looked across to an office building, and down into the alley below. I'd read about Melbourne's laneway culture, but maybe I'd misunderstood something. This looked like any other alley, dark and dumpster-strewn.

Back outside, we headed to the Yarra, where a riverside path wound its way towards the Botanic Garden. We kept a brisk pace,

The Secret City of Melbun

our hands shoved in our pockets for warmth.

'Okay, let me try again,' I said, picking up a conversation we'd been having all week. I cleared my throat. 'Mel*bun*.'

'It sounds weird when you say it.'

'Because I don't have the accent. It'd be like Aussies saying Trawna. I'd expect them to say Tor-on-to.' I suspected we were also mispronouncing Canberra. Steve had inexplicably called it Canbrearra until I convinced him he had too many Rs in there. Still, we both leaned into the second syllable, saying Can*bear*ah, much like we said kooka*burr*a. The worst was Wagga Wagga. Whenever I said it, Aussies burst out laughing at my hard vowels. 'At least Sydney is easy to say.'

'Melbourne's great though.' Steve's tone implied he'd been weighing the evidence and had reached a final verdict.

I scrunched up my nose. 'What do you mean?'

'I just like it. It's better than Sydney.'

I stopped dead and turned to face him. 'We've been here two hours! What are you basing this on?'

He shrugged. 'Two hours and we haven't gotten lost yet. That never happens in Sydney.'

It was true, Melbourne's right-angled streets were much easier to navigate than Sydney's mess of winding curves and dead ends. But this one fact wasn't enough for Steve to stake such a large claim on.

'And? That's it? You like Melbourne better than the city we've lived in for two and a half years because it's easy to read on a *map*?' I waited, feeling irked. Steve didn't respond. 'This river is murky brown, and from what we've seen so far, there's nothing to compare with Circular Quay.'

125

Steve put his hand on my shoulder. 'I bet by the time we leave, you'll like Melbourne better, too.'

'Oh, really?' I took his hand, pulling it around my waist. There was no-one else braving the riverside in the biting chill, and for once, Steve let me lean into him. 'You wanna make that an actual bet?'

He pursed his lips.

'If Melbourne doesn't win me over, you're on chores for a solid week.' We usually split the cooking and cleaning, but I was always scheming for more time to work on my Armenia manuscript.

'And if you think Melbourne is great?'

'I'll bake you a rhubarb pie.'

We shook on it.

The wind along the Yarra cut through our jackets, so we headed back into the city. We stopped at a hole-in-the-wall cafe that didn't seem to have a name, or at least had no sign to reveal it. A chalkboard inside read 'smashed avo!' and underneath 'house-made artisan rye'. Steve sat at one of the mismatched, upcycled chairs. The barista had no beard, which was a disappointment. He wore a black toque and a green flannel button-up shirt, with the sleeves rolled to his elbows, presumably to show off his tattoos. His left arm featured an evergreen air freshener, actual size, solid black. On the inside of his right forearm, the word *serious* was tattooed in a cutesy font. A scattering of tiny hearts surrounded it. Did he love being serious? Or did he take love seriously?

'How're you going?' he asked.

'Yeah, good. Just arrived in Melbourne for the first time.'

'Where're you from?'

The Secret City of Melbun

'Sydney.'

He raised an eyebrow. 'I thought I heard an American accent.'

'Canadian. But we live in Sydney.'

'Melbun's way better than Sydney.' He bobbed his head as he placed his palms on the counter, leaning towards me. 'It's the most liveable city in the world. How long are you in town?'

'Just the weekend.'

He bobbed his head some more. 'You'll wanna move here.'

Was this pride from an Australian? It was refreshing. At the same time, I appreciated the baristas at home, who never boasted about Sydney before I'd had a chance to order. I caught myself thinking of Sydney as home. We were comfortable there, in our apartment, our neighbourhood.

'We've heard the coffee's really good.'

'We have espresso roast single origin or our seasonal blend, and we do a cold drip.'

'A flat white and a decaf capp, thanks.'

He frowned and turned away without comment. I'd been working up the nerve to ask about his tattoo. (Maybe *serious* was his partner's nickname? But why not capitalise it?) Now he kept his head down, letting the fringe that stuck out from his toque hang in his face. He put the coffees on the counter like we'd never spoken.

'You're already losing,' I said to Steve, as I handed his coffee over and we headed back outside. 'The people here aren't very friendly.'

'You're just in a mood.'

I was in a mood. Steve's sudden statement of Melbourne's superiority had thrown me. A knot formed in my stomach, and I dug my fingernails into the fleshy pad of my palm.

127

We walked past Town Hall and through the Block Arcade before popping into the State Library. A glass-paned dome gave the grandiose reading room a gentle glow, and made me wish, for just a moment, that I had an excuse to visit Melbourne more often. But the NSW State Library was lovely, I reminded myself, even if its main reading room was trapped beneath an uninspired ceiling.

We found Ned Kelly's armour standing in a glass case. Other than the letterbox helmet, it had the shape of a dress. The bottom piece in particular hung like a miniskirt, with a stylish asymmetrical point. I didn't understand Kelly's legacy. I filed him away for further reading.

Back outside, we headed towards Flinders Street Station. The temperature was dropping. People shivered and rubbed their arms.

Crossing the Princes Bridge, we admired the city from Hamer Hall. This was the view I'd expected, the bridges framing the city, the setting sun turning the Yarra golden. So maybe Melbourne had one scenic lookout.

'Let's get a drink,' Steve said, after we'd snapped a few dozen pictures. 'Where did Jules suggest?'

Jules had tipped me off about the Hamer Hall vantage, along with a list of places she and Aram recommended.

I consulted the list in my pocket. 'It's on Liverpool Street.'

We caught a tram back into the city. Liverpool Street featured peeling paint, a row of trash bins, and the sort of graffiti that sat at the vandalism end of the spectrum. Piles of cardboard boxes lined one wall. I wasn't sure if it qualified as a laneway.

The Secret City of Melbun

The winter sun had faded fast, leaving us in the dark. Most of the doorways looked like office-type entrances, and few shared their street number.

'What's this place called again?' Steve asked.

'New Gold Mountain. You know, Victoria's gold rush era, when Melbourne was the British Empire's second city? The bar should be ...' I checked my pocket list. 'It should be right here.'

I walked ahead to the end of the alley, then back. There was no signage. We paced the block.

'There's a bike on the wall.' Steve pointed. The bike hung as if an invisible rider were pedalling vertically up the red brick wall above an unmarked door. As far as I could tell, it was headed up an apartment building.

I huffed. The wind tugged at my scarf.

'Is there another Liverpool Street?' Steve asked, giving me a pointed look. 'In Fitzroy or Brunswick?'

'Jules definitely said the CBD.' I was sure of it, but it was 2013, and we hadn't yet bought one of those fancy cell phones with virtual maps. When we were out, we had no internet access, like wild animals.

'It's some stuck-up hipster business with no sign,' I said, after we'd checked every doorway. The city was all around us, and yet it felt hidden and inaccessible. 'You still think Melbourne is so great?' If I won Steve over early, maybe I could get two weeks of chore-free writing time.

He stuck his hands in his pockets. 'Yep.'

~

How to Be Australian

For the next two days, I tried to keep my hardened attitude. I tried to keep it that first evening, when we ended up in Fitzroy, on the rooftop of a bar called Naked for Satan, with its unobstructed view of the city lights. I tried to keep it on Saturday, when a fire truck raced past us on Swanston Street, its siren blaring *pew pew pew* as if the truck were laser-equipped. Steve caught the look of delight that flashed across my face. 'Oh, come on,' I said. 'Where else have you heard laser sirens?' I tried to convince both Steve and myself that I wasn't having one of the most enjoyable meals of my life as we rode to St Kilda on the Colonial Tramcar Restaurant, with its red velvet seats and striped lampshades. The three courses included unlimited alcohol, and I argued this was the reason for my good mood.

I attempted to pretend I wasn't enamoured by Berlin Bar, another of Jules's recommendations, when we eventually managed to find it. Divided into East and West Berlin, one half of the bar was decorated in 'capitalist opulence', the other in 'communist austerity', with portraits of Stalin and Lenin on the walls, and camouflage netting draped from the ceiling. I even tried to hide my feelings when we ended up in Collingwood, at a burger joint built into a graffiti-covered train carriage that perched on top of an otherwise nondescript building.

On Sunday morning, I got up before Steve and lugged my laptop to a cafe near our hotel, intending to squeeze in an hour of writing. It was still early, and the cafe was quiet. Today's barista had a tattoo of an anthropomorphic vacuum cleaner on her arm, and on her lower calf, the words FUCK YOU LIAM. I wished I could be there, decades in the future, when she explained its provenance to her grandchildren.

130

In the past two days, I'd seen smashed avo on so many cafe menus that it must have had a brainwashing effect. I ordered it now. It was pleasingly creamy, and well paired with the crunch of toasted sourdough. But my decaf capp was so bitter, it took three sugar packets to smooth out, and once again the barista had gone weirdly silent after I ordered.

Instead of opening my laptop, I returned to reading Sophie Cunningham's *Melbourne*, one of the same series as Falconer's *Sydney*. As I ate, Cunningham described an afternoon spent learning letterpress at a workshop downtown while listening to AFL on the radio and taking soup breaks to stay warm. 'I realised that I felt about as Melbourne as it's possible to feel. It was a good sensation, one akin to (but colder than) waking up and taking an early morning dip at Bondi Beach and consequently feeling very Sydney.'

Perhaps that was the key distinction. Anyone could rock up, take an early morning dip at Bondi, and feel very Sydney. All it required was finding the beach. The Victorian capital was less fathomable; Cunningham's moment of feeling very Melbourne was layered, and required insider familiarity. Melbourne was a city you had to get to know.

After breakfast, I rendezvoused with Steve. In a brazen effort to win our bet, he'd booked a laneway walking tour.

We spent two hours learning the history of the street art scene, and got acquainted with secret hotspots like Hardware Lane, Croft Alley and Centreway Arcade. We'd been wandering the city for two days – how had we missed these places? All Jules's email had said was 'You'll love the laneways.' Not 'You'll love the laneways once you pay someone to show you where they are.'

Melbourne was a city with an introvert's soul, but like most introverts, it had a rich personality waiting to be discovered.

'This reminds me of Montreal,' Steve said, as we took pictures of Hosier Lane's sprawling murals. 'Not the graffiti, but the rest of it.'

I could see what he meant. We'd honeymooned in Montreal. It was Canada's 'most European' city, and, of all our major cities, the one with the most distinctive personality. Montreal wasn't so coy, however. And in winter, its residents knew enough to wear hats.

'You seem like you're having a good time,' Steve added.

'Maybe.' I wasn't about to admit that I wanted to come back to Melbourne as soon as possible.

'I'm looking forward to that pie.'

I threw up my hands, conceding defeat. Steve laughed, but I didn't join in. His snap judgement about the city was still festering under my skin. Sydney had been good to us. Steve had recently taken a new job with the University of Sydney, and despite the long hours, practically skipped off to work each morning. His blazing career trajectory was why we'd stayed in Sydney, why we continued to stay. It felt traitorous to stroll into Melbourne and declare its superiority.

But maybe my feelings had nothing to do with Steve. I was the one who'd brought us to Sydney in the first place, and even before we'd visited Melbourne, I'd begun to suspect it would have been the better choice. It was more affordable, its arts scene offered more opportunities – and, apparently, Steve liked it better. If I'd suspected we'd be staying in Australia as long as we had, I might have taken the time to figure that out.

I was frustrated with the way adulthood locked you in without warning. I was frustrated with myself.

'I like Sydney, too,' Steve said, as if he could read my mind. 'Melbourne's as nice as Sydney, and it's got right-angled streets.'

'After two days, that's your favourite thing about it?'

He shrugged. 'Pretty much.'

I wondered for the millionth time what it was like to live in Steve's head, and see the world in such an uncomplicated way.

Waiting at our gate at Avalon, I got a text from Jules. *How's Melb? New Gold Mountain is a real trip, isn't it?*

I should have known she'd ask about that. *We couldn't find it.*

What? How'd you miss the bike over the door??

That was the bar?! Of course it was. *Question for you — baristas here will be chatty and then suddenly stop talking to me. I don't get it.*

Huh. What are you ordering?

The usual, decaf capp.

Omg Ash, that's such a nanna drink!

Well, that was one more mystery solved.

12

Worry Box

Our bedroom's industrial beige carpet imprinted its pattern of pockmarked squares on my right cheek as the wet puddle under my face grew. A hammer banged away inside my temples.

Steve sat on the carpet beside me in silence, staring at the wall. This was his standard response to emotional situations. He was like an echidna, curling into a ball and burying his face at the first sign of trouble. He knew if he went to another room, I'd follow him.

It was some hour of the evening, though I had no sense of the time or even the month. A valve had burst in my brain. A neural fuse had blown.

When Steve and I got married, our love was invincible. I was sure we loved each other as much as any two people had ever loved each other. We'd lived in separate countries for nearly three years, and after all that time, still wanted to be together.

Marriage could be challenging, I knew. In the TV shows and movies of my childhood, married couples constantly bickered and sniped. Husbands regarded wives as nagging nuisances, and wives regarded husbands as useless Neanderthals. But obviously real-life couples who constantly chipped away at each other had settled for someone who wasn't right for them. Steve and I hadn't settled, so of course our love would remain as bright and fresh as it had been on our wedding day.

But I was coming to realise that I had a simplified vision of marriage, much like my vision of life in Australia as an endless stroll on a UV-exempt beach.

Things should have been getting easier. We remained in our cosy neighbourhood, Steve continued to excel at work, and I was supposedly doing the thing I'd always wanted to do, writing a book.

But nothing felt easier, especially with Steve. Our list of grievances continued to grow. Mine included several serious allegations:

1. Every time we went on a coast walk or hike, I'd finish my water first, and Steve would refuse to share his. Then we'd return to the apartment, where I'd discover he still had half a bottle left. Every. Time.

2. He used a significant portion of his non-work energy, up to 65 per cent, to religiously follow Winnipeg's hockey and football teams (in other words, ice hockey and Canadian gridiron), though – and this was the part that drove me nuts – not a single player on either team was from Winnipeg. You could slap a Winnipeg Blue Bombers jersey on a sack of mouldy burritos and Steve would follow its exploits.

3. Talking to Steve about the complexity of feelings surrounding my sense of home and identity was like trying to describe a rainbow to the colour blind.

His list of grievances against me were ridiculous, of course:

1. I drank my water too fast. (Yeah, it's hot.)
2. I wanted too many hugs. ('Too many hugs' isn't a thing.)
3. I stopped too long to look at parrots and echidnas and bottlebrush. (Also not possible).
4. I insisted he use 'terrible' suncream. (Sure, it spread like tar, but it was free of toxins.)
5. I worried about everything all the time. ('Everything' was a stretch. I'd never once worried about the Blue Bombers' mid-season line-up.)

Lately Steve had begun using this last point to ignore whatever I said. When I suggested he put on suncream, he told me I worried too much. When I suggested we could afford to spend some money to go travelling because who knew if we'd live to retirement age, he told me I worried too much. When I discovered that alcohol can cause mouth cancer, a cancer I hadn't realised existed, and I'd cut my drinking back to weekends and tried to convince him to do the same, he told me I worried too much.

'That doesn't mean you can ignore science!' I said.

My worries didn't stop there. My master's degree had led to nothing. I was increasingly convinced Steve was plotting to leave me. And lately I'd found myself crying about my parents' deaths.

'Your parents are both healthy,' Steve said, frustration burbling beneath his neutral demeanour. 'They're not even sixty yet.'

'But maybe they wouldn't tell me if they got sick because we're so far away.'

Were my worries reasonable? I thought so, but I was also beginning to have a parallel train of thought: *Is this how you envisioned your thirties? Spending every night crying on the bedroom floor?* If Steve would take my worries seriously, I wouldn't have to worry as much. Instead of fixing things, Steve was pulling away from me. He sat on the carpet at arm's length, as if he couldn't bear to get any closer.

My delusions of invincibility were long gone.

'Remember when we first got to Sydney?' I snuffled through tears and snot. 'And you started to feel terrible?'

'That was because I couldn't get a job interview,' Steve said quietly. 'I don't understand why you …'

'I don't understand either!'

I wished yet again we could move to a new city, a new country. Exploring a new place without the burden of figuring out how to become part of it would distract me from my mental clamour.

But that lifestyle wouldn't work for Steve, and I knew it couldn't work for me long term either.

I was going to have to do something drastic.

~

The psychologist I met was named Linda. She was younger than me, tall and scrawny, with frizzy blonde hair. Also, she wasn't technically a psychologist. I sat in the waiting room, rapping my foot against the chair leg and scrolling through Instagram on my new iPhone. There was Noelle at the Golden Gate Bridge, my American friends with a herd of Mongolian yaks, and my nieces in Canada learning to ice skate.

Finding me in the waiting room, Linda gave a quick, professional smile that betrayed a slight nervousness. I followed her into a small consulting room. It had white walls, a single potted plant, and a street-level window, frosted for privacy. The space was only big enough for a desk and two striped armchairs. When we sat down across from each other, our toes nearly touched. The too-high ceiling made the room feel like a test tube.

I probably should have been seeing some kind of therapist for years, but no-one had offered to provide this service for free. Even if I could have afforded $200 an hour, I'm not sure I would have. Crying on the floor isn't fun, but it is cheap.

Then I discovered the University of Sydney ran a clinic with psychologists in training. Patients paid $10 an hour to see a student who had practically graduated. The session was recorded, and the trainee psychologist reviewed it with a seasoned professional who guided the treatment from behind the scenes. It was two for the bargain-basement price of one.

'What brings you here today?' Linda flashed the same emotionless smile.

'Well.' I shifted in my armchair, interlacing my fingers and squeezing until they throbbed. 'My husband's job is keeping us in Australia, which is fine because we love it here but also hard because every choice we make feels like a last chance now that we're in our thirties, like it's either here or back to Winnipeg, which is a horrible place to live, but we need to make real decisions about the future, especially me because I only have $9000 in my super fund and I'm trying to write this book about genocide that's going nowhere and I think my husband's fed up with me but doesn't

138

know how to say it and any day now he's going to walk out, but that may be because my brain feels like it's spiralling out of control and because we moved away from our friends and family so I don't have anyone here to talk to about things and it's hard to do that over Skype, especially because it crashes every five minutes, so I pretend things are okay except now I'm crying, like, all the time.'

My impression of therapy was – like apparently everything else in my life – formed solely from TV and movies. I assumed I'd spend 95 per cent of my allotted hour telling Linda, in aggressive detail, the worries I only ever talked about with Steve. Right before we wrapped up, she would say something equal parts incisive and reassuring, and over six months of this, she would guide me to a healthier self-perspective.

This was not what was going to happen with Linda. I spent fifteen minutes unpacking a selection of my most pressing worries, Steve's reaction to my worries, and what I wished his reaction had been. I'd barely scratched the surface when Linda cut me off.

'I'm getting a clear picture.' She jerked one palm up, crossing-guard style. I went silent, feeling like I'd been pushed off a podium. 'Let's discuss the worry box technique.'

Linda proceeded to talk for the rest of the hour, emphasising her points with both arms raised, like a loose-wristed orchestra conductor. A worry box, she explained, was a metaphorical box where I could store my worries.

'You put them there, then schedule a time to take them out of the box.'

'Like fur coat storage?'

She looked at me blankly. I supposed most Aussies didn't grow up with a closet full of their mums' racoon and wolf coats that were no longer societally acceptable to wear. In North America, wealthier families had paid to keep their furs in professional storage, then collected them at the start of winter. Unlike fur coats, I doubted that my worries would stay where I put them.

Linda had handouts for me. Multiple handouts, some of them consisting of several stapled pages, which I was supposed to complete at home and return within a fortnight to discuss.

I wanted to point out that TV psychologists never gave handouts. But I felt the same way about Linda as I felt about everyone I encountered, even people I passed on the sidewalk – I wanted her to like me. No, I *needed* her to like me. If I got the slightest hint that she or anyone else might be thinking anything negative about me, it would definitively prove every negative thought I'd ever had about myself.

So I said nothing, collected my stack of handouts, folded them neatly, and left.

It *had* felt reassuring to speak to someone other than Steve, even if I hadn't done as much of the speaking as I'd anticipated. A tiny bit of pressure had been released, the *tsss* of a carbonated bottle cracking open. Maybe Linda could help me. Maybe things would get better.

~

Noelle had texted about arranging a Skype call, and we'd finally found a date. I called from the bedroom. Steve was in the kitchen, banging pans as he made apple cinnamon pancakes, one of his favourites.

Worry Box

'Your hair's so long!' I said, when Noelle popped onto the screen. She was at the desk in her home office, lit by lamplight. The brunch hour in Sydney was early evening across the Pacific.

'When did we talk last, four or five months ago?' She ran a hand through her hair, smoothing it.

'How's San Fran?'

Noelle chatted about her job at Stanford, how Ben was doing, and her family in Chile and Germany. She'd just returned from Santiago – I'd seen her photos on Facebook and Instagram – and was heading to New York next week. 'It's half work, half fun. Ben and I still have tonnes of friends from when we lived there. Anyway, how're you doing?'

No-one but Steve knew about the psychologist appointments. I wasn't trying to hide them; I just didn't know how to bring them up.

'Things are okay. I'm still teaching a couple of classes, and Steve's going well at work, as usual.' The screen froze. 'Can you hear me?' I repeated. After thirty seconds of silence, I hung up and called back, cursing Australia's lousy internet.

'You're back! How's your book going?'

'Slow. I'm trying to organise all my research and interviews into something compelling. The problem is it's all compelling to me.'

'You've been working on it for a while now.'

'I was just starting the first draft when you moved. I can't believe it's been two years! And I saw that Fabrizia got a postdoc in Singapore.'

'Almost everyone I knew there is gone. Elise has gone back to

141

Belgium, too. I guess Sydney is like San Fran – great for a while, but hard to stay. They're both such expensive cities.'

'Yeah, I meet lots of expats, but they keep leaving.' I pointed my finger accusingly at her. Our laughter momentarily soothed my hollowness.

'I thought you were meeting more Sydneysiders?'

'A few. Steve and I joined this public speaking club – he was just elected president, actually.' I'd tried hard to make friends at the club. Steve and I had gone out with Chaoxiang and his wife a few times, but his employment contract had ended and they'd moved to London. 'It's mostly locals who attend, but it's weird. They share these really personal stories in their speeches, about being on a plane that almost crashed or recovering from cancer. But then I invite them over for dinner or out for coffee and it's like pulling teeth. They say they're too busy, but I don't know.'

'Aussies are so reserved. They claim they're laid-back and happy-go-lucky, but it's all marketing.' Noelle smiled. 'Trust me, I used to work in marketing.'

'Why do you think they're so reserved?'

She shrugged and took a sip from her coffee cup.

'You're the one who's lived there three years. You tell me.'

'No idea.' Though, after complaining about Noelle and others leaving, it occurred to me that locals might reasonably feel disinclined to befriend me when I could end up returning to Canada any day. 'Part of the problem is that when I lived in Korea and Peru and Mexico, I expected to feel foreign. Here I don't expect it, even though I should have learned to by now. How do you handle that, after moving around all your life?'

142

Worry Box

'I consider myself a citizen of the world.'

It was an interesting idea, but after a second's thought, I realised I didn't know what it meant. I was about to ask, but Steve knocked on the door.

'Pancakes are hot!'

I apologised to Noelle, explaining about the pancakes.

'That's nice! Ben never makes breakfast for me.'

It was nice, I thought, as I said goodbye and pulled the headphones off. But there were so many things I wanted and needed from Steve, and pancakes weren't on the list.

13

Per Rectal

One area in which Steve and I were skilled was pretending everything was fine. I'd learned from him, and he was a zen-level master. I suspected he could go on chatting about the weather while he was actively on fire. In private this infuriated me, but I appreciated its usefulness at social occasions, like the barbecue we were headed to now.

After more than a year teaching English online and flailing through a draft of my book about Armenia, I suspected I was spending too much time hunched over my laptop, alone. I'd gotten desperate enough to take a casual teaching position at the University of Western Sydney, though the job meant less time to write.

One of my UWS colleagues, Natalie, had invited us to her place for a barbecue. As casual staff, popping onto campus to teach a three-hour class and then heading home, I often only encountered fellow teachers at department meetings. At the latest one, Natalie and I had discovered we lived a few blocks apart.

On Saturday afternoon, Steve and I headed up the street, the February sun crisping our skin.

Per Rectal

'I hope we'll meet some Aussies this arvo,' I said to Steve as we knocked on the front door. Natalie was American, which is what had got us talking, and her girlfriend was from Thailand. But maybe they'd managed to make a few more Aussie friends than we had. Sometimes trying to befriend Australians felt like tracking an endangered species.

I was looking forward to the barbecue, at least as much as anyone with the interpersonal fortitude of a skittish chihuahua can look forward to socialising with a group of strangers. I'd added a slew of barbecue-related worries to my worry box – that no-one would talk to me, that I'd end up standing alone in a corner, that I'd spill pinot noir on another guest. Less than a week had passed since my appointment with Linda, and I'd already filled multiple extra pages and stapled them to my worry box homework.

Considering the national motto was 'no worries', I seemed to be doing it wrong. Once I started writing out my worries, there was no end to them. Steve could die of skin cancer or a thousand other illnesses, or a freak accident, or at the hand of a jealous woman screaming that if she couldn't have him, no-one could. Or he might leave me for someone whose days weren't increasingly consumed by pessimistic prophecy.

Maybe I had misunderstood what Aussies meant when they said no worries. Maybe it was similar to the way they described their friends as terrible when they meant great, the way some people interpreted 'boundless plains to share' as 'fuck off, we're full.' Maybe no worries was an acknowledgement that there was so, so much to worry about – climate change, corporate greed, morally corrupt governments, caramel slice addiction – that the only sane approach was to pretend everything was fine.

Within minutes of popping open the bottle of prosecco we'd brought and settling into a sliver of back-garden shade, it was clear almost everyone at the barbecue was an expat. Removed from our families and longstanding social networks, we tended to congregate.

We introduced ourselves to the strangers who sat down next to us.

'Americans?' the tall guy asked as we shook hands. I pegged him as African American, from Minnesota maybe.

'Close, we're Canadian,' Steve said.

'Hey, me too, from Guelph,' he said. Even as fellow Canadians, we couldn't recognise each other's accents.

'I'm Deon. This is my partner, Carolina. She's from Buenos Aires.' We shook hands with a slender woman, her face splashed with tiny freckles.

Jules had told us that our Australian cultural guidebook was wrong about the impoliteness of enquiring about people's professions. 'I do it all the time,' she said. Confused, I'd asked some Aussie colleagues about it, and discovered that opinions were split. 'What do you do' was either perfectly acceptable or an un-Australian offence. After my ill-fated elevator encounter, I decided it was safer to avoid the question with locals. With Deon and Carolina, however, it was the first thing I asked.

Within a few minutes, we were on the standard expat conversational track: how long we'd been here, what brought us, and inevitably, our visa situations. We were in our thirties, and while we'd escaped the friends at home who sat around discussing

146

Per Rectal

mortgage rates and bathroom renovations, the tedium of adult life had still caught up with us.

'We're on a 457, but we're planning to apply for PR,' Steve said. As fellow expats, we knew they knew these terms, the peculiar three-digits of our work visa, and the two-letter acronym that would come to cast a shadow over our lives.

In this case PR stood for permanent residency. In nursing terms though, PR stands for per rectal, and perhaps this isn't a coincidence.

PR was issued by DIAC, the Department of Immigration And Citizenship, who chose to include 'and' in their acronym, out of fear it would otherwise be too accurate. Despite the name, PR visas weren't permanent; they were valid for five years. The Australian Government has no interest in using words as they're defined in the dictionary (see also: refugee).

Steve and I had heard the PR application process could be challenging. But he was committed to his glowing career trajectory, and I was trying my best to support him. The stability of PR would free some space in my worry box. The deciding factor was that Steve's employer was willing to pay for our application fees and an immigration lawyer. We didn't explicitly need this miraculous opportunity; we could have gone home to Canada and lived our lives. But through immense privilege, the option to stay indefinitely in a city we loved had fallen into our laps.

'We got PR a few weeks ago.' Deon shook his head as if recalling a bad dream.

'I had to get a criminal background check from the police at home in Argentina. Unbelievable, how long it took. The number of times I had to call the police in Buenos Aires, begging for someone to answer my questions.' Carolina waved a hand in the air, indicating the spiralling ordeal the process had become. 'I didn't think it would happen, it was so difficult.'

'From the time we started the paperwork to the time we submitted was a year,' Deon said, like he still couldn't believe it.

To a normally functioning brain, this would imply that the PR process that Steve and I were embarking on would be time-intensive and difficult. My brain ran this guy's statement through its processor and produced this silent response: *pffft, for you.*

For once, my neurons switched to full swagger mode. How bad could this application be? I'd applied for and received multiple visas in my life. It might be tedious and time-consuming, but it was just paperwork. It wasn't like we were trying to fly a plane or transplant a lung or end up in the right suburb after driving across the Harbour Bridge.

And what Carolina had said about getting a background check from Argentina couldn't be accurate. Why would she need that? It was easier to assume she was mistaken. Or maybe lying. That must be it – she was a drama queen, exaggerating.

The conversation moved on to Canadian sports, specifically their superiority to the mayhem of rugby and impenetrable starchiness of cricket.

I took a swig of wine, still thinking about permanent residency, mentally freefalling into a rare burst of dazzling confidence.

~

'I talked to the immigration lawyer today,' Steve said later that week. He'd arrived home from work and was now pouring himself a glass of chardonnay from the box in the fridge. Having recently discovered how much cheaper boxed wine is than bottled wine, he'd become a dedicated convert. We knew it was called goon. We also knew we would never call it that, because 'goon' didn't sound like a product fit for human consumption.

I grabbed a bottle of turmeric kombucha from the fridge and joined him on the balcony. It was one thing to drink at a weekend barbecue. It was another thing to come home on a Tuesday evening and immediately fill a glass. The night before, I'd written MOUTH CANCER in my worry box, then added, 'Steve dying of alcohol-related mouth cancer; choosing a dress for his funeral; trying not to shout "I fucking told you so!" while shaking his coffin.'

I frowned at his wine glass, biting my lip.

'And?'

'I thought the lawyer would complete the application.'

'Isn't that the point of the lawyer?'

'Mostly she checks the application before it goes to the government.'

'How is that worth several thousand dollars?' I asked.

'It's all in how they process the application.' When a lawyer-certified application reaches DIAC, Steve explained, it's processed quickly and efficiently. A do-it-yourself application, however, is processed at the speed of a geriatric tortoise shell-deep in cold porridge.

In effect, you pay the lawyer to do the government's work for them.

'The lawyer doesn't do anything other than check the application?'

'I guess we can ask her questions.' Steve shrugged. 'And she sent me the forms we need to fill in. Do you want to start going through it tomorrow?'

What else did I have to do on a Wednesday while he was at work? My erratic casual teaching hours still didn't add up to full-time. Sure, I was slaving away trying fulfil my professional ambitions by writing a book, but it wasn't like I was getting paid for that.

And so I sat down the next morning with the full intention of calmly figuring out what the application involved.

By the time Steve got home, I was pacing the apartment, waving my arms. My hair was wildly matted, and my eyes bugged out like those of a startled horse. My guts twisted into knots, spreading dread through my body, making me long to curl into a protective ball. The Argentinian's words spun through my brain – *I didn't think it would happen, it was so difficult.*

'There's no way,' I said, before Steve was through the door. 'There's no way we can do all the things they're asking for. I need criminal records checks from Australia, Canada, Korea and *Mexico.*'

Criminal record checks were required from any country you'd lived in for more than twelve months. This meant I didn't need a criminal record check from Peru, where I'd lived for half a year. I could have been arrested in Peru for running an illegal alpaca-fighting ring, murdering a baby and racking up seventeen unpaid parking tickets; the Australian Government will never know because of their arbitrary criminal record check demands.

'Yeah, I read that,' Steve said.

'And you didn't tell me?' It came out as a half shriek.

He exhaled sharply. 'Well, look at you. I thought you'd start with the easy bits, not ... do whatever you've done.' He gestured around the room. Papers were strewn across the table, the sofa and then onto the floor. It looked like a hurricane had blown through an Officeworks.

'There's no way. I have no idea how non-native English speakers can submit this paperwork because I can't understand half of what they're saying.' I wrapped my arms tight around my chest and rocked in place. 'I think I have to apply for the Mexican criminal record check in Mexico.'

Steve rubbed his temples. 'That doesn't sound right.'

'And you have to do the IELTS.'

'The what?'

'The English language exam.'

'No, I don't. I'm from Canada.'

'So maybe your first language is French.'

'It's not.' He looked at me pointedly, as if this resolved things.

'The government isn't going to take your word for it.' My arms flapped in exasperation.

'Okay, calm down. You're acting crazy.' He frowned. 'What happened to your worry box?'

It was my turn to gesture at the mess. 'It got too full and exploded.' A moment passed before I realised what else he'd said. 'And I'm not crazy! I'm just ... my brain's not working well.'

Steve sighed. I took the sigh to mean my brain had never

worked well, and, as far as he was concerned, never would. It was starting to feel that way. Maybe, despite my hard work, I wouldn't find the career success that Steve had. Maybe the psychologist couldn't help me. Maybe I would never feel at home, in this country or anywhere.

I'd achieved my dream of escaping Winnipeg winters. I lived in a beautiful city with a person I loved, a place where handsome monkey birds randomly burst into melodious cackling. Why wasn't that enough? Why did happiness rush away like a handful of water?

14

The Lesser Ocean Road

While we cleaned up the mess of paperwork, Steve suggested taking a trip. It wouldn't resolve anything, but it would distract me from my escalating tension and give us both a break. I started planning that night.

If you take the inland route, the drive from Sydney to Cape Tribulation is a mere 2500 kilometres. We decided to go via the coast. It was a few hundred kilometres longer, but it passed through Brisbane and other places we'd heard of. In our optimistic naiveté, we figured the coastal route would be an extended version of the Great Ocean Road.

By the time we hit Brisbane in our rented Kia, we'd given up hoping for a view of anything other than the scraggly eucalypts that lined the highway.

Rain pounded on the Kia's roof as we made our way through Brisbane's CBD, the traditional lands of the Yuggera people. I'd booked a room in the historic Treasury Building, which was now a hotel and casino, its sandstone columns and arches lit by purple spotlights. Nineteenth-century accountants would have met here to review the state's financial ledgers. I figured Steve would feel at home.

At the hotel bar, Steve ordered a beer. I tried to convince the bartender to make me a decaf espresso martini, failed, and ordered an Aperol spritz. We clinked glasses. As soon as we left home, things were easier between us – another part of the magic of travel.

'What do you most want to get out of this trip?' I asked.

'To not die in a car crash.' Steve propped his elbow on the bar and dropped his head into his hand. 'That was a long day.'

It had been a big deal when the last stretch of the TransCanada highway through Saskatchewan had finally been expanded to four lanes. That had happened years ago, so Steve and I could hardly believe it when, not far north of Sydney, the Pacific Highway had narrowed to two lanes and stayed that way for most of the ten-hour drive. We'd spent the day bracing for impact as oncoming vehicles darted around RVs and trucks. Though I'd attempted to put these worries in my box, I'd failed.

'Also, I do *not* want to discuss our PR application,' he said.

That summed up our progress. 'No argument from me.'

'What are you hoping for?'

'I'm keen to meet some Queenslanders, find out about life north of Brissie.' I rubbed my hands together. 'I have this impression of Queensland as intensely Australian, between the Great Barrier Reef and the crocs and snakes.'

'And white nationalists.'

I'd sent Steve a few articles on a woman named Pauline Hanson. *Am I misremembering*, I wrote, *or is there no equivalent to this in Canada?*

'I'd rather encounter a croc.' I tapped my fingers on the bar. 'We're in a rut in Sydney, not seeing anything new.'

After more than three years there, we'd wrung as much out of the region as we could, with regular daytrips to hike along the Northern Beaches, through Royal National Park and in the Blue Mountains. We'd winery hopped through the Hunter Valley and been anointed by blowhole splashback at Kiama.

'You saw those black cockatoos the other day.'

I had, not far from our place. Three of the huge, mohawk-crowned cockatoos perched in a banksia, munching on seeds. They moved with an unhurried self-possession, a calmness I could only envy, and I'd stood beneath them, transfixed. The sight had transported me outside myself.

'But there's so much more. I want to the see the outback and WA and Tasmania.'

'Well, here's to new Australian experiences.' Steve tapped his drink against mine.

The morning sun broke through the clouds, lighting our view across the Brisbane River to Southbank. We had the day to spend in the city before continuing north.

As I was brushing my teeth, Steve appeared in the bathroom door, mobile in hand. His boss had emailed, needing some financial projections revised.

'Seriously?' I said. 'You're going to work in the hotel all day?' Sometimes it felt like he was in love with his job, and I was a necessary but tiresome task that came between them.

'I don't have a choice.'

I wanted him to be unhappy about it, or at least resigned. He seemed unperturbed.

'What about the Wheel! Of! Brisbane!' I said it with the staccato rhythm of the *Wheel of Fortune* game show theme, clapping along. I wished Wheel of Brisbane was a local version of the show in which all the prizes were cane toads. Instead, it was a Ferris wheel. From our windows in the former Treasury, we could see it across the river.

'You can tell me about it tonight.'

I headed out alone. The morning sun was powerful, and the air hung thick and sultry from yesterday's rain. I walked to the centre of the Victoria Bridge. From this angle, with its yellowish river bordered by freeways, its pedestrian bridges and its cluster of squat office towers, Brisbane looked like a knock-off version of Melbourne.

In search of air-conditioning, I headed for the Queensland Museum. I was expecting to learn some Queensland facts and maybe see some taxidermied snakes. I was not expecting to see the most brutally violent museum display I've ever encountered in my life, but of course I did, because this was Australia.

The display case contained a dried-out goanna that had attempted to shove an entire echidna into its mouth, spines and all. The spines had lodged in the goanna's mouth and throat. 'Unable to swallow or disgorge, this unfortunate lizard choked to death,' the display's sign read. 'Locked together, predator and prey died, then mummified beneath the desert sun.'

The display stood apart from the main fauna exhibition, as if the curators knew it didn't quite belong. The sign concluded with the line, 'This curious exhibit was acquired and displayed by the

156

Queensland Museum prior to 1912.'

'Curious isn't the adjective I would have chosen,' I said, as I recalled the details with Steve over dinner that night.

'You're not Australian.'

'Clearly. I'd like to meet the naturalist who stumbled on the mummified carcasses and thought, "That belongs in a museum!"'

I'd coaxed Steve out of the hotel room late that afternoon, and we'd walked through Southbank's pocket rainforest before finding a restaurant near the Goodwill Bridge, with a view of the city lights. The server brought our meals, gnocchi for Steve and wallaby steak for me. Though I sometimes bought kangaroo mince at the grocery store, this was the first time I'd encountered wallaby as cuisine.

'The thing that gets me most about the exhibit,' I said, because I'd been obsessing about it for hours, 'is that it memorialises the worst mistake that goanna ever made. I'd hate to have the time we put petrol in a diesel engine memorialised in a museum for a century.'

Steve winced. 'How's your wallaby?'

I took another bite. It was melt-in-your-mouth tender, better than any steak. 'Too good. I feel guilty for the wallaby.'

'So you've already achieved your goal of new Australian experiences?'

'Seeing mummified carnage and eating an adorable wallaby?' I pointed my fork at him. 'No, no. You just wait.'

We were on the move, and things felt easy between us again.

~

On our drive north the next day, two barefooted pre-teen boys raced along the pavement, with three surfboards between them. One rode a bike, a surfboard under his arm; the other pushed along on a skateboard, struggling with two surfboards at once. It struck me as the perfect counterpoint to the goanna-echidna tableau, equally Australian, but alive and joyous, and yet still life-threatening, the wind rippling through the hair of their unhelmeted heads.

When we first arrived, I thought Noosa might be the most picturesque spot in the world. We picnicked on the beach with fish and chips, then watched the sun set from a riverboat cruise. It was a fine day, but we could have been in Waikiki or Cancun or a dozen other places.

Walking back to the hotel, I was feeling flat.

'Vacation spot not nice enough for you?' Steve asked.

I didn't reply. Maybe I had set my Queensland expectations too high.

'Would this help?' Steve handed me a bag from one of the souvenir shops. 'I found it when I got the fish and chips.'

The bag held a single item, brown and furry. I pulled it out.

'What is it?'

'A coin purse made from kangaroo balls,' he said, as if describing any ordinary purchase. 'An ad in the store said I'd be nuts not to get it.'

Occasionally, Steve knew how to make my day.

~

The Northern Territory had been my first choice for this trip, but in Steve's appraisal the outback was 'too hot and dry'. The bargaining

158

chip he'd used to dissuade me was a three-day live-aboard Great Barrier Reef excursion that left from Airlie Beach. The shiny marketing pamphlet showed young, attractive people having the time of their lives on a sleek white boat. The night before, our excitement kept us awake long after we'd turned out the motel room lights.

Early the next morning, we abandoned the hire car and boarded the boat with ten other tourists and expats. The first let-down came when the crew introduced themselves. Two were from the UK, the other from Auckland. In hindsight, we probably would have met more Australians driving the inland route.

Grey clouds blew in soon after we set sail, and the wind that brought them hounded us for the next three days, rocking the catamaran relentlessly. Everyone vomited off the back deck at least once a day. We tried to socialise, but Steve's face had a greenish tinge, like he was in the first stage of turning into the Hulk. By the time we reached our snorkelling spot, I barely cared about the reef; I wanted in the water for seasickness relief. I floated facedown in my life vest, letting Steve pull me around by the hand in search of sea turtles.

'Was that a particularly Australian experience?' I said when we arrived back in Airlie Beach. 'When Aussies think of the Great Barrier Reef, does it bring back the taste of vomit?'

'It was the most I've ever paid to throw up,' Steve said, as he searched his bag for the car keys.

We climbed into the dust-streaked Kia and continued north. The bush gave way to cane fields, and for hundreds of kilometres on either side of the highway, there was nothing but sugar cane. I felt restless, chasing some illuminatory experience of Australianness just beyond my grasp.

Soon we'd reach Cape Tribulation, then leave the car at Cairns airport, catch a flight to Sydney, and return to our everyday lives, my classes full of disinterested students, appointments with Linda, the grind of writing, the loneliness that had seeped into our apartment.

For a hard, pounding minute, the landscape flashing past, returning felt unbearable.

~

The world turned leafy green by the time we hit the Daintree River. The muggy air smelled tropical, rich with heat and vegetative decay. Climbing out of the air-conditioned Kia was like stepping into a hot, damp sock.

Steve and I were worn out, not fully recovered from our three days of sea sickness and the 3000 kilometres we'd covered in a too-small car. I'd had to convince him it would be worth driving the extra distance past Cairns.

Still, we exchanged a smile when we boarded the river ferry and spotted the two welcome swallows riding with us. They chirped sweetly, flying off into the thick foliage as the ferry docked.

I'd booked a cabin, one of several set into the jungle. The receptionist, a fellow Canadian on a working holiday visa, handed us a flashlight as she checked us in. The pathways between cabins were no longer lit, she explained. Ants had eaten into the wiring.

'The owners replace it, and the ants just eat it again,' she said with a shrug.

In Sydney, and everywhere else I'd lived, ants invaded kitchens to scavenge for crumbs. In Far North Queensland, they cut the power. That fact alone was worth driving several hundred kilometres for.

The ants hadn't yet managed to disconnect our cabin's electricity. We dropped our bags and headed out.

'So?' I asked, as we navigated to the parking lot with the flashlight. 'Excited?'

'Not really,' replied Steve.

'We're going to see the oldest rainforest in the world! It's older than the Amazon.' I hadn't known Australia had any rainforest before I'd planned this trip, let alone such a distinguished one.

'I don't know if we're going to see very much,' Steve replied. It was 8 pm, the sky was a moonless black, and we'd booked a jungle night tour.

We joined a small group waiting for the tour to start. We'd encountered so many Brits, Kiwis and North Americans working along the Queensland coast that I'd given up on meeting any Australians. Maybe they'd all left to work at Canada's ski resorts. Our two-hour tour through the Daintree would probably be led by a poli-sci graduate from the University of Calgary.

But I was wrong. The guide was a lanky guy named Colbee. He was dressed like a long-haired Steve Irwin, with a black bushranger hat and the sleeves of his tan button-up shirt rolled to his elbows. He might have been playing to the stereotype, but the clothes were worn, with fraying hems and a series of small tears in his shorts, like maybe a freshie had gotten at them.

'The only wildlife I can guarantee you'll see tonight is right here.' He shone his flashlight at a large rock. On top of it sat a monstrous frowning toad, its mouth a long downturned line, its black eyes pointed in different directions. Its shoulders and chest hulked out around its head, like it was on toad steroids. A woman behind me gasped.

'One of our infamous cane toads,' Colbee said. 'This one probably weighs close to 2 kilos, and is about 25 centimetres long, by the look of it.'

He gave us a brief history of cane toads, the error in judgment that had brought them here, the difficulty in slowing their destructive expansion.

'When I was a kid, I'd take a golf club and whack toads into traffic.' He stood with one hand in his pocket, relaxed and unhurried, his other hand holding the flashlight on the still unmoving beast. 'But they're tough. One time I saw a toad get run over by a truck, its guts spewed over the highway. The damn thing picked itself up, shoved its guts back in its mouth, and took off.'

If he was exaggerating, I didn't care. Steve scrunched up his face.

Colbee leaned over and grabbed the toad. It squirmed in his hand.

'There's a law up here that says if you catch a cane toad, you have to kill it. So, everybody, flick off your flashlights.' The darkness closed in. Brush crunched under Colbee's feet. Then we heard a wet thud, and another.

As he switched his flashlight back on, a boy began to cry.

Colbee waved his light around until he saw the boy, who looked

The Lesser Ocean Road

about eight and was holding his mother's hand. 'Hey, kid, you okay?'

'I've never heard anything die before!'

The boy's accent had an Ohioan crispness. Colbee gave the mother an apologetic grimace. The boy continued sniffling, but I felt exhilarated.

Colbee led us deeper into the jungle. Had he switched off his flashlight and left us there, we never would have made it out. We moved slowly, turning off our lights at times to listen to the rustling foliage, the burble of some unseen creek. Then Colbee would illuminate a centipede scuttling up a tree trunk, a scrub python slithering along a branch, or a huge spider. He taught us about mahogany trees, strangler figs, and the spiked wait-a-while vines that hung from tree branches, entangling themselves in our clothes.

We emerged from the rainforest into the harsh light of the parking lot, where the Kia waited to return us to Cairns in the morning. The rest of the group scattered to their vehicles, the traumatised American boy and his mother the first to drive off.

As Colbee was about to turn away, I asked, 'Have you always lived up here?'

'Yep, my whole life.' He tucked his hands in his pockets. 'Tourists always want to know what it's like, you know, like it must be so scary with all the creepy crawlies. I got a bunch of mice in my place last year, so I caught a scrub python. He lives in the house now, takes care of the mice.'

'You just went out and caught a snake?' Steve asked. He sounded as fascinated by this bloke as I was.

163

'I grew up snaking. It's good fun. Snakes don't always like it though. I took a bite from a python one time, ended up with a tooth wedged in my middle finger.' He held up a hand, waggling the finger. 'Couldn't bend it for five months. I worked it out with a knife eventually.'

I could have spent the rest of my life listening to Colbee.

15

Fingerprint Break

I'd never been in a police station before, but I had read a lot of thrillers, and so had often imagined the dramatic inner workings of law enforcement. When Steve and I planned our visit to the Sydney City station, I'd allowed myself to look forward to it. It would be interesting, I'd thought, watching cops prodding people in handcuffs, wondering what salacious, bizarre crimes they might have committed.

Now that we were here, however, my attention was focused on the uniformed officer running the station's front desk. She was short and broad-chested, and I'm pretty sure her father was a megaphone.

'Sit down!' she barked at anyone approaching the counter, finger-pointing them to the stiff plastic waiting chairs lined along the wall, where Steve and I waited, shifting uncomfortably. Every time she opened her mouth, I jumped.

I slipped my hand into Steve's. He pulled away. Right – we were in public, and only teenagers and weirdos held hands in public, even when being acoustically assaulted in the pursuit of paperwork.

How to Be Australian

Two months had passed since our Queensland road trip; it felt like years. Since returning, we'd thrust ourselves back into our permanent residency quagmire. Steve had decoded the worst of the bureaucratese, and we'd chipped away at the paperwork. Now we were about to check off another major to-do.

'What are you here for?!'

Shouty was squinting in our direction. I pointed at my chest with an expression I hoped was inquisitive, but was probably closer to panic-stricken. If Shouty had pulled me into an interrogation room, I would have confessed to anything she suggested.

I looked at Steve, who looked back at me. Our paperwork trembled in my hands.

'We, uh, hi, we're here for, um, fingerprints.' I'd told her this when we arrived, but to be fair that was over an hour ago and she had bellowed at a lot of people in the meantime.

The Australian Federal Police had a relatively humane system of providing police checks. You went to their website, entered your personal information, including every address you've lived at for the past decade, and paid $25. They then posted a printout of your criminal record check to you, and you triumphantly checked that item off your to-do list.

So I could see how the Australian Government thought it was reasonable to demand criminal record checks for every country we'd lived in for more than twelve months. If all we had to do was go on the various police departments' websites and copy-paste our personal info from window to window, it would have been wearisome, but not nightmarish.

But each country had their own unique and zany procedure

166

for providing criminal record checks. Australia's process was at the easiest end of the scale. In contrast, many other nations acted as though the applicant was a lion and their criminal record check was a delicious lion treat only to be earned by jumping through several flaming hoops and maybe being whipped a few times.

The Royal Canadian Mounted Police fell in the latter category, and so we were spending Saturday morning waiting for a NSW police officer to officially fingerprint us.

'You're gonna have to wait!' Shouty snapped, as if this was new information.

Our PR application wasn't going well. Earlier that morning, Steve had phoned the International English Language Testing System office.

'I'm calling to find out if I have to take this test or if there's something else I can do.' For once, he was the one pacing while I sat on the faded cushions of our seafoam couch.

'The thing is, English is the only language I speak. It's absurd to write a test to show that.'

I imagined the poor receptionist, who probably had this same conversation a dozen times a day. Steve tapped his fingertips against the side of his leg, one of his stress-induced tics.

'But I'm speaking English to you right now. Isn't it obvious that –' His head dropped, sagging along with his shoulders. 'Uh huh. Uh huh.'

He hung up.

Knowing he'd have to go ahead with the exam had put him in a bad mood, and sitting in the police station wasn't improving it.

Another half-hour passed before Shouty escorted us into a back room to dip our fingerprints in squid juice and roll them on official forms.

When our inky prints filled every box, Shouty shoved the form back to us. 'You're done!' She started towards the door.

I glanced in a panic at Steve.

'We need you to – we can't, um, mail our own fingerprints and so we need …' I trailed off.

'We don't do that!' The look on Shouty's face implied that I had two seconds to get out of her sight before she tasered me.

'We're not allowed to mail them,' I blurted. 'The Canadian police—' apparently thought we were experts at fingerprint tampering, because it was their strict policy that we, the lowly applicants, did not handle the paperwork after our official fingerprints were inked onto it by a trained law enforcement professional.

'We have FedEx envelopes, addressed and everything,' I added, thrusting the envelopes towards her, along with the rest of our completed, signed paperwork.

Shouty huffed, the force of her breath lifting a chunk of her rust-brown fringe. 'Give them to me!'

The second the envelopes touched her hand, I turned and ran out the door, fearing she'd change her mind.

Steve and I stood on the pavement a few feet from the station entrance, the sun beating down on us. Traffic whooshed past and pedestrians hurried around us.

'She's going to drop those in the rubbish, isn't she?' I said.

Steve shrugged.

'How will we know? And if she does bother to mail them, who knows how long it'll take for a response.'

He sighed and walked towards the bus stop.

I tried to follow, but I couldn't lift my legs. I fought the compulsion to drop to the ground in a heap. My heart raced and my breath came in quick bursts. My lungs felt squeezed, unable to expand. The street spun around me, and my thoughts spun through my head. I wrapped my arms around myself and started to rock. I didn't want to be here on the street in the middle of the day, sinking into fearfulness, this out-of-control feeling. But I couldn't stop.

Steve finally noticed I wasn't with him. He turned back.

'What now?'

'I can't do this, I can't do this,' I said, staring at the ground, willing myself to stay upright. 'We've already spent months on this and gotten nowhere! We don't even have our Canadian criminal records. I'll never get them from Korea and Mexico.'

There were ongoing wars, earthquakes were devastating impoverished communities, and my sister was having another baby, but the permanent residency application had rendered the rest of the world irrelevant. My existence had shrunk to this one impossible task.

I couldn't do the PR application, and more urgently, I couldn't do life. I couldn't bear that if Steve and I managed to stay married, one of us would one day bury the other, that each day we moved closer to that inevitability, that it could strike at any moment, yet in the face of that, and so early in our marriage, we were trapped in the mundane, this endless paperwork, whose turn it was to dust, our taxes, the boring nothingness of adults. And I couldn't bear the goodness of our lives, that we were free to move throughout the world because of nothing but the lottery of birth, and that we moved so breezily through our days, treated with friendliness and respect so often that when a single person raised her voice to us with the slightest impatience, it left me shaking, ashamed of my own existence.

I was afraid. I was inadequate. I was failing at something, even if I couldn't say precisely what. It felt like everything around me was on fire and I was trying to put it out with a flask of gin. I struggled to take a deep breath, managing only quick, shallow gasps. Pain spasmed in my cheek.

I began crying, wailing between choked heaves, there on the pavement outside the police station in the middle of the afternoon, my hands pressed over my face as if I could disappear behind them.

All I wanted was Steve to put his arms around me and say, *It's okay, I love you.*

He took a step back, eyeing me warily. 'Ash, stop it.'

Which only made me cry harder.

16

Welcome to Tits

Months passed in a blur of tears, paperwork and fortnightly appointments with Linda. I'd work at acknowledging my worries and storing them carefully in their box, only for them to erupt, chasing me in circles. My book stalled. I'd transitioned from onset adulthood into what was, apparently, the rest of my life.

Steve and I debated giving up on the PR application. After much huffing, he'd taken the English language exam. He'd been convinced he didn't need to prepare, though I tried to explain that the exam required specific types of responses. I knew what I was talking about, having taught English as a Foreign Language exam prep. Steve figured he'd be fine.

When the results came, Steve squeaked by with a passing grade. An Italian friend who took the exam the same day scored higher.

Our Canadian criminal record checks arrived in the post a couple of months after the fingerprinting debacle. In the meantime, I'd visited the South Korean consulate in Sydney, where the staff provided and endorsed a form for me to post to the police in Seoul. After six weeks passed with no response, I began calling Korea's national police office on a weekly basis only to connect with an automated message in the voice of a perky Korean tween that I assumed was informing me the line was busy.

Still, I eventually received my Korean criminal record check in the post. Counting the Australian one, I had three of four.

All I needed was Mexico.

Except – and here's the funny bit – Mexico didn't provide official criminal records checks for foreigners. For Mexican nationals, sure. But not foreigners.

Instead foreigners had to request a letter in Spanish that, after explaining this double standard, stated, 'We've looked into this person and it doesn't seem like she committed any crimes here, although, let's face it, this is Mexico. She could have been running the Juarez cartel and bribed us into silence. You'll never know.'

It had taken months of calling the embassy, emailing the embassy, calling everyone I knew in Mexico, composing grammatically disastrous emails in Spanish via Google Translate to several Mexican federal departments, and stress-crying until my eyeballs were on the point of bursting to extract this information.

And so, on a bright but chilly Monday in July, I boarded a bus headed to Canberra, traditional lands of the Ngunnawal.

Throughout our time in Australia, whenever the topic of Canberra came up, people derided it. Canberra was the epitome of bureaucratic blandness, a snake-riddled suburbia of confounding roundabouts, especially punishing to anyone stupid enough to try navigating the city by foot.

Disliking Canberra seemed to be a clear Australian value.

Welcome to Tits

In response to this unanimous negativity, I developed a perverse desire to like Canberra (further evidence that my brain's main goal is to sabotage me). *I'll show them*, I thought. *When I visit Canberra, I'll see it from a whole new perspective.*

Now I had my chance.

Scraggly clumps of gum trees flashed past the bus windows as I kept an eye out for wildlife, especially kangaroos. After several years in Australia, the only ones I'd seen outside the zoo were brief flashes of movement in a distant field, or roadkill.

Today all I saw was my own reflection, spontaneously smiling at the joy of heading somewhere new.

'What's taking you to Canberra?' asked an elderly lady across the aisle from me.

I tilted my head. How could I explain that I was travelling to the nation's capital to prove I was myself in order to request a letter that wasn't technically a criminal record check and that, according to our lawyer, the Australian Government may not accept as valid proof of my crime-free Mexican lifestyle?

'Just a short holiday.' As the bus headed along the Hume Highway and Sydney receded into the distance, my excitement built. I began to feel lighter and cheerier than I'd felt in months. Secretly, I was happy to be taking this short trip alone. Lately, there had been nothing but tension between me and Steve, my desperate unhappiness, his emotional withdrawal.

When the bus pulled into Canberra's CBD, I had to admit it looked as dull as everyone had warned. Beige rectangular buildings squatted among wide streets. Despite being midmorning on a weekday, there were no more than a handful of people about.

173

Still, I bounded down the bus steps. It would take more than architectural blandness to quash my enthusiasm. The sun was warm, but the wind cut through me. I shoved my hands in my pockets, wishing I'd brought gloves.

Etched in the glass of a floor-to-ceiling office window was the national coat of arms, the kangaroo and emu proudly facing each other. Someone had stuck googly eyes on each animal's face, proving at least one person in Canberra had a sense of humour.

I'd certainly enjoyed reading about Canberra before arriving. The city's name comes from *nganbra*, a Ngunnawal word that supposedly means 'meeting place', but according to local elders means 'breasts'. I'd learned this from historian David Hunt, who wrote, 'Australians are the only people in the world who would name their national capital "Tits".' This is typical of the tendency to appropriate Aboriginal words without grasping their meaning, he added. To me this made Canberra more, rather than less, appropriate as the name of the national capital.

I'd read conflicting accounts of the city's design as well. The American town planner responsible, Walter Burley Griffin, may have based the layout on occult symbols like Freemasonry or Kabbalah. *National Geographic* observed that, seen from above, Parliament House looks suspiciously like the Illuminati's all-seeing pyramid eye, and some people believe the double ring roads encircling Capital Hill indicate the area is a consecrated temple. *National Geographic* went on to note that these suspicions are baseless, but that's exactly what the Illuminati would want you to think.

Mulling over conspiracy theories gave me something to do

174

while tramping from the CBD towards Capital Hill. The city had a ludicrous spaciousness, as if it were designed for giants.

I'd been here fifteen minutes and I was already reminding myself of my determination to like this place. A stream of traffic passed, but no other pedestrians.

I reached a fork. The right stretch of pavement continued along the road, but the left headed off into the grass. It looked like a shortcut, heading in my direction. Google Maps didn't seem to include the shortcut, but I trusted my sense of direction. After all, this pavement must lead somewhere.

But that is exactly the type of thinking that applies to cities that are not Canberra. I followed the pavement for about ten minutes, deep into a grassy field, until it abruptly ended in the literal middle of nowhere. In the distance were trees, and peering back the way I'd come, I could make out the blur of cars. Surrounding me, however, was nothing. There was no indication there had ever been anything in this spot, and there was no indication of where to go from here. This stretch of pavement may as well have ended with a sign reading, 'That's what you get for walking, you two-legged idiot! Regards, Canberra.'

My mood was significantly less buoyant by the time I found the Commonwealth Avenue Bridge. I shook my head. No, no, this was lovely, the black swans floating on the lake, the sense of serene quiet on a weekday in the centre of the nation's capital. So quiet it was … eerie.

I had time for a quick stop before heading to the Mexican Embassy, and there was one thing in particular I wanted to see. I made my way towards Parliament House.

Front and centre over Parliament's main entrance was a stainless-steel rendition of the Aussie coat of arms, kangaroo on the left, emu on the right, each leaning in to support the shield. According to Justine van Mourik, Parliament House's art curator, when artists submitted coat-of-arms designs during the building's construction, at least one was rejected because the kangaroo was 'not visibly male'.

The kangaroo poised above Parliament now was *very* visibly male. I'd read about this as well, and come to see for myself, thinking it must be a joke. This kangaroo's abstract hunk of maleness was the same size as its snout. Was this roo to scale – or was this a wishful projection on the part of the artist?

Van Mourik offered no explanation for this criterion in Parliament's coat of arms; there's no mention of animal gender in the charter that dictates the design.

Like Canberra's name, this seemed emblematic of Australia in more ways than one. At surface level, it was peculiar and hilarious. But it could also be seen to represent the country's entrenched sexism, this 'visible maleness' hung atop the meeting place of the federal government as if to remind everyone who was really in charge. It could be seen as symbolic of the appallingly sexist treatment of Australia's first female prime minister. Or that, on average across the country, one woman per week was murdered by her current or former partner, and yet that didn't rank among Parliament's top priorities.

And this symbolised, in turn, my own ambivalence towards Australia. There was so much I loved about this country. But there were also so many ways it could do better, for its Indigenous communities, for migrants and refugees, for women – for nearly everyone.

I'd gritted my teeth the past several years, knowing we were paying taxes to a government whose policies and attitudes we profoundly disagreed with. If Steve and I ever managed to get a permanent residency visa, we'd be eligible for citizenship. With citizenship, we'd be able to vote.

I headed off to find the Mexican Embassy with a renewed sense of determination.

~

Parliament to the Embassy would have been a simple walk, but I detoured to find a cafe along Lake Hurley Burley. This again proved more difficult than anticipated, though I eventually got lunch and a half-decent caramel slice.

Now I was back at the lakeshore, the directions to the embassy programmed into Google Maps. Despite the wintery chill, it was the sort of day that, if drawn by a five-year-old, would feature a sun wearing sunglasses. I was trying my best to enjoy it, but all this walking was exhausting. Maybe Canberra's planners had assumed, with the abundance of sunshine and fresh air, that each generation of Australians would grow ever taller, making the capital's spaciousness less absurd.

Google Maps chimed in, instructing me to turn left in 200 metres. I was on an empty road, the lake to the right, bush to the left. I walked on, searching for a side road. I walked back, thinking I'd missed it. Zooming in as close as possible on my phone screen, I discovered the problem. According to the map I was in the centre of the nation's capital. Also according to the map, I was supposed to take a left turn into the bush.

My phone had found a shortcut, a barely perceptible path through the gum trees. I assumed this was an actual shortcut and not another Canberran fake out. I stood at the side of the road, hesitating. Due to being a) not a man and b) a fan of the sort of books in which the remains of women routinely have to be identified by DNA, I wasn't super keen on wandering into the wilderness alone.

I reminded myself that Ivan Milat was currently in prison serving seven life sentences. And surely I'd have heard if he'd escaped. Besides, how much bush could there be in the centre of what was supposedly a major city?

I imagined my worry box as a supermax steel crate with a chunky padlock, able to restrain the most pernicious thoughts. I pictured myself shoving these worries into the box and slamming the lid.

The trail looked like a dried-up creek bed. Browned gumleaves clustered in its crevices. The rocky, uneven ground made for unpleasant walking. Scraggly trees abounded.

After five minutes, I began to suspect I'd been teleported out of Canberra altogether. There was no-one else around, and no evidence I'd ever been in a city. There was nothing but towering, gnarled gum trees and a scattering of scrub and rocks across reddish-brown dirt. I continued to walk in the general direction my phone indicated, clutching my bag compulsively.

A twig snapped behind me. I ducked, like I was about to get shot.

Another twig snapped.

Still hunched over, I risked a glance to the side. A dozen sets of emotionless eyes were fixed on me.

The eyes belonged to a dozen grey kangaroos.

Here was the Australiana I'd pined for on the bus, up close and personal. The roos stood rigid, fanned out as though about to surround me. I didn't note whether the kangaroos were visibly male, because I was busy trying to remember who had told me the males can get territorial and disembowel you with a single kick. Was that a reliable fact or drop-bearish bluster?

I froze, watching the roos watch me, trying to discern which one had murdered before. The largest of the bunch reared up to its full height, its tail creating a tripod configuration. It straightened its ears and rotated them towards me, as if signalling to the others.

Growing up in Canada, you learn that bears will get bored if you play dead, whereas cougars will get scared if you shout and bash large sticks together (but if you get those survival strategies backward, you'll give a cougar an easy snack or piss off a bear). No-one had taught me what do when you stumble upon kangaroos. I'd been so focused on learning how to not die in anticipated encounters with sharks, spiders and blue-ringed octopi, I'd never thought to ask about roo dos and don'ts (i.e. roos and ron'ts). Kangaroos hadn't once made it into my worry box.

If I lay down and played dead, a well-placed leap could burst my internal organs. Maybe I should climb a tree?

I was trying my hardest to commit to this country, to be part of it, but it felt like everything from the government to the wildlife was against me. Or maybe this was what it was to belong in Australia: to feel maltreated by the government, to have heart-stopping encounters with wildlife.

The beefy, towering kangaroo and I continued to stare, the tension so high I could barely breathe.

The *crrrreeeeeeeeeaaaaaaaak* that broke the silence was out of a horror movie, the sound of a door slowly opening to reveal a blood-spattered man in search of skin for his human skin suit.

I jumped into the air as if rocket-propelled, and landed in a pile of bark and leaves, my ankle crunching awkwardly.

Up in the tree branches sat two grey cockatoos. One sported red feathers over his eyes and cheeks, like he was heading to the avian masquerade ball. His crown feathers curled backward over his head in a messy comb-over. The pair wore mischievous expressions.

Now I understood how gang-gangs had earned their 'squeaky gate' nickname.

It was the gang-gangs that had startled me, as if them and the roos had been in on it all along. The roos were acting nonchalant, munching away at the weeds as if nothing had happened. I pushed myself up, brushed off my jeans and cautiously tested my ankle. It would bear weight, though unhappily.

Gang-gangs were one of the things I'd looked forward to seeing in Canberra. Now they were one of the things I never wanted to see again. It was official – I hated this place.

~

I limped towards the Mexican Embassy, pulling leaf detritus out of my hair. I was mentally prepared to sit in an uncomfortable chair or even stand in line for several hours before being turned away by a curt embassy official. If I couldn't convince the embassy to provide this official letter for me, Steve and I couldn't apply for PR, and everything we'd done so far would be pointless. I dreaded going home and telling him that my year in Mexico might block our application, leaving us with the precarity of his work visa and also potentially having to pay back his employer for thousands of dollars in lawyer fees that ultimately led to nothing.

Thinking on it further, I realised the problem was mine alone. Steve could still apply for PR without me and my Mexican dramas. All the more reason for him to leave me.

As soon as I stepped inside the embassy, my mood lifted. This was not the utilitarian, fluorescent-lit, grey formica-inspired decor of most federal offices. The spacious lobby featured Mexican artwork in shadow boxes and the low lighting of a museum. A replica of the Aztec sun stone hung on one wall, the face of the sun god Tonatiuh at its centre, greeting me like an old friend. I felt a swell of longing for Mexico.

I approached the front desk with my thick folder of identity documents and certified copies. The embassy official smiled and I remembered another reason I loved Mexico – its abundance of devastatingly handsome men. This guy looked like a Mexican Chris Hemsworth, dressed in a collared shirt and sharp black tie. I hastily patted my hair down, checking for stray leaves.

'*Hola ¿cómo está usted?*' I said, and he smiled wider.

Speaking the Spanish I'd worked hard to learn in Peru and Mexico also filled me with joy. But my Spanish wasn't sufficient to explain the bureaucratic complexities of my request. I switched to English.

How to Be Australian

Instead of telling me I was in the wrong place, Cristóbal Hemsworth cheerfully talked through my paperwork troubles. He took a moment to consult a colleague, then handed me some forms.

I would have happily stayed and discussed paperwork with him for several hours, but after I completed this latest stack of forms, he pressed his hands together and gave me a final sexy smile. 'The letter, we will post to you within some time.'

'*Muchas gracias*,' I said, and drifted dreamily past Tonatiuh and back outside into the late afternoon sun.

'Within some time' was the epitome of bureaucratic vagueness, but for once, I wasn't worried. If for some reason I didn't receive the letter – well, I'd have a good excuse to return to Canberra.

17

Perthlings

The NSW Government emblem is a red waratah, a tall flowering plant I could identify, though not necessarily pronounce. (Was the emphasis on the *rat*? Wah-*rat*-ah?) The flower is clean and aesthetic, with no sense of narrative. Compare that to Western Australia's emblem, which features two boomerang-wielding roos that have trapped a swan in a tank. The twin roos are ripped, and they gaze towards you, as if they're contemplating trapping you in a tank. The swan has a crown above it, so maybe it's a monarchist who got what was coming to it. Whatever the story, it was an intimidating reminder that WA did things its own way.

Despite the municipal disappointment that was Canberra, the trip had convinced me that I shouldn't wait for Steve to suddenly become interested in exploring more of Australia. I could go on my own. I was always waiting, waiting for Steve to get home from work, waiting for Steve to go travelling with me. Waiting for Steve to announce he no longer loved me.

Maybe it was time to make some decisions for myself.

When I received an invitation to come to WA on an artistic

fellowship, I didn't hesitate. So what if I couldn't pack my belongings and move to Ulaanbaatar or San Francisco? I could rediscover the joy of solo travel. It was something I'd done a lot during my years in Asia and Latin America, but since marrying Steve, I'd stopped.

I'd mentioned to a couple of my colleagues back in Sydney that I was going to Perth, traditional lands of the Whadjuk Nation. One replied, 'You know, I've never been to Perth,' and the other quickly added, 'same'. Asking around, I found this was the case for a lot of New South Welshpersons. I'd likewise never been to the Maritimes, the three smudge-shaped provinces on Canada's Atlantic coast. It was too far, too expensive to get to, and seemed like something I could get around to later, like in retirement. I supposed this was how my Sydney friends felt about WA. As a recent arrival to Australia, however, I thought of Perth as exotic and exciting, so far-flung from the rest of the country that it was practically adrift in the Indian Ocean.

As the Jetstar plane broke through the cloud barrier on its descent into Perth, I pressed my nose against the cold plastic window. I'd pictured Western Australia in that same red, rocky, barren way I pictured the outback. Out the window, the landscape was verdant, no red rock in sight. Scattered amid the forested hills were teardrop lakes, their waters a shimmering turquoise.

A swell of possibility filled me, excitement over the new and unknown Australiana I might encounter here. I was especially keen to experience the near-mythic WA sunshine. Its pure, golden quality infused the landscape with a unique brilliance. Or so I'd read.

Perthlings

Standing alone under an awning at Perth Airport, I waited for a pause in the pounding rain. Apparently August wasn't the ideal time to visit.

~

When the rain let up, I made my way to the CBD. Strolling along the harbour, I felt a surprising rush of familiarity. Perth was an aspiring Sydney in miniature, its skyscrapers proudly clustered around the harbour, its ferries heading off to the zoo. All it needed was a photogenic opera house on the water. I'm not the only one who thought so. An ambitious opera house had been proposed in 2014. The planned building resembled the upturned ribcage of a brontosaurus. Despite this iconic design, nothing seemed to be under construction on my visit.

Regardless of the opera house situation, we reject most cruelly the things that remind us of ourselves. Perhaps their city's Sydneyesque qualities are why Perthlings are obsessed with Melbourne – at least, according to my two WA guides, Viv and Christine.

I was staying in the Perth Hills, east of the city. The name was literal, as I discovered that first afternoon, when I nearly had a heart attack while out for a light jog. The neighbourhood was properly suburban, with no cafes within walking distance, and the only grocery store located in a strip mall 5 kilometres away. The sole blue road sign indicating the direction of notable local attractions read 'Liquor Store'.

For the few minutes each day when the rain stopped, the neighbourhood was glorious, filled with flowering trees and flocks

185

of birds. As well as the familiar galahs, rainbow lorikeets and sulphur-crested cockatoos, there were new birds to get to know, such as the handsome Carnaby's cockatoos and the local 28 parrots. Not 28 parrots because I counted them, but because they're the gangsters of the parrot world, and 28 is their in-your-face gangster name.

'Actually their call sounds like they're saying 28,' Viv told me. She was always Viv, never Vivian, because she was very Australian, and specifically, very Western Australian.

Viv and Christine had also received fellowships. The three of us were temporarily residing in identical, side-by-side cabins on a hillside property with views of the distant CBD. Ostensibly I was here to develop my Armenia manuscript, to somehow weave a narrative thread through nearly 140 interviews and several years of research. I also wanted to discover what made Western Australia unique, other than the brilliant sunshine I hadn't yet seen.

By luck (mine, not theirs), my two companions were both WA born and bred. They were older, Viv with bouncing grey curls and smiling eyes that suggested true inner joy, and Christine still blonde, with a storyteller's enthusiastic gestures. Christine was a Perth local, while Viv lived in Denmark, a town on WA's south-west coast. She often referred to her town by name ('Yoga's popular in Denmark') and every time, I pictured her knee-deep in Scandinavian snow.

They were my guides not in the sense that they had agreed in any way to coach or advise me, but in the sense that I was going to pepper them with questions about WA for two weeks straight. Luckily for all three of us, Western Australians are keen to define

Perthlings

what makes their beloved state and its capital unique. From my first glance, Perth struck me as a charming back-country Sydney, a small town with freeways. To Viv and Christine, Perth was strikingly distinct.

A few days into our stay, the rain still splattering against the windows, the three of us gathered in the main house adjacent to our cabins. Christine had made apricot chicken and rice, and Viv and I had contributed cans of Emu Export. Originally a local beer, it was now brewed in SA and exported across the border with the slogan 'Beer for Western Australia'. Frankly, it didn't taste much like emu.

I asked what it was like growing up in WA. 'For one thing, my mum raised a joey,' Christine said.

'What, in the house?' I asked with delighted incredulity.

'We named her Joanna.'

Her stepfather would go 'roo shooting' to get meat for their dogs. Sometimes he would discover joeys in the pouches of the slaughtered roos, and eventually he brought one home. Christine's mum sewed a pouch for Joanna, and kept the pouch in a milk crate. At first, Joanna had to be fed every four hours with special formula from the vet. (You could argue that it would have been simpler to buy dog food in the first place and not provide round-the-clock care for an orphaned joey. But like I said, Western Australians do things their own way.)

When Joanna was fully grown, she went off into the bush behind their property with the other kangaroos. But she continued to visit, sometimes coming into the house. If Christine's mum went for a walk in the bush, Joanna would accompany her.

How to Be Australian

'Later Mum had an emu named Emily,' Christine said. 'We weren't too creative with the names.'

Hand-raising kangaroos and emus – the animals on the coat of arms! – seemed wonderfully Australian to me. No Canadian I knew had ever adopted a baby beaver, or moose or lynx or polar bear. Not even a deer, despite the enduring popularity of *Bambi*. If I'd tried to bring home a baby deer, my mom would have thrown a dummy. Or whatever that phrase was.

This, I now realised, was part of Australia's appeal – it was so unique, so distinctive. Beavers, moose, lynx and polar bears all lived in the United States as well as Canada. The Rocky Mountains crossed the US border, as did the Great Lakes. Vermont produced maple syrup. What made Canada unique and distinctive was subtle. In Australia, it was in every animal, in the landscape, in the vocabulary, and in the casual way Christine talked about hand-raising emus and kangaroos like this wasn't in any way extraordinary.

Christine, Viv and I were making good progress on my WA orientation. I could now see how Australia's international inferiority complex compounded with WA's national inferiority complex. One of the chief points of evidence offered for this was topographical. Along with Christine and Viv, practically every Perthite I talked to said disparagingly, 'WA is so flat.' Clearly, they'd never gone for a jog in the Hills. I was puzzled by the underlying assumption that mountains equated with worthiness. The only situation in which this point had validity was if you owned a set of skis and felt like paying exorbitant pass rates to see how many bones you could break while acquiring frostbite.

188

We also established that I was an eastern stater, meaning I was from 'over east'. Where specifically was irrelevant; from the WA perspective, it's all east.

'Perth has Melbourne envy,' Viv continued. 'If a new cafe opens up and people like it, we say it's so Melbourne – unless we're being ironic. I think it has to do with the football.'

'And when you say football, you mean ...'

Internationally, football is a useless word. In the UK it's soccer, in the US it's gridiron (a term I'd never heard before arriving in Australia), in Canada it's the local version of gridiron (we have our own rules, they're much more polite), and in Australia it's rugby.

'No, not rugby!' Viv practically leapt out of her chair. 'Rugby is NRL, what you have in New South Wales and Queensland. Footy is what we play in WA and Victoria. It's the only sport that's unique to Australia. In fact, Ashley, I don't think you can consider yourself Australian unless you've at least been to the footy.'

They both nodded emphatically.

'Ha ha,' I laughed nervously, hoping the conversation would move on.

'Hey, the waffle is on this Saturday,' Viv said. 'We could go together.'

By that time, I had successfully lived in Australia for several years without attending any sporting events or watching one on TV. I was not a sportsperson – too graceless and uncoordinated to play, too distinterested to spectate. I knew sport was integral to Australian national identity, but I assumed as an arts person, I'd get a pass. Now, however, Christine and Viv, two fellow arts people, were looking at me the way cult members look at a potential

189

convert, their faces bright and hopeful, their eyes narrowed, intent.

'The … uh, waffle?' I asked.

'The WAFL, the West Australian Football League.' Viv and Christine nodded in unison again.

When I'd arrived hoping for new Australian experiences, going to the waffle wasn't what I'd had in mind. But my trepidation was tinged with delight. I would have gone anywhere with Viv and Christine. Maybe I would have been better off had Steve and I ended up in Perth instead of Sydney. Here were the people I'd been waiting to meet all along, cheerfully sharing their perspectives and memories, as though they were holding open the door and saying, *make yourself at home.*

Just as I was considering whether I'd be better off without Steve, I had a growing sense that Australia could finally start to feel like home.

18

Going to the Waffle

'You'll see how the men pile on top of each other, and there's no protective equipment,' Viv gushed. Rain speckled the windows of our train carriage as we headed towards Perth Station for my initiation to Australian Rules Football fandom. 'When Aussies watch American football with all that padding and their big helmets, we think, "What a bunch of wusses."'

In the Soviet Union, World War II was known as the Great Patriotic War. The name was literal. Soviet soldiers taken prisoner of war by foreign armies were declared enemies of the state, and their wives could be arrested and sent to the gulag. Becoming a POW made you a traitor because soldiers were expected to fight to the death.

Australia feels the same way about their athletes.

Take the story of Aussie cricketer Dean Jones playing in 40-degree heat in India, who became so dehydrated he began vomiting on the side of the field. He wanted to stop playing, which, to my Canadian sensibilities, seemed reasonable. But his teammates made clear there was a sporting match on the line, one that would define Australia in the eyes of the world not only on that particular day in 1986, but also for millennia to come. 'If you can't hack it, let's get a Queenslander out here!' the team captain told him. Jones stayed on the field, scored some points or balls or crickets, dropped seven kilos, and ended up in hospital. *That* is what it means to be Australian.

I'd never be that intensely Australian, much like my disinterest in hockey knocked a few notches off my Canadianness. I was Canadian, but not *that* Canadian.

As the three of us walked through the gate of the sporting complex, my neck and shoulders braced in anticipation, as if the players might come crashing into the stands even before the games began.

'This will be the blind leading the blind,' Viv said. Though she'd dated a footballer years before, she had little interest in the sport. Christine had likewise only been to a handful of games. Neither of my guides were particularly interested in footy, and yet here we were. I shuddered to think what might have happened to me if they'd been actual fans. Waffle boot camp, probably.

On our way to the bleachers, we loaded up with pies, chips and middies of Great Northern. Being from Sydney's Inner West, I preferred roast pumpkin and leek pies, or salmon in white wine sauce. Here, the only option was the Generic Meat Pie – light-brown ooze with crumbs of what I hoped was beef. The pie was daggy, if a food could be daggy. I was still working on that word.

We settled into a row of open seats. I sat tense, leaning forwards, my teeth grinding. I'd hoped the weather might cancel the game, but the deluge had been downgraded. Rain fell with the density of spittle as the players came onto the sodden field.

The night before, Viv and Christine had prepped me for our outing by finding the song 'Up There, Cazaly' on YouTube. They both had fond childhood memories of singing along whenever it came on TV, and they sang along now, their eyes shining. At first I thought they were singing 'up your cazaly' and assumed this was a slang term for ass. Still, the melody was so stirringly nostalgic, for a moment it felt like the song had been part of my own childhood. It played over a promotional video for the Victorian Football League, which a player named Roy Cazaly had starred in decades ago (somehow singing a VFL song was legal in WA). The video featured the exact sorts of incidents I was terrified of seeing live: skulls colliding mid-air, limbs twisting backwards, and players landing on their faces, their necks surely broken.

From the bleachers, I cast a nervous glance over the players below as they warmed up on the grass.

'This is a rugby pitch?' I asked.

'No, it's – forget the word rugby,' Viv said. 'This is the Leederville Football Oval.'

There had been several Saturday afternoon WAFL games to choose from. As none of us had any particular allegiances, we'd eventually chosen based on our preferred shire slogans. Every WA shire had a slogan, many of which resonated like zen koans:

Brunswick Junction: Cream of the South West

Three Springs: Talc and Cocky Country

Wyallkatchem: Strange name, beaut place

Yilgarn: Good country for hardy people (implied: wusses fuck off).

How to Be Australian

Though I was a fan of the Shire of Jerramungup's poetic approach – Break away to Bremer Bay – we decided our team was Subiaco thanks to their intriguingly coy slogan: There's Something About Subiaco. (Later I learned the club's catchcry is 'oobie doobie, come on Subi', so maybe their 'something' is merely an embarrassing catchcry.)

Today Subiaco was taking on West Perth, which had no slogan. Technically it was part of the City of Perth, but they didn't seem to have a slogan either. At one time, licence plates issued in Perth included the slogan 'Perth – a city for people.' It was the blandest, most noncommittal slogan possible, aside from perhaps 'Perth – a city?' We wouldn't be supporting West Perth, that was for sure.

The sun broke through the clouds. With the field backlit and the reflective glare coming off the wet grass, Subi's gold and maroon uniforms weren't that distinguishable from West Perth's blue and red outfits.

The plan was to cheer for Subi, and to see if we could figure out what, exactly, it was about them. But we'd inadvertently sat on West Perth's side.

'We better go for West Perth this quarter,' Viv whispered, glancing at the red and blue clad supporters surrounding us. 'We can move to Subi's side at the break.'

The players started to race around the field. One held onto the neon ball, taking dainty ballet steps before kicking it into the air. Anticipating its trajectory, a dozen players rushed headlong towards each other. I clenched my teeth and squeezed my eyes shut, preparing for the sound of cracking skulls.

It didn't come. I opened one eye slowly. Someone else had the ball and was running backwards, preparing to kick it skywards again, and the men darted and huddled and leapt in frenzied response. This sport was unbridled mayhem.

I tried to focus on the Subi players. What was immediately clear was that I had to go for a team, no matter how randomly selected. Cheering for one group of men over the other meant I could impose meaning on the chaos on the oval. Otherwise, this was just a bunch of sweaty guys squabbling over a ball like a pack of seagulls with a chip. I squinted, trying to distinguish the uniforms. And then I forget which one was Subi.

'So ... what's happening?' I asked.

'There are rules. I know it doesn't look like it,' Viv said.

I nodded non-committedly and sucked in a sharp breath as a threesome of players tumbled through the grass. Two more guys crashed into each other a second later, and moments after that, another dove, grabbing an opponent by the waist. They went down violently, one crushing the other. It couldn't be long before an eyeball would pop out and roll across the muddy grass.

'Who are you going for?' The man behind us leaned over. In his fifties, he sported a West Perth hat and scarf, along with a beer belly that suggested he wasn't playing much footy himself these days.

'Subi – we didn't realise where we were sitting!' Viv said. 'We've brought a friend from Canada to see her first footy game.'

'From Canada?' he said. 'Well, good on ya. How long're ya here for?' Before I could answer, he launched into an enthusiastic lecture about Kalgoorlie's goldfields, where gold was first found in 1893, and which was still one of the largest goldfields in the world. 'They pull $885 million worth of gold out of the ground every year.' He delivered these details like he'd been prepping to meet me for days.

Suddenly something happened on the field. Goldfields interrupted himself to scream, 'That's *ball*! That IS BALL!'

'You lime maggot!' another guy shouted.

Viv pointed at the man in a lime-green shirt dashing among the players. 'Umpire abuse is as much a part of the game as anything.'

'You should have a go,' the second guy said to me. He wore a West Perth jersey. 'Tell him he's got eyes in his arse.'

I broke out in a sweat despite the wintery chill.

'Your eyes are painted on!' Goldfields shouted. 'Like that.'

I laughed my *let's change the subject* laugh.

'What we're really hoping to see is a streaker,' Viv volunteered. I nodded.

'When I was young I thought it was part of the sport,' Christine said. 'One day my uncle was watching a game, and I asked "When does the naked man run across the field?" He said "Oh, you never know when he's going to come on, Christine, it can happen any time." So I'd sit there and wait.'

'Streakers tend to pick the warmer weather. Environmental factors,' Goldfields said. But, he went on, streaking had been on the decline due to fines up to $10,000 and jail time, plus lifetime bans from the sport. 'I don't understand it,' he lamented. 'Streakers should be free to express themselves.'

While I'd heard of streaking at sports matches in Canada, I'd never heard such philosophical discussion of it. I suppose it was a less common practice in the chill of an ice rink. Here was another divide between Canada and Australia. At this point, the two countries had more differences than commonalities. And rather than feeling alienated by them, I was starting to enjoy their discovery.

The teams chased themselves over the far side of the field. The lime-clad umpire interrupted play, returning the ball to Subi.

'Isn't it a little too quiet?' Viv said to the men sitting silent beside us.

'They're across the oval,' one of them replied.

'Oh, you have to save the best insults for when they can hear?'

'Yep,' Goldfields said. 'Like marriage.'

At the first quarter break, men flooded from the stands to join the coach's huddle, crowding the players to overhear.

At 'gridiron' and hockey games I'd been dragged to throughout my life in Canada, I'd never seen the crowd flood into the players' space so expectantly, in the minor leagues or otherwise.

'This seems very ... communal.'

'Isn't it great?' Christine said. 'At half-time, the fans line up on the field to have a kick.'

Play resumed. A man further up the bleachers howled '*goooooooooo* west!' Or maybe it was 'go Wes', or 'girl-less'. What he lacked in intelligibility, he made up for in drama, bellowing like his life depended on West Perth winning. If that was true, he was a goner. West Perth was down 56 to 25 at the end of the second quarter.

As the players came off the field again, Subi's cheerleaders came on. There really was something about Subiaco.

'So you're from Canada. How're you enjoying the footy?' another man near us said cheerfully. 'Our son is a West Perth player, number 17.'

'He's a fan,' the woman beside him said, patting his shoulder. 'I'm here to make sure our son doesn't get hurt. He's a dentist. Footy is his hobby.'

I was relieved to discover I wasn't the only person in the crowd who thought this was all a bit much, and wouldn't it be better if the players sat down on some embroidered cushions and discussed their favourite books. I nodded at her in solidarity, easing back in my seat an inch.

'Do you come to every game?'

'We do.'

'No better way to spend a Saturday arvo,' her husband added. And surveying the little community of strangers chatting happily with each other, I caught a glimpse of what he meant.

We felt so warmly embraced by the West Perth crowd, we forgot about moving to Subi's side.

A few dozen spectators trundled down to the oval for their chance to 'have a kick'. Viv, Christine and I got another round of Great Northerns, and the players jogged back onto the grass to resume tackling and crashing into each other.

Despite the rain-slicked field, no-one took a cleat to the face. I found myself leaning back in my seat, anticipating the next cheer when the ball entered the vicinity of either set of uneven poles.

'The WAFL is like its own church,' Viv said, and I could see this, too. People coming together through a liturgy of umpire abuse, the wine and bread replaced by beer and pie, and everyone praying

198

Going to the Waffle

for a miracle, whether that was a West Perth win or a dentist who'd survive to drain another abscess.

In the final quarter, with Subiaco up 84 to 36, a double rainbow arched over the field, framing the action at the West Perth posts. They scored again, and the Subi flag-waver gave it his all. Christine, Viv and I cheered. By that time we were cheering for everyone.

I never shouted 'you lime maggot' at the umpire. Raising my voice in public would normally be as inappropriate as spitting on the maple leaf, and deep in my core, I was still very Canadian.

But in the fourth quarter – perhaps with the joy of having made lovely new friends and spending an arvo surrounded by such amiable people, and flushed with relief that the players had made it through the game without shattering any bones, but more likely because I was well into my second beer – when the fans took up their chorus against the umpire, I joined in, revelling in a moment of pure Australianness and shouting with glee, 'Up your Cazaly!'

19

Welcome to the Wet

Steve still dismissed the Northern Territory as 'too hot', but a few months after my Perth trip, I had a good excuse to visit. An American friend had recently married a Darwinian (the geographic variety) and moved from Sydney to be with him. I had a Top End couch to crash on.

And there was more buoying my mood. Before I left for Darwin, Steve and I finally submitted our permanent residency application.

The 'some time' my Mexican Embassy heart-throb had referred to, in describing when I would receive my we-don't-issue-criminal-background-checks-for-foreigners letter turned out to be two months. In all, it had taken us a year to compile and submit our permanent residency paperwork. Just like the Canadian–Argentinian couple we'd met at the barbecue had warned us.

The week we submitted, a PR applicant in New Zealand was making headlines. The government had rejected his application because he was, to quote the official medical report, 'too fat'. The applicant had no health problems, but the immigration officer had

Welcome to the Wet

decided that, based on the man's girth, he'd probably develop some, and used that as grounds to reject him.

Steve and I were keeping our fingers crossed. Our lawyer had warned us of possible issues with our application, my Mexican letter chief among them. There was nothing we could do now though. I closed my eyes and imagined dropping my PR concerns into my worry box.

I was relieved to be travelling again so soon. Keeping control of my worries had grown easier the more I got out of Sydney, and I felt most at home in myself when I was travelling. Perhaps because as a traveller, there was no expectation of feeling at home.

But mushrooming in a dark corner of my thoughts was a new, insidious worry. Which aspect of my solo travelling was most helping me – the travel? Or the solo?

~

Tomorrow I was finally going to see the outback. In the meantime, I had a day on my own to contemplate Australianness from a Top End perspective. Unlike me, my Darwinian mates had to show up at their jobs five days a week. They drove me into town, then kindly handed over the keys to their Ford Fairmont.

The morning sky shimmered, thick with humidity. Although the Larrakia people, the region's traditional landowners, distinguish six seasons, Darwin is commonly described as having only two. In the Dry, from May to October, the humidity eases and the temperature lowers, and it's more suited to popular activities such as breathing. Like my visit to Perth in the wintery rain, I'd kept my tradition of booking the cheapest flights I could find, which

201

meant I'd arrived Darwinside in the season known as the Wet, when the humidity stays in the triple digits and monsoon-type rain is frequent. I struggled to suck enough oxygen out of the woolly air. How many times would I have to learn that there's a reason it's called low season? Eventually this was bound to kill me. I'd book a flight to Kansas and stroll off the plane and into the path of a tornado. I'd die happy though, knowing my epitaph would read *The flight was such a good deal!*

Darwin was less a city and more a loose collection of suburbs arterially connected by highways and unified in the belief that the height of architectural sophistication was corrugated iron. I passed a Darwin apartment complex that had managed to be constructed entirely without corrugated iron – until the architects had realised their faux pas and slapped on strips of wavy steel as an aesthetic flourish.

Superfluous or not, corrugated iron seemed like an odd choice in a place susceptible to tropical cyclones, a point emphasised by the Cyclone Tracy exhibition at the Museum and Art Gallery of the Northern Territory, where I headed first.

Cyclone Tracy had ripped through Darwin on Christmas Eve 1974, flattening much of the city and killing sixty-six people. Through the museum's news clippings, photos and survivor testimonies, I gained a sense of the full extent of the devastation. The most affecting part of the exhibition was the recollections of a boy who'd witnessed his sister's arms sliced clean off by a piece of airborne metal.

The museum also featured a 5-metre, 780-kilogram taxidermied crocodile named Sweetheart. His gaping mouth was more spacious than the interiors of some modern cars. Sweetheart had been accidentally killed in an attempt to relocate him, deemed necessary because of his increasing propensity to attack boats.

Between Sweetheart, the cyclone exhibition, and a museum collection that introduced me to yet more toxic Australian fauna and flora, including a type of poisonous seaweed, a more accurate name for the museum would be Ways to Die and/or Be Maimed Horribly in the Northern Territory. Which, to be honest, is exactly what I'd expected.

On the way out, I stopped in the gift shop, and paged through a copy of a book stacked in tall piles. Darwin's capacity for self-reflection seemed best represented not by the quiet, low-lit museum, but by this book, *What a Croc!* It collected front pages from the *NT News*, and featured headlines including 'Man stabbed with fish,' 'Man bashed by prawn' (juxtaposed with a photo captioned, 'This dog thinks he's a chicken'), and, for an article describing a mysterious outback crop circle, 'Aliens' circle work'.

The museum offered sharp insight into the territory's perception of itself as a tough place full of resilient people. *What a Croc!* built on that insight, adding another essential aspect – irreverence. Canada's frozen northern territories demanded toughness and resilience as well. But if I visited Nunavut, I'd find no *What a Narwhal!*

I was about to close the book when I flipped a page and saw the headline, 'Why I stuck a cracker up my clacker.'

I turned the phrase over in my mind. I had no idea what it meant. How could I have lived here four years and still encounter entire sentences out of which I could tease no meaning? I assumed cracker wasn't a savoury biscuit. In Canada we also used cracker for what I'd heard here was a popper, those decorative cardboard tubes that are placed on the Christmas dinner table to be yanked apart and thrown in the bin. But then what could a clacker be? I could hazard a guess from the context. It made vague sense that someone might insert a Christmas popper in his ass, or awkwardly attempt to. But why this would be front-page news, even in the NT, raised questions of its own.

I could have accepted my popper theory if not for the photo accompanying the headline. It captured a twenties-ish, shirtless white guy, half-empty beer bottle pressed to his lips, and, dangling from the beer bottle, a green patterned snake the length of the guy's torso.

Was the snake the clacker? Was the snake the cracker? Either way this was a case of animal cruelty. Was the white guy the clacker, and he'd shoved a snake up his butt? Was this photo taken pre- or post-insertion? As a hopefully soon-to-be permanent resident of Australia, these were the kinds of mysteries that reminded me I was a stranger here.

I took a photo of the *NT News* clacker spread and texted it to Jules back in Sydney.

What does this headline mean?

She replied within seconds. *Aussie to English translation – 'why I stuck a firework up my arsehole.'*

Why is it called a clacker? I asked. *And what does the snake have to do with it?*

Good question. Google says it's from the Latin word cloaca, i.e. sewer. The snake is probs some macho shit.

I pondered this. *The snake is a red herring?*

Yeah, I reckon it's bogan show-ponying.

If the headline did mean 'Why I stuck a firework up my asshole' (and I never doubted Jules's tutelage), the subheading, like the snake, remained a mystery: 'Victim reveals all, p2'. What exactly was he a victim of? His own stupidity? And had literally nothing more significant happened on 31 July 2012 in all of the Northern Territory?

Maybe not, I concluded. What a marvellous place.

~

It was only mid-morning, but when I opened the Fairmont's door, heat roiled from inside the car.

I felt jubilant to be exploring on my own. Why had I waited so long for Steve to want to travel here? He would have been bored in the museum and crotchety in the heat.

At home, when I thought about Steve leaving me, I couldn't imagine how I could live without him – how empty and pointless life would seem. But travelling to Canberra and Perth and now Darwin reminded me that I'd had a life before Steve, and if I needed to, I could have a life after Steve. He said he loved me, but his actions – like backing away from me on the street while I cried – made it hard to envision a future together.

My worry box broke open, a constant, niggling fear rearing up – would my marriage last?

My breath started to come too fast.

I focused on the steering wheel burning my hands, the rumble of the car's aircon, and the sun's glare off the windshield. I shoved the worry back in the box; it was too hot to think about important life decisions.

What I most wanted to do in this cloying heat was go for a swim. At the thought, a shiver of doubt raced through me. I'd never been swimming without Steve – and I wasn't sure I was ready. I took a deep breath and imagined myself adding all thoughts of swimming to my worry box for later, along with my indecisions about Steve.

Within minutes I'd arrived at Darwin's historic Fannie Bay Gaol, a collection of single-storey stone buildings with barred windows and corrugated metal roofs built in the late 1800s. I wandered the grounds until I found the infirmary, where the last executions in the Northern Territory had taken place in 1952. Beneath the gallows, a pit in the floor featured a trapdoor. Since the gaol's repurposing as a historic site, a glass barrier had prevented tourists from falling into the pit. But the rusty lever that operated the trapdoor had remained accessible, enabling visitors to act out their professional executioner fantasies.

I touched a finger to the lever. Then I went outside.

The final two men executed in the NT were Czechoslovakian immigrants, convicted of the murder of a taxidriver. They were buried outside the infirmary, imprisoned forever in the gaol grounds. I found the painted concrete plaques that marked the spot. I wondered what I was supposed to make of this history. That the nation had progressed, perhaps. That it had moved on from the barbaric punishments of the past. That it was capable of change.

Exhausted by the heat, I drove to East Point Reserve, a bayside park on the city's outskirts. No-one was around. From a bench,

Welcome to the Wet

I stared across the water to Darwin's squat skyline. Were there any people in this city? Maybe everyone was smart enough to stay inside. The Wet was getting wetter. The air had thickened to aerosolised sweat, and my body felt steam-cooked.

I pulled a now-warm Paul's Iced Coffee from my bag. My friends had insisted this beverage was part of the Darwin experience. It wasn't only their opinion. The venerable *NT News* described the drink as 'a true NT icon', stopping short of comparing it to a liquefied equivalent of the Sydney Opera House. Paul's marketing built on this status, insisting in large text imposed over an outline of the NT (which was conveniently milk-carton shaped), 'You can tell a true Territorian by the Iced Coffee they knock back.'

I took a sip. Paul's Iced Coffee was mostly sugar, and only made me thirstier. In a place where diabetes rates were reaching epidemic levels, marketing a doubly addictive beverage as an intrinsic part of local identity should have been illegal. Instead, the marketing team had probably won an industry award for Best Caffeinated Beverage Slogan. Territorians loved the drink so much that shortages made the news. Its subsequent return to shelves inspired the *NT News* staff to run a photo of two tradies joyfully splashing Paul's Iced Coffee over themselves.

If I'd grown up in Darwin, would I have believed that drinking a certain brand of iced coffee made me a truer Territorian? If I'd grown up in Perth, and was given the opportunity to express my identity through the joy of consumption, would I have splashed an icy can of Emu Export over myself?

Travelling was reminding me of the essential truth that

there was no one Australia, no single way to be Australian, or any nationality. My childhood had ground that lesson into me. Six weeks after I was born an Albertan, we moved to Winnipeg, Manitoba. A few years later, we moved to Moose Jaw, Saskatchewan, staying until I was ten, when we packed up and resettled on Vancouver Island. I'd arrived thinking life would be much the same; we were still in western Canada. My grade five classmates didn't see it that way. They asked where my cowboy boots were, why I wasn't out milking the cows. I told them I'd never worn cowboy boots, that I didn't come from a farm. They ignored me. I struggled to make friends.

I was fourteen when the Canadian Air Force transferred my Dad back to Winnipeg. I'd looked forward to the move. My Vancouver Island peers had made it clear that I belonged on the prairies, and I anticipated being warmly accepted by my classmates.

My family arrived in Winnipeg the day before high school started. On the first day of grade nine, my peers branded me as a weirdo interloper from the west coast. I gave up trying to make friends.

No wonder I still felt like my identity was up for grabs.

20

The Platypus Gene

Sweat dripped into my eyes, blurring the view from my bench in East Point Reserve. The cool blue waters of Fannie Bay spread out in front of me, glimmering like a sea of diamonds. I contemplated Darwin's skyline from East Point. The city itself might not be much to look at, but the surrounding landscape was postcard-perfect: golden coastline, sparkling turquoise water and waving palm trees.

A think piece I'd read on the flight, written by an Aussie, bemoaned the disinclination to live along Australia's coastal north. The rest of the tropical world – the Bahamas, Thailand, Hawaii – was in high demand, so why not Australia? I wondered if the writer had ever been to Darwin, or anywhere above the Tropic of Capricorn. Unlike the Bahamas or Thailand or Hawaii, it's 6700 degrees Celsius in Darwin and, aside from the $7-entry-fee Wave Lagoon, the water is chock-full of box jellyfish and giant saltwater crocodiles and poisonous fish and toxic seaweed. Darwin was fascinating to visit, but unless sweating was your all-time favourite activity, it would be a torturous place to live.

Canada struggles with its own under-populated northern territories. Media stories regularly warn that if Canada doesn't get more people at the North Pole, Russia or America will glide in on their militarised snowmobiles and snatch it. Still, there's no patriotic rush to relocate along the Arctic coast, and no-one wonders why.

Dropping my bags off at my friends' apartment that morning, I'd noted the kidney-shaped pool in their car park. It was the size of a decent puddle and about as deep.

'It's not worth going in,' Kim had warned. 'It's as warm as a bath. But you could swim at Lake Alexander.'

Swimming was bound up with my burgeoning Australian identity, and in Darwin's peaking mid-afternoon heat, it seemed the only sane thing to do.

~

At seven years old, I believed I could swim. The fact that I'd never been swimming was irrelevant. I'd seen people do it, mostly on TV. 'I know how to swim,' I announced to my parents from the back seat, as my dad drove us to the community pool.

'Okay,' Dad replied, sharing a smirk with my mom.

I'd show them. When we emerged from the change rooms, I strode to the edge of the pool, leapt in, and immediately sank to the bottom, flailing wildly and gasping mouthfuls of water.

What was happening? Was this swimming? It looked easier on TV. I kicked my legs and windmilled my arms, succeeding only in ramming my head into the pool's tiled wall. I didn't know where the surface was. My lungs started to burn.

The Platypus Gene

Dad stood on the edge a few extra seconds, making sure the lesson would stick with me. Then he jumped in, hauled me out, and whacked me on the back until I started breathing again, which, circa the 1980s, was the proper procedure.

After that, Mom signed me up for swim lessons. The Red Cross swimming levels were graded by colour, like karate belts: yellow, orange, red, maroon, blue, green, grey and white.

It was well known among primary students that maroon separated the dog-paddlers from the future lifeguards. In maroon, you had to tread water for five minutes, swim ten laps, and dodge killer jellyfish while collecting gold coins in a timed underwater obstacle course. Or maybe that was Super Mario Bros 3. Either way, I thrashed through yellow, orange and red, but didn't bother to enrol in maroon.

Mom accepted this decision, perhaps because the prairies offered limited places to potentially drown. Assuming you didn't want to swim in a urine-filled pool with 37.5 children per cubic metre of water, your only choice was to drive out to one of Manitoba's plentiful lakes.

Canadians have a bad habit of calling any stretch of water-adjacent land a 'beach', even if it that land is nothing more than a wide stretch of foot-piercing stones. But through a geological quirk, Manitoba's largest water body, Lake Winnipeg, has a few beaches that feature genuine, Australian-quality sand. They're popular during the few months that they aren't buried under snow.

For Steve's 26th birthday, during my last year of uni, we drove the hour north to spend the day at Grand Beach. I'd barely got my towel spread over the sand when Steve splashed into the polite, lake-sized waves.

'Come on in!' Steve, genetically part seal, finds water irresistible.

My child self, so eager to leap in the water, had grown into an adult happier to stay on the beach reading Douglas Coupland.

'C'mon, the water's great,' Steve called before diving under. Sighing, I closed my book.

We splashed around like children, chasing each other through the shallows and laughing. He was right, the water was great.

Except that it was infested with E. coli bacteria. I woke up at 2 am convinced someone was stabbing my eardrum with a flame-tipped spear, and ended up in the emergency room. (As is typical in our patriarchal society, Steve did not get an E. coli infection, despite swimming in the exact same water for way longer.)

That was the last time I went swimming in Canada. By the time I arrived in Australia, I might have been able to thrash with enough proficiency to save myself from drowning if I fell off the Manly ferry, but for all practical purposes, I couldn't swim. In Manitoba Steve had accepted my inability to swim and general reluctance to get wet. Once we were in Australia, he was not having it.

Our Camperdown apartment complex featured two attractive pools where Steve often swam, always keen for me to join. On weekends, we frequented beaches with concrete ocean pools. Steve would swim while I sat on the edge, legs dangling in the water, Coupland replaced by Helen Garner. He'd cajole me until I relented and eased myself into the water up to my armpits, keeping

212

The Platypus Gene

my feet firmly planted. Sufficiently cooled off, I'd retreat to dry land.

'Let me teach you to do breaststroke,' Steve said for the hundredth time one afternoon in Curl Curl's ocean pool, treading water beneath me. 'You don't have to put your head under.'

'Not interested.'

'C'mon, we could swim together.'

'Why would I want to make exercise more unpleasant by submersing myself in a cold pool first?'

'It's fun, you'll like it. Here, I'll hold you up.' Steve held his arms out, just below the water.

We'd been having this conversation throughout the three years we'd been in Australia, and my resistance was waning. Not because Steve was so convincing, but because I was surrounded by people who had an impressive ease in the water. From the treadmill at the gym, I'd watch our neighbours stride up to the pool and jump as if into a pile of feathers. They didn't stand on the edge, dip a toe in, pretend to do some stretches, shiver, prevaricate for twenty minutes, then ease themselves in, their faces contorted in agony. They just got in the pool and swam like they were one-tenth platypus. They did this at the beach, too, striding into the water like they were carrying a goddamn trident. The beaches also featured one of the most Australian sights I'd seen: hordes of 'bubs' in matching swim shirts sprinted headlong into the surf, a chaotic approach to swimming lessons that terrified me. I wondered how many bubs were lost, on average, per lesson.

Running on the treadmill one day, I watched two women standing in our apartment's indoor pool. They kept up a friendly

213

chitchat while one of them repeatedly shoved a baby under the water. The baby was newborn-tiny, and every time the mother pushed it under, it would bob back to the surface, its face glowing with delight. Then the woman would put her hand on its bald head and shove it back under, never breaking eye contact with her friend. This baby was mere days out of the womb and it was already a more confident swimmer than me, a thirty-year-old with her red swimming badge.

Thinking back to that oh-so-Australian baby, I finally cracked. Grimacing, I eased myself into the contained surf of Curl Curl's ocean pool and onto Steve's outstretched arms.

'Now sweep your arms and frog-kick your legs!' Steve said. 'Um … okay, now maybe at the same time.'

'I am!' My limbs moved jerkily. I swept and kicked without enthusiasm.

'No, I mean—'

'I AM!'

'Okay, I'm going let go.'

'No! No!' It was too late. He pulled his arms away and I began to sink like a breached submarine. Pure animal terror electrified my brain. I beat my arms with hummingbird intensity, the water around me frothing into a localised typhoon. Still I was barely keeping myself from plummeting.

This was the bit I'd never understood. Swimming was a battle against drowning – how could it be fun? Every time I tried to swim or tread or float or in any way relinquish a firm connection to solid land, I started to sink.

'Nope, no, I'm not a swimmer.' I stalked out of the pool.

214

The Platypus Gene

'If you practice, you won't sink.' Steve said this the way some people insist Jesus is your personal friend.

Through that summer and into the next, Steve cajoled me into practising breaststroke. He'd pester me and hold out his arms until I'd relent and go through the motions to reiterate how hopeless his crusade was. Every time he let me go, I'd sink, panic, and stomp out of the pool with the graciousness of a drunk elk.

And then one day, I didn't sink. I was frog-kicking and arm-sweeping and I was *swimming*! This was more than preventing my imminent death by drowning. It was a whole new way of moving, a grace I couldn't achieve on land. I was freed from gravity.

In Sydney that summer, my favourite thing became catching the ferry to Watson's Bay and heading along the coast to Parsley Bay, which cut in abruptly from the harbour. Its narrow shape made for calm waters. Grandmothers and toddlers would push past me while I lowered myself into the chilly water inch by torturous inch. But once in, I could tread water endlessly and swim lazy laps, sometimes outlasting Steve.

It had taken twenty-five years, but I was finally ready to get my maroon swim badge.

Well, almost; I still refused to put my head under, and I'd never been swimming without Steve.

But every time I stretched out my arms and glided across the water, I did feel a sliver more Australian.

~

Now that I was a swimmer – even if I only knew breaststroke – all I could think about in Darwin was getting in the water. On Kim's

215

suggestion, I'd brought my bathing suit to East Point Reserve, to swim at Lake Alexander. It was man-made, just large enough that it couldn't be called a pond.

The place felt deserted. Still, I practised the Aussie 'make your own change room' trick of using one hand to hold a towel around myself while I struggled underneath it with the other hand, inadvertently flashing a wallaby.

Lake Alexander had an uninviting brownish tinge, but still, I'd been roasting in my own sweat since I'd arrived. I hid the car keys in a shrub, then headed for the water.

Standing on the lake's edge, I engaged in my ritual of dipping a toe in. It was warm – so warm, it was unpleasant.

Stepping from rough grass onto slick mud, I waded in, thinking the water would be cooler further out.

Up to my thighs, the water remained the temperature of fresh urine. I sighed loudly, startling a rainbow bee-eater out of the trees.

Flicking my hand through the warm, brown water, I headed back up the grassy slope to search the shrubs for Kim's keys.

~

On my last day in the Top End, Kim and her Darwinian husband, Garry, escorted me to Litchfield National Park. This was it – I was finally going to experience the outback.

'Litchfield isn't as famous as Kakadu, but it's just as good,' Kim said as we headed out of the city. In her Fairmont, Litchfield was also much more accessible than Kakadu, most of which required a four-wheel drive.

The single-lane highway wasn't edged, but instead roughly gave

The Platypus Gene

way to a shoulder of earth that grew increasingly rust-red. Finally, here was the outback of *Crocodile Dundee*, that iconic aspect of Australia I'd managed to spend years in the country without seeing.

In Litchfield, we stopped first at the impressively two-dimensional magnetic termite mounds, and then at the imposing cathedral termite mounds, which were more conventionally shaped in their three-dimensional lumpiness, and stood taller than most buildings in Darwin. This seemed worthy of its own tourism campaign. *Welcome to the NT – marvel at our termites!*

We pushed on through the rippling mid-morning heat to Florence Falls, which plunges out of the Litchfield bush, over a cliff of rust-red rock, and into the shady calm of a basin below. A set of stairs gave a full view of the falls.

At the basin, we joined a jostling crowd. It seemed this was where everyone was waiting out the Wet.

'Is this a billabong?' By now I'd learned that billabongs weren't the lesser cousin of the boomerang, which was a disappointment.

'Nah,' Garry said. 'This is a rock pool. Still good for a dip though.'

Stripping to our swimsuits, the three of us waded over water-slicked rocks into the basin.

I felt a pang of longing for Steve. He would have hated every minute of Darwin – the humidity, the museum, the colonial history. But he would have leapt from the still-moving Fairmont to swim at Florence Falls.

Kim and Garry swam across the basin to where the water cascaded noisily from the rocks above.

In the past I would have made excuses and stayed cautiously

217

pinned to the rocky edge, watching them go on without me. Today still, I let them go ahead.

'I'll catch up,' I called.

Unlike Lake Alexander, the water here was cool, and for once that felt lusciously inviting. As I eased into the water, my core temperature dropped. It was instant relief.

Kim waved to me from across the water. I stretched out my arms. Out of reflex, I glanced back to check that Steve was watching for me. *Right*, I remembered. *I can do this on my own.*

Taking a shaky breath, I pushed my arms ahead of me and swept them back, amazed by how comfortably I could move through the water. Here I was, swimming – swimming! – in one of the most picturesque places I'd ever visited.

Water from the falls splashed onto my face like droplets of pure joy. I swam past Kim and Garry, waving, then circled the basin again.

I'd overcome my goat-headed stubbornness about swimming because of my desire to feel a sense of belonging in Australia. But I had Steve to thank for teaching me the actual technique, and for repeatedly forcing me to practise despite my tendency to swear at him during the process.

Steve was frustrated by my unpredictable mental health. But so was I, and I was doing what I could to manage it. He wasn't the husband I wanted him to be. He wasn't going to say 'I love you', or put his arms around me in public, or have long, involved conversations with me. He'd done these things while we were dating, when we lived in separate houses and then on separate continents. But since we'd been married, he'd gradually stopped.

The Platypus Gene

Had I been convincing myself that because Steve didn't act certain ways, it meant he was growing fed up enough to leave?

There was another way to pose the question. Would someone who didn't love me spend two years teaching me to swim?

21

Further Down, More Under

In late 2014, four months after applying for our permanent residency visas, we received an email from our immigration lawyer. It came while Steve was at work.

'I am very pleased to advise your visa has now been approved and you have been granted permanent residency. Congratulations!!'

The double exclamation marks offset the blandly administrative language of the attached notification letter, a PDF from the renamed Department of Immigration and Border Control. Receiving the email was dissociative – the visa was a bureaucratic construct, an administrative detail; the visa was significant to the shape of our future, and thus ourselves. Knowing I could stay in Australia made me realise how much I wanted to. I'd worked hard to feel at home here, and bit by bit, I was succeeding.

I called Steve in an attempt to acknowledge the moment, but as usual he didn't answer. He texted later to say he was stuck at the office.

PR gave us most of the benefits of citizenship but, like prison inmates, we couldn't vote. I wanted to call myself a citizen of the

Further Down, More Under

place I'd devoted years of my life to, the place where we were saving for a deposit to have the privilege of spending a million dollars on a one-bedroom unit. And I wanted to vote. We could keep our Canadian citizenship, so we planned to apply for Aussie citizenship as soon as possible to ensure we'd never have to complete a visa application again.

Waiting for Steve to return from work, I started planning a celebratory trip. Returning from Darwin, I'd told him I needed to travel more, and I wanted him to come with me. 'Sure,' he replied. 'As long as it's not somewhere hot.'

His wonderful Australian job included two weeks of office shutdown every Christmas. The problem with these two miraculous weeks was that they happened when Australia was sweltering. While nothing compared to the misery of a minus 40 winter, neither Steve nor I enjoyed the oppressive furnace of plus 40 summers.

I didn't want to squander our two magical weeks of freedom in Sydney, marinating in our own sweat while tourists swarmed the city like locusts. Over previous Christmases, we'd tried Cairns (voted the top holiday destination by box jellyfish), Thailand (hello monsoon season), and, of course, back to Winnipeg (welcome home, it's minus 32). It's a First World problem to complain about the travelling I've done, but I have a larger point: December is a terrible time for holidays. Let's all agree to reschedule Christmas and New Years in September, and give everyone some time off when the weather is not so murderous.

While we were stuck with Christmas in December, I determined that Tasmania sounded like an ideal holiday destination.

How to Be Australian

Tassie was a mountain paradise laced with hiking trails, and most importantly, its summers were cool.

As I booked our Tassie holiday, I resolved that this year I would push myself to be better. I was going to master my anxiety, and when I received my citizenship, I'd feel confident that this new aspect of my identity was more than bureaucratic – it would be integral to who I was and how I understood myself.

Part of what drove my impression of Australians as happy and carefree was that, before moving here, I'd read that the country had the highest rate of skin cancer per capita in the world, but also the highest recovery rate. The article attributed this to the cheerful, easygoing, no-dramas national attitude. This conclusion may not have been scientifically accurate, but it enforced what I already believed, which made it true to me. And if the average Aussie could manage skin cancer with optimism, surely I could stop handling the banalities of life by lying face down on the floor in a puddle of tears.

I was in the process of becoming an actual Australian – it was time I started acting like one.

~

A few weeks before we were due to leave, I texted Jules asking for any Tassie recommendations.

You're going to The Vagina?! she replied.

Is that what Aussies call it??

Well, guys shout things like 'show us your map of Tassie,' so that's what I call it.

It's a credit to my seventh-grade geography teacher and the

Further Down, More Under

entire Canadian education system that before moving to Australia, I'd assumed Tasmania was one of the South Pacific islands, most likely a sister of Tahiti.

I wasn't the only Canadian who found Australian geography murky. Skyping with my great-aunt in Canada, I mentioned our upcoming holiday to Tasmania.

'It's one of the Australian states,' I added.

'Yes, that's right, and isn't Timbuktu there on the south coast?' This was a genuine question.

'What? That's in Africa.'

'Are you sure? I was certain it was there on the south coast of Australia.'

'Definitely Africa.'

'I'll have to ask your cousin.'

According to my great-aunt, the most credible source of Australian facts was my fifteen-year-old prairie-dwelling cousin, a trustworthy provider of information due to his ability to multiply six-digit numbers in his head and memorise entire atlases at a glance. Whereas I, who'd lived in Australia for four years, was a font of bullshit.

I wondered if my cousin, with his head full of random facts, would also inform her of Tasmania's nickname.

~

Within an hour of arriving in Tassie, Steve and I managed to find National Highway 1. We were cruising south to Hobart, the traditional lands of the Palawa people, heading through the island's forested heart, our hired black Commodore straddling the narrow lane. Steve gripped the wheel. His body tensed with the effort of driving on what we still secretly felt was the wrong side of the road.

'Why do you want to climb this mountain?' he asked. 'I can think of hundreds of better things to do for New Year's.'

I waved a pamphlet at him. 'According to Tourism Tasmania, it's one of the state's 60 Great Short Walks.'

At six to eight hours, the Cradle Mountain summit seemed long for a 'short' walk, but that was exactly what I wanted. An ambitious one-day hike on 1 January with the definitive reward of a summit struck me as exactly what I needed to kickstart 2015, and exactly what I felt Steve and I needed as we entered a new phase of our life in Australia. New Year's Day would set the stage for the entire year and our lives ahead. And the sheer grandiosity of our Cradle Mountain achievement would make up for the fact that the entirety of our New Year's Eve plan was to be in bed by 9.30 pm, like a couple of octogenarians who understand that counting down to the new year is the same as counting down to the inevitability of one's own cold grave.

'You want to wake up at 5 am, drive two hours, hike all day, then drive back?'

'I want to start the year by doing something really Australian.'

'Then let's go to a pub,' Steve said, glancing at me from the driver's seat, 'get a schoonie, watch some horses run around a track.'

'I don't think anyone says schoonie. Look, I've got the whole trip planned. We'll spend time in Hobart over Christmas, then we'll celebrate New Year's with the Cradle Mountain summit and spend a few nights in Lawche ... Lounse ...' I still couldn't wrap my mouth around Launceston.

224

Further Down, More Under

'Lawnchester,' Steve said. We stuck with that. (Later though, we'd successfully learn to pronounce Bicheno, when a local suggested the helpful homonym *bitch, no*.)

'We're hiking Cradle Mountain, no more debate,' I said.

~

Hobart was an unpretentious city, stretching from its historic waterfront centre to the base of Mt Wellington, which provided a majestic backdrop. Like Darwin, Hobart had a dwarfish skyline and a small-town feel, but its coniferous trees, mountain vista and deep-blue water made it feel like a tiny, sunny version of Vancouver.

'Hobart seems nice,' Steve said, after we'd stopped for flat whites, scallop pies, and a wander through the CBD. 'But wasn't it supposed to be cooler here?'

I wiped my forehead on my sleeve. It had been 32 degrees when we'd landed in Lawnchester, and Hobart was hotter still. We'd come here specifically to avoid the hellfire summer heat that tourism campaigns had convinced me wasn't a feature of Tasmania's climate.

I thought back on how I'd come to this conclusion. 'The tourism marketing campaign I read about may have been ... outdated.'

'Uh huh,' Steve said.

At the Mt Wellington lookout, we stood against the rail with the breeze in our hair, the city spread beneath us. The River Derwent carved its way through the hilly suburbs below.

'Maybe we should have moved here,' Steve said. Perhaps because he'd spent thirty years on the pancake-flat prairies, he was strangely impassioned about mountains, much like everyone in WA. I was

How to Be Australian

less enthusiastic, preferring palm trees and turquoise waves to ominous peaks and brooding waterways. Still, standing at the Mt Wellington lookout, I had to admit it was nice. Like Perth, here was another charming Australian city that, had we ended up in, I probably would have come to love as much as Sydney.

'You know what's great about being up here?' I asked. 'It's cool.' At the top of the mountain, the temperature had dropped several degrees. A refreshing breeze ruffled our clothes.

Throughout our trip, the brutal heat remained. There was no escape because there is very little to do indoors in Tasmania. In fact, there is very little indoors in Tasmania, period. Aside from one day set aside for cultural fulfilment at the Museum of Old and New Art, we'd planned to spend our two-week holiday outdoors, revelling in the cool temperatures. It seemed no matter where I was in the world – in Winnipeg, Sydney, Darwin or Hobart, the weather found a way to torture my pathetic constitution.

Christmas Day was 36 degrees. We had a Christmas luncheon with a fellow writer I'd met at an author talk and her Sydneysider parents. They fed us barbecued salmon, and we were in their debt for such a touching, quintessentially Australian holiday experience.

But after, they invited us to Kingston Beach, where they were intent on remaining on the boardwalk, appreciating the beach without touching it. The refreshing water, so blue it was practically navy, beckoned cruelly from across the wide expanse of sand. Sunscreen-laced sweat ran into my eyes, making me blink red and resentful.

The second our friends released us from their company, I turned to Steve.

226

Further Down, More Under

'Swim?'

'I'm melting,' he replied, as the twin sweat patches spreading from under his arms met in the middle of his T-shirt.

We rushed back to Kingston Beach and stripped to our swimsuits. Confident of my swimming prowess, I raced ahead of Steve and plunged into the water – then leapt out, screaming.

The water was like icicles slicing through my skin. I expected a polar bear to float past on an ice floe.

'What is this? Antarctica?!' I stood ankle-deep, struggling to cajole myself back in.

Learning from my mistake, Steve waded in gradually, taking five minutes before he let the water reach his waist.

'My nuts are gone,' he said, which is as close as he ever got to being romantic.

The freezing water was slightly less unpleasant than the scalding sun, and we eventually submerged ourselves.

Like a Christmas miracle, our bodies went numb.

I swam the length of the beach as kids and dogs chased each other on the sand and other people, most likely fellow tourists, shrieked as they tried to get in the water. As I swept my arms and frog-kicked, I counted down the hours until we packed up the rental car and returned north. This trip – my life – was all about Cradle Mountain.

~

Finally it was New Year's Day. After the two-hour drive from our Lawnchester hotel, Steve pulled into a parking spot at Cradle Mountain National Park. I sprang out of our hire car, slinging on

227

my daypack. It hung heavy with my lunch, snacks and multiple litres of water.

At 8 am, the heat was already building, but it would be cooler as we headed upwards. All the more reason to get going.

'Hey,' Steve said as we each propped a foot on the bumper to lace our hiking boots. 'How about we do the Dove Lake trail? It looks nice.'

This was about the eighth time he'd suggested Dove Lake.

'I told you already, it's mostly flat. How is walking in a circle around an oblong lake going to set me up for a success-filled year of Australianness?'

'It'd just be nice.'

I shook my head. 'Follow me.'

On the trail, we bypassed the cerulean calm of Dove Lake and its forested surrounds. Steve looked dejectedly over his shoulder as a pack of downy ducklings waddled into the lake.

Bushwalking (or 'hiking' as we still preferred) wasn't out of character for us. We thought of Aussies as outdoorsy people that liked getting out to surf, swim and hike, and this was one of the few ways we genuinely fit in.

We also understood Australians to be fearless daredevils. The first Australians Steve had ever met confirmed this impression. On his first trip to Europe, Steve had stayed in a hostel with several Aussies who invited him to go hang-gliding. In the Alps. They'd already been rappelling, bungee jumping, whitewater rafting, parachuting and bull-running, and frankly, if things didn't get more interesting, they were going to have to bicycle the wrong way down the Autobahn, blindfolded. (As it turned out, one of them

Further Down, More Under

slept with a local's wife, and they had to clear out of town abruptly when the husband rounded up a posse to demonstrate just how interesting Germany could be.)

Our impression was confirmed when we moved to Sydney, where barefoot toddlers flew downhill on scooters into traffic, and beyond the bright yellow signs with NO SWIMMING – RIPS or pictures of deadly jellyfish, there were always, always people in the water. It was like the whole country had some kind of joyous death wish, the national survival ethos writ large.

Steve and I, in contrast, had insurance on our insurance. We weren't sure we could ever adapt to the carefree recklessness of Aussie culture, just like we still asked where to find the entire bathroom instead of just the toilet, and, despite having it explained to me several times, I couldn't distinguish between a mole and a deadset mole. None of this bothered Steve, who had devoted himself to building a successful career and could barely start a new role before he was promoted again. For me though, chipping away at a fifth draft of my Armenia manuscript, fitting into Australia had become the keystone of my adult identity.

If I pushed myself, I thought, I was sure I could be more Australian. And to do that, I needed to look danger right in its steely eyes and dare it to blink first.

That said, despite some online reviews ('I thought I was going to die'), I assumed the Cradle Mountain hike wasn't dangerous, just strenuous. I was seasoned at great walks, both short and long. I'd hiked on five continents, including the four days and 4215 vertical metres of the Inca bloody Trail. I could handle whatever this 1500-metre Vagina rock had to throw at me.

The trail veered right, headed up an outcropping of white stone marked by deep ridges. Chains ran along steel poles, which were drilled into the rock at regular intervals. Using the chains, we hauled ourselves up hand over hand. This seemed to be the only way to get up for anyone who wasn't a mountain goat.

'This trail isn't much fun,' Steve said.

'That's' – *huff* – 'not' – *puff* – 'the point!'

'Don't drink your water so fast,' Steve called. He still preferred the camel method of water consumption, which was to store his water in a hump on his back (usually called a backpack) and not share it with anyone, especially his parched wife.

We continued, sweating at a rate that would soon leave us dehydrated, if not dead. The sun bore down. It was 35 degrees again.

Despite the heat and sweat, I was feeling peppy. I couldn't see the top, but it felt like we were making great progress. My Year of Australianness was off to a smashing start.

With one last all-consuming burst of energy we heaved ourselves the final few steps onto what I could only assume was the summit.

There, in the distance, was what appeared to be another mountain. A completely separate mountain from the one we were currently standing on. This new behemoth stood by itself against an empty sky. A sign next to us, pointing helpfully upwards, read 'Cradle Mountain'.

I couldn't believe it. 'Is that Cradle Mountain?'

'I guess so,' Steve said.

'I thought we were on Cradle Mountain!'

230

Further Down, More Under

Our current mountain had features such as vegetation and a trail and thoughtfully installed chains to aid in climbing. The beast ahead had none of these things. It was a barren pile of rocks with thrusting upper ridges that looked like the inspiration for Mount Doom.

'We could go back to Dove Lake. It's a lot shadier – and it has ducks.'

My pep was waning, but determination drove me on. I wouldn't be tempted by shade or ducks. I steeled myself and continued forwards. This would be my defining moment.

As the trail curved upwards from the new mountain's base, it lost all the qualities normally associated with the term 'trail', such as being a surface suited for walking on, having edges, and guiding you in a particular direction. A stark metal pole every 50 metres, indicating roughly the direction you might want to head in, was the only sign that any human had been here before us. Before we'd heard cicadas buzzing and native scrubtits chirping. Now there was no sign of life beyond the lichens on the brown rock that made up the mountain. A hot breeze whistled over the barren landscape.

We were walking on apple-sized rocks and then we were stepping over watermelon-sized rocks and then we were lost among prize-winning-pumpkin-sized rocks. This was less a mountain than a towering pile of loose stone. It had obviously been solid long enough for lichen and moss to grow, and that took, what, hundreds of years? Regardless, the haphazard jumble felt moments away from an avalanche, as though one load-bearing rock could let go and Cradle Heap would collapse into the valley below, with our bodies crushed among the debris.

231

How to Be Australian

I was thinking that uncomfortable thought when the rocks around me became larger still. These were refrigerator-sized rocks, and all pretence of walking was gone.

We started climbing. Conscious of how easy it would be to slip and plummet, I placed my feet and hands with a cautiousness normally reserved for holding newborns. We were several hundred metres up now, but the sun continued to bake the mountain face like the crust of a scallop pie. If I didn't tumble off the rocks, I would pass out from heat stroke. Either way, I'd make a ghastly corpse, my hair matted with sweat, my skin peeling with sunburn, one of my eyeballs dangling out.

Despite becoming delusional, I was making steady progress up Cradle Cliff. Steve was 30 metres ahead, his athletic build making it easy for him to clamber over the stones. I stared daggers at his receding back. He was an accountant who often sat at his desk for sixteen hours at a time; the most exerting physical activity he experienced on an average day was tabbing through spreadsheets. Clearly, Steve had mountain climbing in his genes, whereas mine leaned more towards self-doubt and crying.

To avoid looking down, I craned my neck up. My heart raced and the whole mountain seemed to sway. Fear threatened to choke me.

A couple came scrambling down, two fit young people in brand-name workout clothes and trainers – not even proper hiking boots. They jumped from rock to rock like they'd been bit by the same radioactive spider as Steve.

'Hey, did you make it up?' I called. 'How far is it?'

The guy shrugged. 'Maybe thirty minutes?'

232

I nodded, clinging to the edge of the rock face to let them pass.
I can handle thirty minutes.

Five minutes later, I asked another lanky guy the same question.

He looked at his watch. 'Been about an hour since I left the top.'

There was no longer any sort of slope, just a cliff face of boulders. My brain was determined to reach the summit – Year of Australianness, symbolism, etc. My body, however, did not give a scrub's tit about symbolism. My body knew I shouldn't be climbing a chaotic mess of appliance-sized rocks over a 500-metre drop. It knew I'd been out in the heat with limited water for more than three hours. And it knew I was an accident-prone klutz who had, back in Canada, often attempted to break multiple bones by slipping on patches of ice that I bloody well knew were there.

Based on that evidence, my body decided that if couldn't override my brain by broadcasting its increasing fear, it was going to shut this expedition down the only way it knew how: full-blown panic attack.

I started hyperventilating. My legs and arms trembled.

'Steve,' I called. 'I don't think … I don't think I can do it.'

He turned to look down at me, hanging one-handed off a boulder with the grace of a shaved orangutan.

'Are you sure?'

I started to sob.

At that moment a fit and energetic couple with three young boys appeared below us. The oldest boy might have been twelve and the youngest seven or eight. One was wearing thongs. They were scampering up the rocks like they were black belts in parkour. Their parents called to the boys in robust Aussie accents, instructing them to wait without expecting them to do so. Both parents showed the level of exertion you'd expect from – well, from people on a great short walk. Mum and dad didn't look or smell like they'd poured a bottle of last week's sweat over themselves. They didn't seem overly concerned that one of their kids might tumble from this cliff face to an abrupt death below. And what I particularly noted was neither of them was clinging to a rock ledge weeping because their whole year was over before it started.

Steve worked his way down to me. We waited while the parents clambered past us, chatting cheerily. Other hikers made their way down, their beatific faces broadcasting the joy they'd felt on reaching the summit, taking in the 360-degree view and achieving a meaningful personal goal.

These were Australians – fearless, physically fit, blissfully unconcerned over their children's daredevil antics. No matter where they were from, in that moment, on that mountain, they were Australian. And I, definitively, was not.

Sitting on the cliff ledge, I cried for a while.

Steve patted my hand. 'It's not a big deal.'

I sniffled. 'It's not like I'm into sports or have an Australian accent or can make Anzac biscuits. The one time I tried, they ran together into biscuit goop that stuck to the pan. I thought I could climb a mountain, but apparently I can't even do that. I've never quit halfway up a mountain before!'

'Why do you think it's so Australian to climb this mountain?'

'It's the national character – tough, resilient, outdoorsy.' This is what I'd thought I was signing up for that morning. I should have suspected that part of the appeal of this 'walk' might be surviving

234

Further Down, More Under

it. You had to be tough to make it up this mountain, you had to get over yourself and get on with it.

Steve was quiet for a few minutes, contemplating the expanse of mossy green beneath us, and the rumples of mountains beyond.

'Who's the most Australian person you know?'

'Jules.'

'Has she ever climbed this mountain? Or any mountain? Do we know anyone who's climbed this mountain?'

I sighed. Steve patted my hand again, then reached into his backpack and handed me his water bottle.

Since coming home from Darwin, I'd paid more attention to the ways Steve expressed his love, and less attention to the ways I wished he'd express it. In a back corner of my mind, I recognised this as one of those moments. It wasn't brazen or overt. His love was a quiet pat on the hand. It was the loyalty to come and sit beside me while I dripped my messy emotions everywhere, when he could have continued to the summit without me.

'Do you feel like things were easier, before we got married?' I asked.

'Between us? Yeah.'

'Why did things get so hard? We live in a comfortable home, we've made nice friends, and since you got a job, everything's worked out well. Except it never feels that way.'

Steve tapped the fingers of his free hand against his thigh. 'I'm like a cat – I like to be left alone a lot of the time. And you're like a dog. A nervous dog that needs a lot of affection.' He must have noticed the dismay on my face because he quickly added, 'But a good dog.'

I rested my head against his shoulder. 'I'd feel better if I got more affection.'

'I know. I'll try to work on that.'

'So you're not planning to leave me?'

'Where do you get these ideas?'

I rubbed a scrape on my left hand, noticing for the thousandth time the absence of my wedding rings. 'I'd be okay if you left me. For the record.'

'Geez, it sounds like you're the one planning to leave me.'

I gave a sarcastic scoff. 'Where do you get these ideas?'

Below us, a dozen tiny figures made their way across the rocks. I wondered how many of them would reach the summit.

'Steve, I'm glad we're talking about this. But sitting on the edge of this cliff is making me nauseous.'

Slowly and carefully, we headed back down. I resolved that this year would probably be like every other year, a mix of good and bad, with days when I'd feel confident and others when I'd struggle. It was probably going to be like that the rest of my life – even if I had managed to summit Cradle Mountain on New Year's Day.

22

Tasting Notes for Australia's Worst Beers

'How many cans did you get?' I asked.

'Tinnies!' Jules said. 'You have to say tinnies. How long have you lived here?'

It was a golden Sunday arvo in mid-September, and Jules had arrived to spend it on the balcony with me. Lorikeets darted and chattered, and the breeze carried a hint of the salty harbour. In the distance, a ship horn bellowed.

When Jules had learned I was applying for citizenship, she decided we needed to mark the occasion by doing something very Australian.

Like me, she preferred sparkling wine and $20 cocktails. Because I was embarking on the final step of my citizenship journey, however, Jules had planned a special afternoon of beer tasting.

Beer drinking is the country's 'greatest national pastime', according to the book *Life's a Beer*. 'To sink a few cold ones with the blokes is both an escape and a confirmation of belonging,' the author, Australian journalist Rennie Ellis, wrote. He didn't offer an equivalent confirmation of belonging for the sheilas, so we'd have to make do with the beers.

Earlier at the bottle-o, Jules said, when she'd brought her selections to the counter, the cashier had raised an eyebrow and asked, 'Did you go through the shop looking for the worst beer, and then you couldn't decide so you bought them all?'

Now she lined up her selections on the table: VB, Fosters, XXXX Gold and Toohey's Extra Dry. I'd heard of these brands, but had never tried them.

Jules gestured to the arrangement. 'I present an assortment of liquid cultural cringe.'

'People have cultural cringe over beers?'

I was still puzzled by cultural cringe. It often came up when I asked what it meant to be Australian. For some people – notably those without Southern Cross tattoos – it was as if to be Australian was to cringe.

There are things we're not proud of in Canada, such as Alberta's increasing Texanness and our cracked, heaving highways. And there are things we cringe at, like Nickleback. But if you ask what it is to be Canadian, the most common response involves a quiet superiority to the United States. *Look how much better we are*, we think to ourselves, *with our universal health care and our gun control and our stylish flannel*. Our Rocky Mountains stand taller than those south of the border. And whenever any Canadian hockey team wins against the US, whether it's an Olympic team or the Junior Pipsqueaks Division, Canada takes

Tasting Notes for Australia's Worst Beers

this as cosmic confirmation of our superiority.

Even our beer is superior. If you wanted a random sample of terrible beers in Canada, you'd buy American brands. The most mass-produced, generic Canadian beers – Molson's, say, or Kokanee – are a step above the average American variety. Despite my cocktail preference, I knew that as gospel.

Maybe Australia's geographic isolation had resulted in some self-esteem issues. It also couldn't have helped that the country spent so many decades trying to be English, rather than embracing its own uniqueness. Maybe if Australia felt better about itself, it could treat others better – its Aboriginal population, and refugees, say. Or maybe if it treated others better, its self-esteem and sense of identity would improve. Either way, there were things worth cringing about, and domestic beer was the least of them.

Jules popped the tab on a VB. Its slogan read, 'For a hard-earned thirst.'

'I suspect it's the worst,' Jules said, grinning wickedly as she handed one to me. 'Here's to becoming Australian!'

I laughed as we tapped our tinnies together. 'We still have to pass the citizenship test.'

'What's the test like?'

I wasn't sure. 'I've heard you have to know Bradman's batting average.'

Jules looked shocked. 'I'd totally fail.'

'I can memorise his batting average, his team name, the year he won the Golden Cricket Cup. I can memorise anything. I'm just not sure what Bradman's batting average tells me about being Australian.'

Jules shrugged. 'Apparently some of us like sport.'

I grinned, knowing Jules, much like myself, wouldn't notice if all sports suddenly ceased to exist.

'I'll have you know I attended a genuine waffle match in Perth. There was a ball and everything.'

'Well, cheers, you're already Aussie in my books!' She laughed, loud and brassy. We clinked tinnies again, then both took a sip. Jules frowned. She took another sip.

'That's fine,' she said, surprised. 'I would drink that again.'

The sun reflecting off the table glass gave the balcony a warm glow, contrasting perfectly with the cold beer.

'Have you found many differences between Australia and Canada? Other than the weather.'

I gave the slow nod of the afternoon drinker. 'More than I expected.'

'Such as?' She arched an eyebrow.

I thought for a moment. 'Canada has no equivalent to bushrangers.'

It had taken some effort to wrap my head around the concept of bushranging. I was still unsure whether Canadians were simply more law-abiding, or if our history did feature escaped criminals who had wandered the woods, occasionally turning to cannibalism (like Australia's Alexander Pearce, originally transported for the theft of six pairs of shoes and later alleged to have eaten eight of his companions in escape attempts), but who for whatever reason never entered our national mythology. More likely any Canadians attempting to bushrange ended up freezing to death before they could establish much of a legacy.

Tasting Notes for Australia's Worst Beers

But it went deeper than that. Canada's relationship to law and order is different to Australia's. One of our national symbols is the Royal Canadian Mounted Police. We're proud of our Mounties, and not only because of the hit 1990s TV show *Due South*. They figure into our mythology as much as the cop-murdering antihero Ned Kelly figures into Australia's.

This was yet another way I couldn't align myself with Australia, or at least with its mythology. I was, at my core, deeply law-abiding. And, on reflection, so were all the Australians I knew. I thought I understood why Kelly's actions resonated with his contemporaries, but I couldn't grasp his relevance in modern Australia.

'Does the Ned Kelly story feel like a CD stuck on repeat to you?' I asked. 'I mean, there was that time he was arrested for putting calf testicles in the post, which ranks him among the nation's great criminal masterminds. But still ...'

Jules waved a dismissive hand. 'Yeah, nah, a bloody foreigner like you wouldn't know a true-blue Aussie if he shot you in the head.'

I froze, thinking for a half second that her cold tone conveyed the depth of true feeling. But I caught the subtle smile in her eyes. This was one of those moments where, in typical Aussieness, she meant the opposite of the words coming out of her mouth.

It irked me, but I knew I was supposed to let it pass. I smirked and tipped my tinnie towards her.

'There are heaps of more interesting bushrangers anyway,' I continued. 'Like the Birdman of the Coorong in SA, that tiny Irish guy who rode around on an emu stealing gold necklaces.

241

They think he had a million dollars' worth of jewellery, and he wore it around his neck while riding emu-back.'

'What! I've never heard of this.'

'He got away with it for years because the Coorong is sandy marsh. Horses struggled over that terrain, but his emu could tear across it. Then one day he was shot and rode off into the Coorong, wounded and trailing blood. He was never seen again. They think his jewel-clad skeleton is still out there somewhere.'

'You're starting to know more Australiana than I do.'

When I'd first arrived, I wanted to stuff my head full of Australiana. I was surprised to find I still felt that way. Though sometimes confusing and other times infuriating, Australia was also endlessly fascinating.

The mildness of our VBs made for quick drinking. We moved on to the Foster's. The blue cans featured a patriotic kangaroo.

The 'Foster's: Australian for beer' commercials were a staple of Canadian TV. In the ads, actors purported to be Australian through their rugged handsomeness, pub-based drinking and proximity to frothy pints of Foster's. Discovering that Foster's was mainly an export beer felt like a sham. Next they'd tell me the platypus was a hoax, just like the naturalists back in England had suspected.

'I'm surprised you could find Foster's,' I said. 'I thought they didn't sell it here.'

'It wasn't on display. I had to dig around in the back.' Jules took a drink. 'That is ... far less nasty than anticipated.' Her look of confusion deepened. It was like we were exposing a great lie.

At that moment, a kookaburra somewhere in the trees began

Tasting Notes for Australia's Worst Beers

laughing. My breath caught and I turned my face to the sound. Instead of pausing in proper appreciation of the auditory joy, Jules talked over it.

A jolt of shock coursed through me. I was on the verge of chastising her before I caught myself.

Of could she didn't understand the reverence kookaburra laughter deserved. She'd grown up with it as everyday background noise.

'Well, what's next?' I managed, embarrassed for myself, and sad for Jules. 'XXXX?' I pronounced each X.

Jules laughed and shook her head. 'It's called Four X. Which reminds me, one time I met a German guy at a hostel in Byron Bay, and he asked "Why do Australians call their beer Four X?"' She popped the top on one of the tinnies. '"Because they can't spell shit."' She paused. 'Seriously though, XXXX is the beer of people who voted for Pauline Hanson.'

'Well, it smells like beer.'

'And it tastes like … Foster's plus yeast.'

I nodded in agreement.

We ended with the Toohey's Extra Dry, which, like the others, tasted like beer, though with a slightly hoppier flavour.

Jules gestured towards the empty cans lined up on the table. 'I've learned something today. I would drink any of those again. I mean, except the Foster's.'

'I don't know anyone who drinks Foster's at home either, despite the ads.'

'You still say "at home". Have you noticed?'

'Yep. And when we visited our parents in Winnipeg last

243

Christmas, Steve and I kept saying, "When we get back home …" about Sydney.'

'How long have you been here now?'

'Five years, nearly.'

'Do you feel Australian?'

'You know, when I lived in Mexico, I dated a guy there briefly, and at one point I looked into long-term visas. To apply for Mexican citizenship, all you have to do is live in the country for five years. For a while I thought maybe that's what I'd do, stay in Mexico. But I never thought I'd *be* Mexican. It's the conflation of ethnicity and nationality, I suppose.'

'That's the promise of Australia and Canada – there's no ethnic requirement. At least, not officially,' she said with a shake of her head.

Past the balcony rail, the breeze rustled the palm trees, jacarandas and gums. An ibis glided past. What did being Australian feel like? What did being Canadian feel like? I'd ruminated on this for years, dragging myself around the country in pursuit of an answer.

Being born in Canada, I'd never had anything to compare it to, in terms of personal identity. I was Canadian, my parents were Canadian, my friends were Canadian. My family heritage was a muddle of Irish, Scottish, Polish, German and Armenian; I'd felt little connection to those places growing up, and little connection still to the physical territory Armenia occupied today. I'd grown up in small towns and Winnipeg's far-flung, uncosmopolitan suburbs. My peers came from varied cultural backgrounds, but we lived in the same daily milieu, watching the same pre-internet TV,

Tasting Notes for Australia's Worst Beers

suffering the same weather. Growing up in those parochial places, I was Canadian by default. I didn't appreciate the grain bin next to the train tracks as a quintessential prairie tableau because it was just the place I walked past every day. I didn't get excited by chickadees and robins because they'd been hanging around since I was born. The Canadian prairie became the default baseline against which I compared all future experiences.

Australia was a choice. Not just the original choice to move here, but the choices I made every day to pay attention, to interrogate what Australianness was, to move through my life like a bowerbird, collecting bits of Australiana and weaving them into myself.

I'd made progress. I said 'Cans' without thinking 'Cair-ns', asked 'how're you going' as a reflex, and had conceded that maybe 'sport' could be singular.

But I didn't fit seamlessly into the daily fabric of Aussie life. I refused to eat iced vovos, I had to restrain myself from taking pictures of the Opera House every time I passed, and I felt a shiver of indecency on the rare occasion I used the word 'bush'. Ibises still gave me a secret thrill, and I suspected I'd forever feel effervescent joy whenever I heard a kookaburra. And there was my damn accent, which would always be more Winnipeg than Wagga Wagga.

If they overlooked the accent, would Aussies recognise me as a compatriot? I'd experienced Darwin in the Wet, footy in the rain, and the unforgiving face of Cradle Mountain in the searing heat. If Aussies reminisced about disgusting share houses, I could tell them about the thin layer of cardboard that once stood between me and a torrent of pigeon faeces.

245

I'd come here hoping for a year of easygoing, beach-centric happiness. I'd learned instead that wherever I was, I brought my internal turbulence with me. My struggles and my response to them, more than anything else, formed my true identity. My project of becoming Australian was as much about gaining that perspective as about feeling at home in a new culture.

Jules was watching me, waiting for an answer.

'Honestly,' I said, 'I feel like someone who just drank several beers rather quickly.'

~

Home alone Monday afternoon, I steeled myself and looked up the citizenship application. The process was simpler than the permanent residency one, although we'd need to provide our passports, birth certificates, marriage certificate and other documents for the fourth time, as if the federal government had no previous record of us. What were they doing with all the certified hard copies we'd given them? From Steve and me alone, they had enough to wallpaper Parliament inside and out.

The test was a series of multiple-choice questions taken from the study booklet material. I downloaded it. A tide of worry rose in my brain. What if I couldn't pass? What was the fail rate?

I let the worries crystallise, acknowledging them, then edging them aside. When I'd gone to my first psychologist appointment with Linda, I'd assumed there was a way to eliminate my anxiety, as though it were an infection that could be fought off. During my six months with her, I'd adjusted my expectations. Anxiety was about ongoing management. Despite my scepticism, the tools

246

Linda gave me had helped. My worries were still there, but instead of verging on a mental rampage, they stayed contained, with effort.

The front door swung open and Steve walked in.

'Hey, I've downloaded the citizenship application,' I said. 'Maybe we could start on it tonight?'

He took off his shoes and put his laptop on the table, moving slowly. His face looked worn, like he'd aged several decades since leaving for work that morning.

'My mum's turning seventy this year,' he said.

'And your dad soon, and both my parents are turning sixty and their fortieth wedding anniversary is coming up. And you're turning forty. It's a big year.'

He sank onto a kitchen chair, tapping his fingertips against the table leg like a woodpecker.

'What's up?' I said, taking a seat beside him.

He put his hands on the table and sighed, a huff of mingled sadness and stress.

'One of my staff … his dad has cancer.'

'Oh, that's terrible.' I took his hand, sandwiching it between mine. I couldn't remember the last time I'd seen something shake Steve like this. He leaned his head on my shoulder. 'What's the prognosis?'

'It's one of the bad cancers. I can't remember which. It's been going on for a while. But he's in England. The dad.'

'Which employee is it?'

'Pranav. He's the nicest guy.'

'So he's flying to England?'

'He was in London for a month. He got back to Sydney two

weeks ago when they thought his dad was on the rebound.' Steve pressed his thumb and forefinger against his temples. 'Things took a turn for the worse. Pranav left again today.'

When my student visa had expired four years earlier, one of my main concerns about staying in Australia was how far we were from our families. That we were effectively orphaning ourselves. And that, if we stayed, we couldn't be there for our families when they needed us. Steve had shrugged this off, as if our parents would live forever.

I squeezed his hand. I could tell he was imagining himself in Pranav's place, worrying about his own parents and the long journey to Winnipeg, the difficulty of keeping up with his work from abroad.

'I've been thinking that … maybe we should move back,' he said, his eyes on the floor.

I dropped his hand and leaned back to stare at him. We'd invested all this time in Australia, had made it our home, had made it part of us. This felt like a betrayal. *If you'd listened to me four years ago*, I wanted to snap. *I warned you this would happen.*

It was like I'd spent years painstakingly building a house, nailing in each board, and now Steve was standing on the porch with a jerry can of petrol and a match.

My mouth gaped open and shut a few times before I managed to speak. 'Do you really want to move back?'

He turned his face away, levelling his gaze at the floor. 'I started looking at jobs in Canada.'

23

It's the Vibe

If you have $25 and can cajole someone literate to complete the online visa form, you are allowed to enter Australia even if you know absolutely nothing about it. You can think that the national language is Portuguese and that koalas are endangered because they make such tasty taco filling and 'the outback' is a CIA conspiracy.

As a tourist, you're also permitted to leave Australia not knowing anything. Nobody checks your comprehension on the way out. You can present yourself as an authority on Australia by reason of time spent within its borders even if you believe Bondi is in Dubbo and Alan Jones is the prime minister and vegemite is safe for human consumption.

If you apply to stay permanently, you still don't have to know anything except how to complete a lot of paperwork without murdering your spouse.

If you want to become a citizen, however – if you want to call yourself Australian and have some legal paperwork to back up your claim – then you have to know some things. Specifically thirty pages worth of things, with another fifty pages of recommended but not testable things.

The provided study booklet reads like a parody. It includes a section on 'Compassion for those in need', which is a hilarious joke considering Australia's current refugee policies. There's also a section on equality, emphasising that men and women have equal rights, such as access to employment, while conveniently ignoring the gender pay gap and many other instances of nationwide inequality. And though part of the testable material does reference Indigenous history and culture, it's summarised in less than five paragraphs.

After you submit your citizenship application, you receive an email from CTMSEmailReturnsSydney, which is obviously not spam. It will announce your test time as 02:40:00, because apparently that's how Australians write time, and you managed to live here for five years without being aware of this.

You misread your test time and arrive at the immigration office at 2 pm. This means you have to sit through forty minutes of an employee telling everyone who comes into the office, 'DON'T take a number!' The numbered ticket dispenser is a complex machine and only trained professionals are permitted to operate it. This is a matter of Occupational Health and Safety, which Australia takes very seriously.

Sit down, mate. Your test time was scheduled to the hundredth of a second, but the man whose entire job is to press the ticket machine button will give you a number when he damn well feels like it.

It's the Vibe

~

I arrived at the citizenship testing office alone. It was a blazing December afternoon, but inside the aircon was set on shiver. The requisite twelve months had passed since we'd received our PR. I'd never envisioned being here without Steve.

Rows of chairs filled the room, and along the back wall ran six cubicles, each with a different colour of tinsel hung haphazardly over the grey felt dividers. A mixed-age crowd from across the ethnic spectrum filled the seats, everyone dressed for summer, their exposed skin goose-pimpling. I took one of the few free seats.

As the situation with Pranav's father worsened – pancreatic cancer, little chance of recovery – Steve dug hard into his intention to move back. He spent his evenings browsing real estate websites for Ottawa, a city I'd never been to and only agreed to consider begrudgingly, and by default. Steve refused to live in the smog and congestion of Toronto, I refused to live in rain-soaked Vancouver, and neither of us spoke enough French to get by in Montreal. Ottawa was the only city left worth considering.

The knot of tension in my jaw, caused by my clamped teeth, had faded away over the past year. I hadn't noticed its absence until now, when it returned, pulsing with pain. I massaged it with two fingertips. To me, the time for moving back had passed. Our professional networks were here, our friends were here, and, I felt, our future was here. Even the book I was submitting to publishers offered an Australian perspective on modern Armenian history, and would have to be rewritten yet again if we moved away.

But seeing how affected Steve was by the slow, torturous death

251

How to Be Australian

of someone he'd never met made me think perhaps it would be better to move back to Canada in readiness. All four of our parents were still relatively healthy, and I recognised that as incredible good luck, a lottery we'd won. We called our parents every week. We visited every second year, and cajoled them into visiting us. I wondered though – if we lost one of them suddenly, would we look back on the years we'd spent abroad with regret? Were we being selfish, living a fantasy life in Australia with flamboyant parrots and stunning coast walks and excellent coffee while our ageing parents dug their vehicles out of the snow each winter?

Despite the unbearable weight of knowing Steve wanted to leave Australia, of knowing it was probably the right thing to do, of knowing that all it would take would be for me to say *okay* and we'd be back in Canada within three months – I wasn't curled up on the bedroom floor crying at night. And I hadn't once considered that maybe this meant the end of our marriage. Whatever happened, we'd go forward together.

Regardless of our uncertainty, I'd convinced Steve to apply for citizenship as soon as we'd been eligible. We'd come this far, I'd argued, had paid a queen's ransom in taxes, and had nothing to lose by finalising our citizenship. Maybe we could retire here. When I thought about retirement, the most likely scenario seemed to be climate devastation, economic collapse and mass starvation. If we were going to spend our final years living in a cardboard box, at least we could do it on an Australian beach rather than in a Canadian snow bank.

If we had citizenship, the door would always be open to return – and maybe in that way, I could cope with leaving.

Steve and I had submitted our applications at the same time, but had ended up with different assigned dates for our citizenship tests.

More people filed into the office every few minutes, joining the listless crowd. They mostly looked impatient, rolling their eyes around the room in search of distraction, heaving the occasional sigh. No-one looked nervous. I felt nervous for Steve, though his test wasn't for a few weeks. He found tests stressful, and was struggling to memorise the citizenship material. I wondered if he was psychologically resisting the test. While I'd invested myself in overt efforts to develop an Australian identity, he'd invested himself in his job. He had full citizenship to Accountingland, a place where he never doubted his identity. Maybe he now felt as dislocated in his Australian life as I had when we first decided to stay.

The irritable employee finally waved me over, pushed the button on the ticket machine and handed me a number. I waited long past 02:40:00 before another man called me to his padded cube. With an officious nod, he took my documents – the same documents that I'd submitted with my permanent residency application, then again with my citizenship application – and photocopied each of them. With the sheaf of copies sitting on his desk, he then scanned each of my documents.

Next he explained that he was going to take my photo, despite the fact that I'd provided him with a number of photos as instructed.

'Turn to face the camera, don't smile.' His voice was robotic.

Was this the test? Was I being tested on my willingness to submit to bureaucracy, no matter how inane and redundant? If I protested, if I pointed to the stack of certified photos I'd handed

How to Be Australian

him, if I questioned the tedious scanning of each document, would my citizenship application be rejected? I sat in silence, bewildered.

'That's the first time I've seen a marriage certificate from Manitoba,' he said, seeming to break out of his routine script. He flashed a tiny smile while gazing at the certificate with its bison emblem.

'You're about the 4800th person I've processed,' he said, his voice warmer now, like he'd just noticed that the thing across his desk was an actual person and not a mannequin. 'That's me personally. There are people here who have done a lot more.'

'It must be fascinating seeing all these different people.'

'It would be if I had time to talk to them, but I have to process you and move on. Everyone has a story to tell though. In this job, I often meet people at the end of a long journey. For some it's been a terrible struggle. For others, it's been easy. For me, it was an accident.'

I leaned in, keen to hear how one accidentally becomes Australian. But his human face vanished, like a flipped switch.

'The next swearing-in ceremony in your area will be sometime in April,' he said in a monotone, and directed me down the hall to the testing room. I stood up, swept back into the bureaucratic tide.

The only person in the testing room was the employee in charge. She smiled and directed me to any one of the roomful of computers, each separated by the same padded grey cubicle walls, but without the festive tinsel. The only sound was the hum of computer fans.

I sat in front of a screen. I had forty-five minutes to answer twenty questions.

It turned out that Bradman's batting average had been part of an earlier version of the test. The latest version had done away with sports trivia to focus on two main objectives. First, to ensure the applicants knew what we were getting ourselves into as citizens – that we had to vote and could be called for jury duty or into military service, like in Canada. Applicants also had to understand the big-picture details of Australia's government and recognise its symbols. It made sense for citizens to know the deal between the PM and the Queen, which was the head of state and which the head of government. Having a clear grasp on the Governor-General's role, on the other hand, didn't seem like an essential part of being an Australian citizen. But according to the test material, it was, and now I was staring down the question on my screen. I selected b) the signing of bills passed by the Australian Parliament – just like in Canada.

Being Canadian had made the governmental questions easy; as Commonwealth siblings, our systems of government were fairly similar. I raced through those. Fifteen per cent of the questions were about Australia's flags. The government is very concerned that new citizens can identify all three flags (when I mentioned this to Aussies, they often responded, 'Wait, three?'). I flew through these questions, too. I knew my flags, including the blue, green, black and white of the Torres Strait Islanders'. Instead of 'What are the colours of the Australian flag?' a real challenge would have been putting the Australian flag next to New Zealand's and asking, 'Which one, mate?'

In four minutes I completed the Australian citizenship test, with a score of 100 per cent.

Jubilation filled me. The test was excessively bureaucratic, but I'd been tested in so many ways leading up to this moment – and here I was. I'd been asked to prove myself as Australian, and I'd done it.

Then I caught myself, and shrank my thoughts down to average poppy height – *the test went okay*, I repeated.

The testing room employee shook my hand in congratulations. As far as the federal government was concerned, I couldn't be more ready to be Australian. All that was left was for Steve to get through his test – and realise we were better off here.

~

Jules arrived wearing cherry-red lipstick, her hair pulled into a high bun. She handed me a bottle of prosecco and a DVD. It was a sultry January evening. The aircon's hum competed with the chirruping crickets.

'How's the book going?' she asked, handing me the icy cold bottle as I ushered her in.

'Just got knocked back by a publisher.' It'd taken me several weeks to work up the nerve to mention this to anyone. The unkindly worded rejection had spiralled me into a mess of doubt and tears for seventy-two hours, and then I'd shoved my fears into a mental box and started a new draft.

'You'll get there.' Jules winked.

'I hope so. We donate to refugee organisations, but sharing my great-grandparents' story feels like a more personal way I can advocate for others. I feel so helpless about the refugee situation here.'

Jules grimaced. 'I guess that's part of what it means to be an Aussie these days.' We both stared at the floor for a moment. Then Jules's gaze flicked across the apartment. 'How 'bout your man, where is he?'

'At work, like usual.'

'Aram, too.' She threw up a hand. 'Is he ready for the big test?'

'Nope. I'm hoping he'll study on the weekend. The test is next week.'

'Well, congrats on *your* test!' She slapped my shoulder cheerfully.

The prosecco bottle gave a resounding pop as I prised it open, the cork bouncing off the ceiling. Normally I wouldn't crack a bottle on a Tuesday evening, but the more I hung out with Jules, the more I drank. I realised suddenly that I hadn't thought about mouth cancer in months. I wished I could thank Linda, shake one of her loosely flopping hands, but the clinic had never told me her surname.

'How's it going on your quest to be Australian? Other than feeling disgusted by the government.'

'I've been thinking about something lately.' The prosecco threatened to bubble over as I filled our glasses. We took quick sips. 'When I was teaching English in Canada, I gave a seminar on small talk and professional networking opportunities to new migrants who were restarting their professions in Canada – teachers, engineers, accountants. At the end, the first question was "Where is the lake?" And everyone in the room started nodding, they all wanted to know. Their colleagues and neighbours were always talking about going "to the lake", which was baffling to

How to Be Australian

them because Manitoba has thousands of lakes.'

'And everyone says "the lake" like there's only one?'

'I'd never thought it about before. So many people have a family cabin on a lake or go visit friends or family at one of the lakes that the city empties out in the summer. Steve still says, "My parents are at the lake this weekend." And I know he means Lake of the Woods, where they have a cabin.'

'That's super confusing.'

'I asked why the students hadn't simply asked people what they meant. And this woman from the Philippines said, "It felt like I should know what they were talking about." Then I asked how many of them had visited one of the lakes around the city. Almost none had. We ended up having a 20-minute discussion about lake culture. It was such an ordinary thing to me. To them, it was like the big secret of how to be Manitoban. At least in the summer.'

'Speaking of figuring out the locals ...' Jules held up the DVD she'd brought, shimmying it. 'You're telling me you haven't seen this?'

I pulled a few cheeses out of the fridge and arranged them on a board with some crackers and fig paste. 'I'd never heard of it till you mentioned it the other day.'

Her mouth gaped. 'How have you lived here so long and not even heard of *The Castle*? You're going to have to watch this again with Steve-o when he passes his test, because this is *the* quintessential Australian movie.'

The case claimed the film was from 1997, but the cover looked like a family photo from the 80s, the mum in a daggy sweater, the dad moustached and pot-bellied, with five adults who might have

258

been their kids. An unremarkable house filled the background. There didn't seem to be anything particularly Australian about it.

I didn't voice my scepticism as I slid *The Castle* into my laptop.

I never should have doubted Jules. The Kerrigan family's struggle to save their house from demolition was instantly endearing. Jules had the film memorised, and echoed her favourite lines five or six times.

'Okay, so,' she said, emptying the last of the wine into my glass as the credits rolled. 'What'd you think?'

'When you told me this was the quintessential Australian movie, I was picturing something different.'

'What, *Crocodile Dundee*?'

'I can't help it, that's the image of Australia I grew up with. *The Castle* is so … ordinary. I mean, it's hilarious. But it's just about this family and their house. It feels like it could take place in Canada — except, it couldn't.'

'It captures the Aussie spirit,' Jules said, her eyes sparkling. 'Most people just want a little place to themselves, you know, the opportunity to get away sometimes and appreciate the landscape, and to get on with their lives and let others do the same.'

'But where were the larrikins? The one brother was in jail, I guess, but that wasn't celebrated.'

'Aw, what would you know anyway, mole?' Her voice had a sudden hard edge, and the comment cut into me.

She grinned in a sly way that said she was kidding. I could have laughed it off like other times, but it got under my skin. I was earnestly — still too earnestly, after all these years — trying to understand this confounding country and getting insulted for it.

259

'Why do Australians do that?'

She looked surprised. 'What, take the piss?'

'It's like Steve with his bloody Englishness. He'll never say how he feels, he'll just click his teeth and tap his fingers against his thigh and make me guess what he's thinking. So Australians inherited that and then took it one step further – it's like it's too painful to say how you feel, so you go the opposite way and insult people you care about.' You could learn to be Manitoban by visiting a lake. In Australia, you had to purge your emotions and fill the void with needling sarcasm.

Jules leaned back. Instead of her usual quippy remarks, she pursed her lips.

'Sorry,' I said, 'it's just – I don't know how to be cool with that.'

She reached over and put her hand on my shoulder. 'Just wait for the day I start calling you a dopey cunt.'

24

Welcome to Australia

On a Sunday morning, Steve and I packed our towels and suncream and headed to the beach. Not Bondi, because it was January and we now understood that Bondi in summer was a swarming infestation of the worst sorts of tourists. Instead, we went to Camp Cove Beach, a nook on the Watson's Bay peninsula. We brought our beach umbrella, so we could stay in the shade. Steve carried an extra bottle of water for me. We went late in the arvo, after the worst of the day's extreme UV had faded. I still couldn't go outside without thinking about skin cancer, but I could usually prevent anxiety from hijacking my day.

At Camp Cove, we set up our umbrella and beach chairs as our shadows stretched across the sand. A warm salt-scented breeze brushed over us. In the harbour, the Manly Ferry glided past, its passengers waving at sailboaters, who waved back.

I took a moment to appreciate the view. Then I pulled out the citizenship test preparation booklet. Part of figuring out how to enjoy the beach meant accepting that I wasn't the type of person who enjoyed idle time. Idle time was like opening my worry box

How to Be Australian

and shaking its contents loose, inviting my anxiety to run riot. If I was going to sit on the beach, I was going to do so productively.

'Alright, Steve. Which of these is a role of the Governor-General? The appointment of state premiers? Or the signing of bills passed by –'

'I don't want to do this now.'

'Your test is tomorrow morning!' My voice rose to a squeak.

'You said it was mostly flag-based.'

'I said 15 per cent of the questions that I answered were about the flags. You'll get different questions. And you need 75 per cent to pass.' My jaw twinged in pain. I was clamping my teeth again.

'I know the flags. The main two and the other one.'

'The Torres Strait Islander flag.'

'Right.' He paused. 'Where is the Torres Strait?'

That seemed like the type of thing I should know. 'North-ish?'

'Shouldn't that be on the test?' Steve raised his sunnies to give me a pointed look.

'Debating the test questions won't help you pass, mate.' I tried to smile while fighting back the stress flaring through my chest. It didn't matter if he failed on Monday, I reminded myself. He could retake the test another day.

But would he? Or if he failed once, would he decide he couldn't be bothered with citizenship? Would that be what pushed him from bookmarking Ottawa job openings to applying?

Steve interrupted my spiralling thoughts. 'Any there any practical questions?'

262

Welcome to Australia

'What?'

'You know, like identifying live spiders? Performing snakebite CPR?'

'You think the test should have a practical component?'

'It's not like I'm going to have anything to do with the Governor-General. There are lots of aspects of life here that the test doesn't mention.'

I could have spent the day worrying. I could have accused Steve of not taking things seriously. I could have gotten stressed to the point of tears.

That was what I would have done in the past.

Instead, I chewed on my lip and thought about the years we'd invested here, and how we could be leaving soon, likely for good – forever.

If Steve found a good job in Ottawa with a compelling salary, it would be foolish to stay and then, in years or months, find ourselves flying back and forth, desperately stressed and exhausted, coping with a family health crisis.

Could I convince him to stay? Should I? I didn't know.

'Okay,' I said. 'What would you put on the test?'

'Seriously?' Steve said, catching on to the cheek in my voice. 'Where do I start?'

We spent the rest of the afternoon brainstorming a much better test, one that we wouldn't necessarily pass on the first go, but that highlighted a few of the more precise challenges of being Australian. It was the best possible use of our afternoon.

263

Ashley and Steve's Improved Citizenship Test

1. Pronounce these words: Cairns, Wagga Wagga, Canberra, Melbourne, Launceston.
2. Intimidate a tourist with casual discussion of the deadliness of creatures found in your backyard.
3. Eat a vegemite sandwich without making that face.
4. Stride up to a swimming pool and jump in (points deducted for testing the water temperature, prevaricating, flinching).
5. Go for drinks with nine other people and determine the precise moment it is your shout.
6. Attempt to beat former prime minister Bob Hawke's Guinness World Record for drinking a yard glass of beer in under twelve seconds. You won't succeed, but keep trying.
7. Demonstrate competence in the making of fairy bread.
8. Go for dinner with nine other people and split the bill among yourselves.
9. Arrange from smallest to largest: middy, glass, schooner, pot, pint, seven, pony, handle, imperial pint. (Note: ponies are now rare, presumably because they encouraged too many five-year-old girls to start drinking.)
10. Draft a ten-step spider-preparedness plan.

Essay question: The Harold Holt Memorial Pool – is it a joke? Note that the United States features no John F Kennedy Memorial Firearms Warehouse or Jimmy Hoffa Commemorative Concrete Factory. Is the pool's name supposed to serve as a warning – swim carefully or you'll end up like Holt? Or does it celebrate the wise choice of swimming in a pool as opposed to the liquid orgy of death that laps at Australia's shores? Show your work.

~

Later, we sat at Robertson Park, eating takeaway fish and chips as the sun set behind the cityscape, a deep purple seeping across the sky. Seagulls clustered around us, alert for dropped chips. The air smelled of fresh-cut grass. Gentle waves splashed against the ferry wharf.

'I talked to my parents this morning,' I said, dipping a piece of fish into my tartar sauce.

'What's up at home?'

'You know how it's been so cold? The water pipes to people's homes have started freezing.'

Steve's eyes widened.

It was a surprising event. Neither of us had ever heard of the city's water pipelines freezing before, and neither had Mom, who had lived through a lot more Canadian winters than we had. Even the brutal, miserable winter when I slipped and fell into a snow bank and decided to leave Canada for good, the winter when it was minus 40 for three months, I hadn't heard of anyone's water pipes freezing.

'Mom's worried about it. Several hundred homes have lost their water. The city is trying to dig through the frozen ground to thaw the pipes, but it's a slow process. They can only do a few every day, and there are about 1500 houses with frozen pipes already. Some families have had to move into hotels.'

In the tree branches above us, a cockatoo gave a pterodactyl shriek.

'Are you still looking for jobs in Canada?'

Steve sighed. 'We never planned to stay here forever.'

'But do you actually want to leave? It's January at home and it's so cold, the water pipes are freezing.'

'*Some* water pipes,' he said, as if this made the idea more bearable.

Part of me knew we should return to Canada. And if Steve decided now was the time, I'd go with him, just like he'd come here with me. But if it were up to me, I knew what I wanted.

'Besides,' I said, 'there's so much of Australia we haven't seen. We need to visit South Australia, and swim in a billabong – and I want to take the Ghan across the Nullarbor.'

'That super expensive train? No way.'

'What if there's a great deal on Ghan tickets?'

'Or we could take the Canadian Pacific north to Churchill and see the polar bears,' Steve said.

'I'm not sure if you know this about me, but I'm not a big fan of snow.'

'We've never toured the Maritimes. There's lots we could do.'

I rubbed my feet in the grass, struggling to keep my desperation out of my voice.

'Steve, I lived in four other countries before this. I never felt like I belonged anywhere.'

'You tried to convince me to leave Australia because you felt like you didn't belong here either.'

'I don't feel like I belong in Australia, but I do feel like …

I want to. Figuring out how to belong here has meant a lot to me, despite the national neuroticisms. When we lived in Canada, I spent half of every year counting down the weeks until winter was over.'

Steve took my hand. 'What about our parents? You were the one who said we shouldn't be so far away from our families. I didn't think about it much a few years ago, but now …'

It was the one question I had no answer to. It was expensive and arduous to visit. Now we had three nieces and a nephew we barely knew. If we stayed, we might never really know them.

We both stared at the water.

'I guess no matter what we do,' I said, 'there are no easy answers.'

~

In January, Steve took the citizenship test. He passed on the first go.

A few weeks later, I opened the mailbox to find two immigration letters welcoming us to Australia.

My thrill of excitement was cut short when I glanced at the bottom of the letters and saw the signature – Minister for Immigration, Peter Dutton. Seeing his name made my stomach heave. A xenophobic man with a villainous smile, Dutton was making headlines that week for calling a female reporter 'a mad fucking witch'. He had refused to attend PM Kevin Rudd's national apology to the Stolen Generations, and had warned against having compassion for refugees and asylum seekers. He was also determined to change federal policies to make it harder, if not impossible, for lower socio-economic migrants to ever have

How to Be Australian

a chance of receiving the very letter I was now holding in my hands. Dutton was the physical embodiment of everything rotten in Australia. After Ivan Milat and Martin Bryant, he was one of the last people I wanted to welcome me anywhere, let alone to a nation I was pledging allegiance to.

It was fitting for the political reality of Australia to sour this moment. It was a reminder that as a citizen, I couldn't be complacent. That I had to agitate for the people who needed these letters far more than I did. Especially the people who, like my great-grandparents after the genocide, had no home to return to.

The citizenship letters made us 'proposed citizens' – Australia had popped the question, we'd said yes, and all we needed was a ceremony to make it official. (It's a wonder 'proposed spouse' hasn't replaced fiancé.)

As proposed citizens, we were captives. We weren't allowed to leave Australia until we had Australian passports, and we couldn't get Australian passports until after we were confirmed as citizens – which would be at our swearing-in ceremony, in three months.

'What do they think will happen?' I asked, when Steve got home from work. 'That we'll visit a better country and change our minds about citizenship?'

'With this government, I'm already tempted.' He pulled off his tie and tossed it over the back of a chair.

'Governments change though. There's a federal election coming up.'

He sank onto the couch, the one we'd bought second-hand shortly after moving to Camperdown, its seafoam fabric now sun-faded, its cushions going lumpy with age. I still hoped to one day put wheels on it and ride it down a hill, ideally while drinking a VB.

'Even if the government changes, will you actually be happy here?'

I sat beside him. 'I'll never be that person I imagined when we moved here. I think I'll always be working at happiness, working at feeling at home. Australia is a rewarding place to do that.'

Steve tapped his fingers against his thigh. Delia Falconer had described Sydney as allergic to earnestness; it was an apt description of Steve as well.

'Canada is home for me,' he said. 'Australia is just a place I live. I like it, and having citizenship will make a lot of things simpler.'

There was a *but* coming. He was about to tell me he had an upcoming interview for a job in Ottawa, or that he already had an offer and was seriously considering it. My body tensed as if I was back clinging to the sheer face of Cradle Mountain. I squeezed my eyes shut against the prick of tears.

'But if moving back to Canada is going to make you unhappy …' Steve faltered. 'I know you've been working hard. You've been calmer this year.'

'What about your parents?'

Steve nodded slowly. 'It's like you said. Wherever we are, something will be difficult.'

From my face down to my toes, my muscles relaxed. I realised I'd been bracing since Steve first told me he was considering jobs in Canada. It was as if my body expected to step out into winter any minute, to end up back in that snow bank in the dark, shivering wildly to slow the onset of hypothermia.

269

I pulled myself into Steve's lap. He pressed his face into my neck and wrapped his arms around me. We sat together like that, listening as magpie calls echoed through the dusky sky. The sound, once foreign, felt like home.

25

Citizenship Sizzle

Three years after seeing Aboriginal pole dancer Matty Shields at Down Under Burlesque, I was still thinking about his performance. It represented the best of what Australia could be, honouring the past while forging something new and distinctive.

I was discussing this one day with a friend, another writer I'd met as I started connecting more with Sydney's literary scene.

'Matty Shields? I know him,' she said. 'He's housemates with a friend of mine.'

I met Matty at a pub in Newtown. I recognised him the moment he walked through the door. He clocked me by the way I leapt out of my seat. The close-cropped beard he sported made him look older, but he was two years younger than me. His dark curls, which he wore long on top, reminded me of many Armenians.

We got drinks and grabbed a seat. Matty propped his arms on the table and folded his hands together.

'Thanks so much for meeting me,' I said. 'Your performance gave me a whole new perspective on Australia.'

'Oh, thanks.' He gestured, a little wave expressing typical

Aussie demure, as if it was no big deal.

A Kamilaroi man, Matty grew up in Walgett, a rural NSW town of about 2000 people. He started dancing at age nine, when his teachers encouraged him to join a traditional Aboriginal dance group. In high school he learned jazz, ballet and hip hop, dancing to Britney Spears and S Club 7.

Matty was sixteen the first time he came to Sydney, when he performed among thousands of students in the Schools Spectacular.

To him, the city was 'a vast empire ... I was in awe,' he told me. It was the first time he'd seen buildings over two storeys tall. 'I was profoundly overwhelmed by how many different types of people there were in Sydney.' He liked listening to different languages and learning about other countries and cultures. In Walgett, most people were Aboriginal or white. Sydney was his first exposure to Australia's full diversity.

Matty then received a scholarship to St Joseph's College, a prestigious Catholic school. Living in Sydney and travelling back to Walgett was like having his life split between two worlds, 'the world of the white and privileged, and the world of a kind of poverty.' While Sydney was fascinating, Matty struggled to feel at home. He felt like an outsider because of his accent, his colloquialisms, and even his table manners.

After moving to Bronte in his mid-twenties, he found himself walking past a door with a hot-pink sign reading Pole Dance Academy. His first thought was that it must be full of naked women walking around in stilettos, G-strings and lace.

After passing the sign every day for a week, he got curious

and looked up pole dancing videos on YouTube. The strength and grace of the women amazed him.

'I got up the courage to go and walk into the studio, which was upstairs above a funeral parlour.'

In that first class, he learned a move that involved hanging upside-down, his legs extended, arms bracing. 'I couldn't believe I could do that with my body.' A trace of astonishment lingered in his voice as he recalled the achievement. That one move convinced Matty that pole dancing was for him.

Soon he was at the pole studio most days, and eight months later, he competed on *Australia's Got Talent* in a comedic pole routine. His first performance received a standing ovation, and he made it to the show's semifinals. He went on to compete in the 2011 World Pole Dance Championship in Budapest, placing third in the doubles division.

Matty discovered pole dancing at a difficult time in his life, when he was grappling with loneliness, wondering how his culture fit in the world, and struggling as a minority in the gay community.

Performing on national TV, however, he felt embraced. 'It was phenomenal.'

Matty had been pole dancing for three years by the time I saw him in Down Under Burlesque. When he was invited to take part, he knew it was a comedic show billed as tracing Australia's history, and that his role as the opening act was to represent Australia's Aboriginal past. He considered doing a satirical performance. 'I can be very satirical about my culture. You know, Blackfellas, we all make fun of ourselves.'

Instead, he composed a routine to Emma Donovan's 'Miminga', a song about Mother Earth. The soulful music inspired him to give a serious performance, to offset the rest of the show and share a deeper message.

He described the performance as 'contemporary Aboriginal dance infused into the pole'. Matty used ochre, both to sprinkle on stage and as body paint. It adds a spiritual aspect to the performance, he explained, because of the intrinsic connection between Aboriginal land and culture.

'I wanted to make people recognise that Aboriginal people are beautiful, that we come from an ancient past.' He gave a thoughtful nod. 'The greatest message is "don't forget us." I think a lot of people forget that Aboriginal culture is a very sophisticated, complicated culture that existed for a long time. It's not as simple as we're being taught in schools.'

He reflected on the stereotypical image of pre-colonial Aboriginal life as a man posed on one leg, balancing against a stick. 'I think about my great-great-great-great-grandfather, living a traditional life – something that I'm very envious of – but I have a new identity now compared to that.' It's an identity that he spent years working hard at. Particularly when Matty was facing racism in the gay community, he said, 'the only way I could express myself was through pole dancing. It gave me new confidence to talk to people. I wasn't invisible anymore.'

I was straight, white and middle-class, and still struggled with identity and feeling at home in the world. I could only begin to imagine how much more challenging it was for Matty.

I tried to convey the impact his performance had had on me.

'You created something totally new, and found a creative and powerful way to express both who you are now and where you come from. If more people did that, think about how amazing Australia would be.'

'Thanks. I love it, and I am very creative.' Then quickly he added, 'I'm not talking myself up.'

It's okay, I wanted to tell him, *Australia could use a few tall poppies like you.* Instead, I asked Matty if he thought of himself as Australian.

'I am Australian, yes,' he said, giving another of his thoughtful nods. 'There's no doubt about it. And I love that we have a multicultural country. But my true identity lies with me being Kamilaroi.'

Matty still navigated the tension of living in two worlds. In Sydney, he worked as a nurse, had begun studying to be a midwife, and had the pole dance community, where he felt respected and free to express his true self creatively. Walgett still didn't have any buildings more than two storeys high, but it was where Matty's family was. More than that, it was his traditional homeland – his country.

In this way he was like many Armenians I'd interviewed who lived outside of Armenia, often for pragmatic reasons, but who maintained a deep connection to their homeland.

People like Noelle and I were cut adrift, our feelings of home severed from any particular land. If, like her, I'd lived in four countries before I'd finished grade school, I might have considered myself a citizen of the world. But the world was too immense for me to locate my identity in. It was as unhelpful as describing

How to Be Australian

myself as a citizen of the solar system.

Instead, I was about to become a citizen of Australia, a place where I'd come to feel at home in part because of people like Matty.

~

Steve joked about wearing shorts and thongs to the ceremony, but I convinced him to dress up. As we joined the entry queue at Town Hall, I straightened the jaunty teal pocket square he'd paired with his grey sports coat. Five years and two months had passed since we'd arrived in Sydney. His face was starting to look sun-worn, and grey patches had appeared at his temples, but otherwise, he looked much as he had when we first stepped off the plane, fit and professional. He'd run half marathons across the Harbour Bridge and through the Botanic Garden, he'd swum in beachside pools, and he'd had four promotions. Thanks to our public speaking club, he was now so comfortable giving speeches that he was often asked to emcee town hall meetings in front of hundreds of staff. He'd found the club so helpful, he'd started his own version at his office, which was growing in popularity. He'd worked hard, and Australia had treated him well.

Scanning the crowd of fellow proposed citizens, I hoped they all could say as much. Behind me, two men joined the queue. They wore sharp suits and turbans, one sky blue, the other a royal purple that matched his tie. I wondered how different their citizenship journey had been from ours, but also in what ways it might have been similar. Had they also mistaken the vegemite scrolls for chocolate?

Citizenship Sizzle

Along with a black and white patterned shift dress, I was wearing my new wedding rings. They were identical copies of the rings I'd lost on Bondi Beach, made by the same Winnipeg jeweller. It had taken a few years, but Steve had contacted the jeweller to have the rings remade. Earlier that week, he'd presented the unwrapped box to me with nothing more than a cheery, 'Look what finally arrived!' If this were Hollywood, he would have planned a re-enactment of our engagement. He could have at least taken me out to dinner, wrapped up the box, and made this an opportunity to celebrate our relationship.

That wasn't Steve. He was steadfast, loyal and hardworking, and also pragmatic and unsentimental. I was learning to accept that he would never be comfortable with public displays of affection and, now that our engagement and wedding were fading into the past, that sort of overt romance would never be how he expressed himself.

And none of that meant he loved me any less.

After we'd officially checked in, Steve and I followed the crowd inside. I'd expected the ceremony to take place in Town Hall's grandiose main chamber with its towering organ, once the largest in the world. Instead, the day's festivities were in the basement.

A backdrop painting of the Opera House in an Aboriginal art style decorated the stage. In the corner, a jazz trio played a snazzy version of 'Waltzing Matilda'. I hoped their selection would be entirely Australian songs, but after Matilda, they reverted to 'Moondance' and other non-Australian jazz standards. I waited, but they played no AC/DC, no INXS or Kylie Minogue.

Along the side wall, servers were filling flutes with Australian sparkling wine and stacking lamingtons, Anzac biscuits and miniature pavlovas onto silver trays. Kiwi slices topped the pavlovas, perhaps a subtle acknowledgment of the pavlova's true origins across the Tasman – though, as a proposed citizen, I knew better than to say that.

We filed into our assigned seats, surrounded by people from what felt like every ethnic background across the world. Two Aboriginal men came on stage to welcome us to Gadigal land. Though I'd seen many Welcome to Countrys, this one felt especially significant. Leading up to the ceremony, I'd resolved to read more Aboriginal authors, and today had a copy of Bruce Pascoe's *Dark Emu* in my bag. Its revelations about the extent of Aboriginal agriculture, housing and permanent communities, drawn from the accounts of European settlers and explorers, were giving me a new perspective on Australia's vast history. It was the kind of material that should have been on the citizenship test, along with a screening and discussion of *The Castle*.

Sydney's Lord Mayor, Clover Moore, strode onto the stage wearing a bulky necklace of gold medallions, the city's coat of arms at its centre.

'Welcome to our proposed citizens,' she began. 'Today, 178 people from 24 countries will become citizens.'

The detail filled me with a warm glow, reminding me I was officially being inducted into something much bigger than a legal construct forged by white Englishmen centuries earlier. Australia had citizens from over 250 countries, more than currently existed, which must have placed it among the most diverse communities in the world's history.

'This is the start of a new journey,' Clover said. 'Each of you has something unique to contribute to Australia.'

It wasn't very Australian of me, but I was beaming. I leaned into Steve. Instead of shifting away, he put his arm around me.

We were staying in Australia, at least for now. Like so much else, it would be an ongoing negotiation. Life, I'd come to learn, was never resolved. My marriage, my mental health, and my identity were ongoing processes, not moments frozen in time.

Still, I knew in my heart this place was home to me in a way that Canada wasn't. I was Canadian by default. I was Australian – not only on paper, but also in spirit – because of the effort I'd put into moulding myself to the culture in ways that made sense for me. When I sat in the shade of a Moreton Bay fig tree listening to the lorikeets, I felt Australian. When I rose early to sip a flat white before swimming through the surf at Bondi, long before the UV was blazing and the tourists were awake, I felt both Australian and very Sydney. And when, in the months after I'd failed to climb Cradle Mountain, I turned the experience into a self-deprecating anecdote about my lack of Australianness, I felt very Australian. At the same time, I knew my Australianness was urban, white, and middle-class, and that it was only one of myriad ways to belong in this country.

Clover asked us to stand with our hands to our hearts, a gesture of unabashed earnestness.

'From this time forward, I pledge my loyalty to Australia and its people,' I echoed. When I'd repeated my wedding vows, the moment held a storybook quality, a feeling of acting out a scene I'd witnessed a thousand times in movies and on TV. I was twenty-six years old when Steve and I got married. An adult, but not really. Now I was thirty-two. An ocean separated my new Australian self from the person I'd been when Steve and I exchanged wedding rings. Pledging my loyalty to Australia felt very adult. It was also a moment I was free to interpret anew, having rarely, if ever, seen it played out in all my media consumption.

I squeezed Steve's hand. My wedding rings pressed into my finger as he squeezed back.

Once we were seated again, Clover wrapped up her speech with a toothy smile.

'Today we'll be presenting you with a sample bag, so you won't just be Australian, you'll *feel* Australian.' Her comment had the undertone of a threat. What could be put in a sample bag that had the power to make someone feel Australian? A handful of Bondi sand that would inevitably end up in your underwear? Your skin cancer biopsy results?

'It's a vial of Barnaby Joyce's blood,' I whispered.

'It'll be a tiny Australian flag on a plastic stick, made in China,' Steve said.

The bag contained a City of Sydney pen, a single serve of Vegemite, a postcard-sized photo collection of Sydney (as though perhaps we didn't have our own pictures of the Opera House) and an electoral enrolment form. After the years of paperwork it had taken to reach this stage, the fact that the government gifted us more paperwork was probably the best indication of what they thought it was to feel Australian.

Steve and I queued again, this time to receive our citizenship certificates. On stage, Clover shook our hands as she handed us

Citizenship Sizzle

our documents. My stiff card-printed certificate featured the coat of arms, its kangaroo and emu both gender-neutral, I noted with relief.

I tried to savour the moment, but it passed in a blur. We turned to face a camera, a flash blinked twice, and we were ushered away. Clover had a long queue to get through.

We beelined for the dessert spread and each took a glass of sparkling wine. I held mine up. 'To being Australian.'

'Cheers,' Steve said as our glasses clinked.

I piled a napkin with Anzac biscuits and pavlova. As with iced vovos, desiccated coconut had long made me avoid lamingtons. I might be officially Australian now, but some things would never change.

I snapped a selfie with the dessert spread and texted it to Noelle. She and her husband had recently bought a house in San Francisco. And even my American friends had left Mongolia, returned to Washington, and had a baby. Maybe everyone settled down eventually.

Officially Australian now! I wrote.

She texted back immediately. *Congrats! But where are the caramel slices?!*

They weren't the only baked goods missing. 'I can't believe there's no vegemite scrolls here, geez.' I laughed as Steve curled up his nose.

'Did I tell you my boss suggested we hold a can of Foster's and a twig of wattle for the photo?' Steve asked.

'Ha,' I said, my mouth full of meringue. 'We should have done that. Wait, no – we should have done *that*!'

I pointed to the stage. Clover was handing a certificate to a tall, rail-thin man with an ear-to-ear smile. He didn't have a wattle twig or a tinnie, but he was wearing a large, jaunty hat.

'That guy's wearing a drop-bear hat!' I exclaimed.

'What?'

As the man shook Clover's hand, the camera flash lit up the dangling corks that framed his smile.

'You know, the hat that protects you from drop bears. They won't drop on you because the corks scare them off.'

'I'm pretty sure they call it a cork hat,' Steve said. 'And I think it's for the flies.'

It seemed this country would always have something new for me to learn.

'Whatever it's called, that guy must feel really Australian.'

~

'I can't believe how long the line is,' Steve grumbled, leaning to get a better vantage. How many people are ahead of us? Fifty?'

'At least we're not standing in the baking heat.'

The July morning was crisp and sunny, laced with the distinctive scent of golden wattle. We'd thought we were arriving early to our polling place, but apparently everyone in our neighbourhood was keen to cast their votes in the federal election. The queue wound out of the primary school gates and halfway down the block.

We made our way inside the school hall and I received my ballot. I could have wrapped it around my body and worn it as a dress. Every Australian election must deforest a small country.

Citizenship Sizzle

'This is as long as my arm!' I whispered to Steve. It was covered in dozens of names, like a phonebook had vomited on it. A thin line divided the top third from the rest of the page. 'And even more complicated than I'd imagined.'

Steve regarded his own giant ballot with consternation.

We headed to our individual voting booths, cardboard dividers set up on rows of trestle tables. I looked over my shoulder. Steve had vanished into the maze of booths. The ballot curled up the sides of the cardboard divider as I tried to wrestle it onto the table. I broke out in a sweat despite the room's chill.

I loved Australia, but that statement came with an asterisk. I loved it – but I could love it so much more if it stopped indefinitely imprisoning refugees, if it acknowledged the traumatic legacy of Invasion Day, if it would join the 21st century and legalise same-sex marriage. These were federal government matters, and I knew other Australians – it was so strange to use that phrase – felt the same. I had to make sure my vote counted among theirs.

I took out my selected 'how to vote' instructions and compared it to the labyrinth of names on the ballot. I started numbering the boxes above the line, awkwardly writing on the side of the cardboard wall.

After escaping the ruins of the Ottoman Empire, my Armenian great-grandparents had arrived in Canada in 1920, and must have received citizenship at some point. But I didn't know when or if they'd ever voted in a Canadian election. If they had, I imagined their sense of privilege at participating in a country's democracy would have been infinitely greater than mine now – and mine was pretty powerful.

Folding my ballot like bureaucratic origami, I shoved it into one of the collection boxes. There was no way to be sure I'd done it right, but it was done.

I headed outside to find Steve. There was one more important part of election day to take part in.

'It doesn't matter if you understand the details,' Jules had said, when the four of us had gone for dinner a few weeks earlier. 'What matters is you get a snag.'

'What, an election sausage?' Steve laughed, assuming she was joking.

'They're called democracy sausages. There's even a website.' Aram pulled out his phone. 'Here, look.'

A map of Australia filled the screen, dotted with green checkmarks and sausage icons. Some places also had a cupcake icon.

'Election day is a nationwide barbecue?' Steve asked.

I'd never heard of anything like it. Election day in Canada was pure procedural seriousness, devoid of culinary tradition. 'I love this country.'

'Geez, tamp down the pride there, mate,' Jules had said, flashing her cheeky smile.

Now, Steve and I walked across the schoolyard and joined the crowd at the grill, the smell of roasted onions and snags filling the air. We handed over our gold coins and took our sausages, topping them with tomato sauce, then tapping our buns together like champagne glasses.

'Cheers,' Steve said, smiling.

We'd done it. I wanted to reach back in time to that version of

Citizenship Sizzle

myself in the snow bank, squeeze her hand, tell her things would get better. And maybe, somewhere in the future, a version of me had finally gotten my book about the legacy of the Armenian genocide out into the world, in one form or another. Even if it took another five years, it would be worth it.

As we bit into our snags, a kookaburra began to laugh from the schoolyard trees. Quiet at first, the jaunty chortling grew more robust, echoing across the playground-turned-polling station, where our oversized ballots sat in their collection box, waiting to be counted among millions of other Australian votes.

The instant the kookaburra call reached me, my eyes met Steve's. We straightened up and stopped chewing. If there was a better mindfulness practice than this, I couldn't imagine it. Our mouths full of democracy, we turned in unison towards the sound, our faces joyous.

I was scanning the trees, trying to spot the laughing kookaburra, when a blur of movement startled me. A huge creature came out of nowhere and swooped past my face, its feathers brushing my nose.

I shrieked. Steve jumped back. My snag tumbled out of its roll and landed on the bitumen, sauce splattering my shoes.

'What was that?' I shouted. But I could see it, settling on a tree branch a few metres away. The kookaburra, part of my roll clutched in its beak, stared back at me, steely eyed and undaunted.

From the surrounding trees, the laughter of the birds continued.

Acknowledgements

I acknowledge the Traditional Owners of country throughout Australia, and in particular the Gadigal people of the Eora Nation, on whose land I wrote much of this book. I recognise their continuing connection to land, waters and culture, and pay my respect to their Elders past, present and emerging.

My immense thanks to Steve, for everything, including his total support for this book. And to my parents, for a lifetime of love and encouragement.

My feelings toward Winnipeg formed in the late 1990s and early 2000s. The city has improved since then (although the weather hasn't). You should visit! And I'm not just saying that because my dear friend Cody Chomiak is the marketing director for Tourism Winnipeg.

Some amazingly talented people provided feedback on early drafts. All that's best in this is thanks to them: Luke Ryan, Jacqui Dent, Fiona Robertson, Adele Dumont, Ellen Holtzman, and my incredible writers' group – James Watson, Simon Veksner, Jonathon Shannon, Amanda Ortlepp, Andrea Tomaz, Ren Arcamone, Andrew Christie and Michelle Troxler.

I owe huge thanks to the authors and editors who have

supported my writing career, especially Emily Maguire, Lee Kofman, Ashley Hay, Toni Jordan, Claire Scobie, Vicki Laveau-Harvie, Katherine Collette, Kate Mildenhall, Linda Funnell, Jean Bedford, Catriona Menzies-Pike and Bronwyn Mehan. Special thanks to Marcelle Freiman and the Macquarie University English Department.

I couldn't have written this book without all the wonderful people I've met since arriving in Sydney, and our countless conversations about Australia. I've drawn on the humorous observations of many friends. My enduring thanks to Carol Neuschul, Marije Nieuwenhuis, Richard Heersmink, Helena Klanjscek, Fran Giudici, Fran Jakin, Eleanora Bodini, Alexandra Berlioz, Valentina Baú, Oldooz Dianat, Sheila Pham, Rhonda Kaidbay, Michelle de Souza, Matthew Woolaston, Dash Maiorova, the Galoyan family, Kim and Garry Jennings, Sherry Landow, Cassie Watson, Bridget Lutherborrow, Rosie Evanian, Kate Dilanchian, Leo and Marion Dent, Lindsey Wiebe, Rachel Ramberran, Sarah Hodges-Kolisnyk, Alyona Morozava and Arminé Nalbandian.

I was also lucky enough to meet and learn from Ruth Rinot, Laura Setyo, Erin Colgrave, Clare Schnelle, John Dale, Adrian Revell, Paul Curtis, Joanna Robinski, Mith Selvendran, Whiter Tang, Mike Santos, Olivia Peckowski, Lara Mathers, Simone Conchin, Michael Geng, Sally Rippingale and Dawn Tuften.

My fellow writers are a constant source of inspiration and encouragement, including Arna Radovich, Cass Moriarty, Christine Scuderi, Nicole Hodgson, Mark Keenan, Eva Lomski, Robin Riedstra, Sharon Livingstone, Georgina Ballantine, Shae Millward,

Andrew Patterson, Rivqa Rafael, Rebecca Chaney, LA Larkin, Zohra Aly, Judyth Emanuel and Wai Chim.

The extraordinarily excellent people at Writing NSW deserve special mention: Jane McCredie, Julia Tsalis, David Henley, Claire Thompson, Sarah Mott and Lou Garcia-Dolnik.

Thanks also to all my family, including Pam and Rick Blunt, and Kerry and Janet McLuhan.

I'm enormously grateful to Walter Mason, the most generous and supportive person anyone could have the pleasure of knowing, who will receive a signed copy of this book as part of the 2020 #AuthorsForFireys campaign.

Thanks are also due to Varuna and KSP Writers' Centre, who supported the writing of this book through fellowships. Earlier versions of certain chapters appeared in *Griffith Review*, the *Big Issue*, and the *Lane Cove Literary Awards 2017 Anthology*. I'm also grateful for the support of the Consulate General of Canada in Sydney.

And finally, huge thanks to the Affirm Press team, especially Martin Hughes and Coco McGrath, for bringing this book into the world and making it the best it could be.